The 9/11 Terror Cases

LANDMARK LAW CASES & AMERICAN SOCIETY

Peter Charles Hoffer
N. E. H. Hull
Series Editors

For a complete list of titles in the series go to www.kansaspress.ku.edu

ALLAN A. RYAN

The 9/11 Terror Cases

Constitutional Challenges in

the War against Al Qaeda

UNIVERSITY PRESS OF KANSAS

Published by the University Press of Kansas (Lawrence, Kansas 66045), which was
organized by the Kansas Board of Regents and is operated and funded by Emporia State
University, Fort Hays State University, Kansas State University, Pittsburg State University,
the University of Kansas, and Wichita State University

Library of Congress Cataloging-in-Publication Data

Ryan, Allan A., author.

The 9/11 terror cases : constitutional challenges in the war against Al Qaeda /
Allan A. Ryan.

pages cm — (Landmark law cases and American society)

Includes bibliographical references and index.

ISBN 978-0-7006-2132-3 (hardback)

ISBN 978-0-7006-2170-5 (paperback)

ISBN 978-0-7006-2161-3 (ebook)

1. Trials (Terrorism)—United States. 2. War on Terrorism, 2001–2009.
3. Constitutional law—United States. I. Title.

KF221.P6R13 2015

345.73'056—dc23

2015023666

British Library Cataloguing-in-Publication Data is available.

Printed in the United States of America

10 9 8 7 6 5 4 3 2 1

The paper used in this publication is recycled and contains 30 percent postconsumer waste.
It is acid free and meets the minimum requirements of the American National Standard for
Permanence of Paper for Printed Library Materials Z39.48-1992.

"By the protection of the law human rights are secured; withdraw that protection, and they are at the mercy of wicked rulers, or the clamor of an excited people. The founders of our government . . . secured in a written constitution every right which the people had wrested from power during a contest of ages. Those great and good men foresaw that troublous times would arise, when rulers and people would become restive under restraint, and seek by sharp and decisive measures to accomplish ends deemed just and proper; and that the principles of constitutional liberty would be in peril, unless established by irrepealable law. . . . The Constitution of the United States is a law for rulers and people, equally in war and in peace, and covers with the shield of its protection all classes of men, at all times, and under all circumstances."

Justice David Davis, Supreme Court of the United States, *Ex Parte Milligan* (1866)

"The laws and Constitution are designed to survive, and remain in force, in extraordinary times. Liberty and security can be reconciled; and in our system they are reconciled within the framework of the law."

Justice Anthony Kennedy, Supreme Court of the United States, *Boumediene v. Bush* (2008)

CONTENTS

EDITORS' PREFACE

As Allan Ryan tells us on the very first page of his brilliantly argued account of the Guantanamo cases, no one old enough to remember 9/11 will ever forget that day. In the coming years, however, new generations of Americans will come to adulthood unaware of all the military, political, and legal ramifications of that day. The war in Afghanistan was undertaken with the understanding that the attack was a virtual declaration of war by a worldwide conspiracy of terrorists and terrorist-harboring states. The incarceration of hundreds of suspected terrorists and enemy combatants in US military facilities, principally the naval base at Guantanamo, Cuba, followed from a more complex understanding of the attack. To the federal courts then came questions that neither direct military action nor fraught political rhetoric could untangle. What was the basis for the continuing imprisonment of the suspects? Were they prisoners of war? Were they criminals? Did they have the procedural rights that prisoners in American jails exercised? Would they be tried at all, and if so for what offense, in what venue and jurisdiction?

Ryan, whose expertise in military and constitutional law covers all of these bases, follows the story case by case and transforms the complex and confused into the clear and explicable. He brings to life a remarkable cast of characters in the executive branch, the courts, and counsel for the detainees. Most important to readers in the coming generations, he writes with genuine understanding of the pressures on all the policy makers and the lawyers. For these cases were more than the resolution of the fates of individuals—they were a test of a nation's commitment to a rule of law when faced with enemies whose conduct was the very opposite of the rule of law. Could American justice overcome the panic and fury 9/11 engendered?

As Ryan closed his account, Guantanamo was still open, and though the number of prisoners had drawn down, the lessons of Guantanamo were still there. Even when, as seems likely in the near future, the containment facility will close its doors and the last detainee depart, historians and jurists will debate the legality and the policy of the detention. Ryan's splendid account will be a central part of this debate. For as he concluded, the use of Gitmo as a containment facility and the determination to try its prisoners by military commissions "were ill conceived to begin with and they have proven to be failures. Worse, they have been failures that have contorted American ideals, polarized American politics, repelled American allies, and radicalized America's enemies."

On September 11, 2001, early on a pleasant late-summer morning, nineteen men from Saudi Arabia and elsewhere in the Middle East, in groups of four or five, acting in concert, routinely passed through airport security in Boston, Newark, and at Dulles airport in northern Virginia. They boarded four United and American Airlines flights bound for the west coast: big planes, loaded with flammable fuel. Soon after takeoffs at about 8:00 a.m., the men overpowered the flight attendants, forced their way into the cockpits, killed the pilots and took control of the aircraft. The two planes from Boston flew into the north and south towers of the World Trade Center in Manhattan. The plane from Dulles flew into the Pentagon, headquarters of the US Department of Defense, across the Potomac River from Washington, D.C. Passengers on the fourth plane, from Newark, fought the hijackers and deterred its course, believed to be to the United States Capitol or the White House; it plummeted into a field in rural Pennsylvania. Everyone aboard all the planes, and many more on the ground—nearly 3,000 people in all—lost their lives on that sunny and tragic day.

It was immediately clear that the attacks were the work of al Qaeda, a radical Islamist organization then based in Afghanistan and led by Osama bin Laden, the forty-four-year-old son of a wealthy Saudi Arabian family. Al Qaeda's earlier work included a truck bomb in the World Trade Center in 1993; the bombing of the US embassies in Dar es Salaam, Tanzania and Nairobi, Kenya in 1998; and an attack on the US Navy ship *Cole* in a harbor in Yemen in 2000.

It was the most destructive act on American soil in the country's history. Beyond that, there was no telling what further violence and carnage might be imminent in the days and weeks and months ahead. American military forces throughout the world were placed on high alert. Civilian flights were grounded in the country for a week; only military planes flew. Americans were gripped by fear and grief, and much of the world—though certainly not all of it—reacted with outrage and sympathy. For anyone in the United States old enough to realize what had happened, September 11, 2001, can never be forgotten. As President

Franklin D. Roosevelt said of the Japanese attack on Pearl Harbor sixty years earlier, it is a date that will live in infamy.

President George W. Bush, in office eight months, summoned the country to respond with force and determination. It was an act of war, he said, and no effort would be spared to find and defeat the enemy, to kill them or to bring them to justice. In his call lay a clue to much of what was to come: 9/11 was inarguably a crime—indeed, a cascade of crimes—that was also taken by the president, and most Americans, as an act of war.

What followed over the next dozen years was one of the most tense, turbulent, and controversial periods in American legal and political history. It brought two presidents, the Congress, and the Supreme Court into repeated confrontations that called into question the very meaning of the Constitution of the United States: the separation of powers, the authority of the president in war, the due process of law, the role of the Supreme Court and the nation's federal courts, and the balance of military and civilian control in a government ordained under the rule of law. Not since Roosevelt's New Deal of the 1930s had such fundamental principles come into such sharp conflict, not since the Civil War had they done so in a time of war. The four cases decided by the Supreme Court from 2004 to 2008, and the response of the president and Congress, are the focus of this book.

Much of that turbulence and controversy has centered on a backwater US naval base on Guantanamo Bay, Cuba, which the Bush administration turned into a detention camp for nearly 700 aliens captured by, or handed over to, American military forces that invaded Afghanistan weeks after September 11. President Bush also ordered that those who were behind the attacks be brought to trial, not in federal courts but before military commissions—ad hoc tribunals of military officers, operating under rules specially written for them. The rules departed, markedly and quite intentionally, from the legal and constitutional provisions that govern both civilian and military courts. In addition, the Congress enacted laws to prohibit Guantanamo detainees from going to any federal court to seek a judicial ruling on the legality of their imprisonment.

These actions inevitably created sharp and prolonged disagreement on what it means to be a nation under the rule of law. The President of the United States, Commander in Chief of its armed forces and chief executive officer of the nation, implemented policies that the Supreme Court of the United States, the nation's highest judicial authority, repeatedly rejected. The Congress of the United States, the embodiment of democracy, enacted laws that sought to overturn the decisions of the Supreme Court and circumscribe the jurisdiction of all federal courts. After a new president was inaugurated in 2009, it sought also to restrict his authority to deal with the complex issues that emerged so viciously from that September morning.

As this is written in the first weeks of 2015, the turmoil of United States law in what can aptly be called the post-9/11 era is not over. That conflict has abated in some respects, but it has not been resolved, and may not be for years to come.

The Supreme Court, its nine justices divided on fundamental questions of the constitutional balance of powers in the American system, decided four crucially important cases from 2004 to 2008 but has been silent on the conflict for seven years since then. A president twice elected to bring about change has continued the policies of his predecessor in some respects, altered and ended others, and faces an obdurate Congress that has frustrated his attempts at further change. And Congress, riven by partisan division, has shown itself unable to accomplish little of importance that requires cooperation or compromise.

Still, it is not too soon to chart the course of American law during this momentous period, to illuminate how it has both preserved and reshaped fundamental concepts of the due process of law, the separation of powers, and presidential authority. That is the purpose of this book. My focus is primarily on the cases decided by the Supreme Court in 2004, 2006, and 2008, arising out of lawsuits filed by lawyers representing the Guantanamo detainees as they sought judicial review of their captivity, and relief from the procedures of trials by military commissions that controlled life and death for some of them. But these cases did not arise in a calm political environment, nor did the confrontation among the three branches of our government by any means subside after 2008. The decisions of the Supreme Court resolved some issues, in some respects, but in almost equal measure they left others undecided, returning them to the Congress, to the president, and to lower federal courts. That process continues.

Any examination of the Supreme Court's terror cases, therefore, important as those cases are, must also take account of the response of the president and the Congress both to the decisions of the Court and to the issues that the Court left undecided. The best lens for this examination is the foundation of the US Constitution: the separation of powers. That principle can be simply described, as it has been throughout our history in countless classrooms. The Constitution creates a national government of limited powers, some of them quite specific and others indistinct and ambiguous, reserving all else to "the States respectively, or to the people" in the words of the Tenth Amendment in the Bill of Rights.

To both create and limit the government, the Constitution vests the national government's powers in three branches, each with its own authority and the ability, through a system of checks and balances, to restrict the other two branches from exceeding the powers given to each of them. To those who wrote the Constitution, no principle of governance was more important than this. "The accumulation of all powers, legislative, executive, and judiciary, in the same hands, whether of one, a few, or many, and whether hereditary, self-appointive, or elective," James Madison wrote in *Federalist* No. 47, "may justly be pronounced the very definition of tyranny." Thus, "the preservation of liberty requires that the three great departments of power should be separate and distinct." The framers had no use for the parliamentary democracy of Great Britain, in which the prime minister and others in the executive were drawn from the elected members of the legislature, and the highest judicial authority was that body's House of Lords. Invoking "the celebrated Montesquieu," the French lawyer and philosopher, Madison was emphatic: "Where the WHOLE power of one department is exercised by the same hands which possess the WHOLE power of another department, the fundamental principles of a free constitution are subverted" (Madison's emphasis).

Ordaining a separation of those powers in the Constitution was thus necessary, but not enough. A "mere demarcation on parchment of the constitutional limits of the several departments," Madison wrote in *Federalist* No. 48, "is not a sufficient guard against those encroachments which lead to a tyrannical concentration of all the powers of government in the same hands." For the separation to be effective, it would need teeth, and so each branch of the government was allocated certain limited but effective controls over the other two, so as to "divide and arrange the several offices in such a manner as that each may be a check on the other." Madison quoted Thomas Jefferson, in his *Notes on the State of Virginia*: "An ELECTIVE DESPOTISM was not the government we fought for; but one which should not only be founded on free principles, but in which the powers of government should be so divided and balanced among several bodies of magistracy, as that no one could transcend their legal limits, without being effectually checked and restrained by the others."

These checks and balances could be realized, Madison (or perhaps it was Alexander Hamilton) wrote in *Federalist* No. 51, only by "so contriving the interior structure of the government as that its several constituent parts may, by their mutual relations, be the means of keeping each other in their proper places." He went on to explain, "It may be a reflection on human nature, that such devices should be necessary to control the abuses of government. But what is government itself, but the greatest of all reflections on human nature? If men were angels, no government would be necessary. If angels were to govern men, neither external nor internal controls on government would be necessary. In framing a government which is to be administered by men over men, the great difficulty lies in this: you must first enable the government to control the governed; and in the next place oblige it to control itself."

The primary separation of powers is simple: Congress enacts laws; the president implements them; the courts interpret them by resolving disputes that arise over their meaning and application. Each branch operates independently but they must also act interdependently. The president nominates judges to the Supreme Court and lower federal courts; the Senate confirms them, or not; the judges, once confirmed, have lifetime tenure by which they decide disputes free of political control or any direct accountability, yet their decisions can define and restrict the powers of the other two branches.

But this simple summary only opens the door. "Checks and balances" is a nice way to say "tension and conflict," and the Constitution is notably sparse in its details of how tension and conflict are to be resolved. The Constitution is clear enough that Congress "constitutes tribunals" (that is, it creates the lower federal courts and defines their scope and authority); that the president commands the armed forces; and that the Supreme Court decides cases and controversies arising under the Constitution, the nation's treaties, and the laws enacted by Congress. Yet the Supreme Court's most profound authority, to invalidate congressional or presidential actions that exceed constitutional powers, is found nowhere in the Constitution itself. It was declared to exist by Chief Justice John Marshall in 1803, as a necessary aspect of the Constitution's limits on government authority. In the terror cases, and in the response of the president and Congress to those cases, each branch of this government, relying on its constitutional powers, was thrust into confrontation with each of the other two. How those confrontations arose, how they were addressed, and how they have been resolved—to the extent they have been resolved—is the subject of this book.

One may reasonably ask why another book on the consequences of 9/11 and the "war on terrorism" is needed, especially from one whose military and government service concluded well before the events. There have been dozens of books written about this period, some of them quite good and most of them by those who bring their personal perspectives formed as military, political, and intelligence officials; academics; journalists; and lawyers. Many of these works are decidedly partisan, seeking to justify the author's actions or perspectives and to persuade the reader of the rightness of that course or those insights. Such works are essential to the public dialogue and to the often messy compilation of history by contemporary generations and succeeding ones.

But the dialogue, and the compilation of history, also require contributions of those who have no particular turf to defend and seek instead to examine the facts as objectively as they can. No account, however brief or lengthy, can be perfectly objective; what one chooses to address or to leave out is the first step off the path of complete objectivity, if such a path exists at all. And how one recounts what is addressed is a further step off that uncertain path. Still, as someone who has taught constitutional law and the law of war to law students and to undergraduates during this post-9/11 era, who has followed those events closely and incorporated them into my teaching, and who has been pressed by students and colleagues to explain and defend my views, I believe there is a place for a concise, readable, and relatively objective account for readers who are not necessarily lawyers or law students but who want to understand, in some depth, how American law was tested and how it responded during this tumultuous period, so as to draw their own conclusions. In the account that follows, I do not shy from presenting my own opinions, or from criticizing the actions of individuals and political institutions—two presidents and their administrations, the Congress, and the federal courts—and the reasons for those actions. But I have tried to make my own analysis evident, and not to tailor my account except to show the reader what I believe is important to an understanding of what has happened, and how it has affected the fundamental principles of our Constitution and our democracy.

A glossary (p. 193) and a chronology (p. 197) follow the text.

ACKNOWLEDGMENTS

I want to thank, once again, my longtime friend and colleague, former Marine Corps military judge Richard D. Sullivan, who read each chapter as it was written with an acute and knowledgeable eye and made valuable contributions to its accuracy and clarity. William Banks of the Syracuse University School of Law read the manuscript and provided helpful comments. I am grateful also to Boston College Law School, which offered me the opportunity in 1989 to teach what was reportedly the first course on the law of war in a civilian law school, where I have taught it every year since, and to the Harvard University Summer School, where I have taught a similar course to undergraduate and graduate students since 1997. Michael Briggs at the University Press of Kansas encouraged me to write this book. Above all, my wife, Nancy, supported me unfailingly in this endeavor, as in all others, with limitless patience, understanding, and good humor.

The 9/11 Terror Cases

CHAPTER ONE

Guantanamo

In early October 2001, on orders of President George W. Bush, American military forces invaded Afghanistan, augmented by a robust number of civilian operatives of the Central Intelligence Agency, and soon joined by some military units of the United Kingdom and other "coalition partners." The immediate objective was to depose the Taliban, the country's fundamentalist Islamist government and a protective host of the al Qaeda network as it planned and carried out the attacks of September 11. Al Qaeda was led by Osama bin Laden, whose stated objective was to rid the Arab world of Western influence. His followers were Muslims from many nations, some of whom had initially come together to repel, with American arms and aid, the Soviet Union's invasion of Afghanistan in the 1980s and had maintained their cohesion despite the Soviet Union's dissolution in 1991. Many of them were skilled in the construction and use of missiles, bombs, and other weapons, but they were not conventional military forces. Their strategy was terrorism—attacking targets, some of them military but many not, without warning. If this was war, the al Qaeda network acted with no regard at all for the international laws of war, formalized in the Geneva Conventions, that prohibit attacks on civilians and other noncombatants.

Al Qaeda operatives had detonated a truck bomb in the garage of New York's World Trade Center in 1993, killing six and injuring more than a thousand, a crime for which several of them had been convicted in federal court in 1995 and sentenced to life imprisonment. That carnage, and their subsequent attacks on the US embassies in Tanzania and Kenya in 1998 and the Navy's guided-missile destroyer USS *Cole* in Aden harbor in Yemen in 2000, had made al Qaeda well known to the US government, enough so that the Central Intelligence Agency had an office whose sole job was to find and kill bin Laden. Whether the administration of George Bush, inaugurated in January 2001, should have been more alert to signs that bin Laden was planning a major attack on the United States led to recriminations, some of it along partisan lines, in the wake of 9/11, but there was near-universal popular support for the invasion of Afghanistan and the destruction of al Qaeda.

Working cooperatively with anti-Taliban Afghan elements of the Northern Alliance and with its coalition partners, US forces succeeded in overthrowing the Taliban within a few months of the invasion and taking some of its fighters into custody, but getting at al Qaeda proved difficult. Bin Laden and his councilors were thought to be hiding in the almost impenetrable terrain along the Afghan-Pakistan border, undisturbed by Pakistan's military, which supported the Taliban. Unwilling to confront that sometimes helpful but always uncertain ally, the US military offered lavish cash rewards to anyone in Afghanistan who turned over a member of the Taliban or al Qaeda. The locals produced captives with enthusiasm, but whether they were actually hostile combatants proved to be another question.

From a standing start, the United States in little more than four months had carried out a difficult military invasion of a mountainous and landlocked country halfway around the world and had held its position, however tenuously. The swiftness of the action and the elusiveness of al Qaeda created any number of challenges, but two were especially pressing. The military forces in Afghanistan had few places to hold those who had been captured on the battlefield or turned over for bounties. And, back home, US political and intelligence officials were desperately trying to figure out what al Qaeda was planning next. Both needs were to be answered in one of the most unlikely places imaginable: the US Naval Base at Guantanamo Bay, in Cuba.

The United States knew Guantanamo well. In 1903, when Cuba had gained its independence from Spain after the Spanish-American war, it gave the United States a perpetual lease of a naval fueling station on its southeast coast. The United States had been there ever since, notwithstanding Fidel Castro's overthrow of the government in 1959 and his subsequent alliance with the Soviet Union. The base was an isolated American enclave run by the US Navy and stoutly fenced off from the rest of this Communist country. There were no diplomatic relations, no trade, no direct communications between the two governments and so no US worries about bothersome interference. Where Guantanamo was concerned, the American policy was simple: Castro didn't like it, and America couldn't care less. Apart from the Cuban Missile Crisis of 1962, when civilian dependents were evacuated from the base, nothing of great consequence happened there anyway. Most Americans knew Guantanamo, if they had heard of it at all, from the 1992 movie *A Few Good Men*, a court-martial drama starring Jack Nicholson.

How Gitmo, as it was commonly known in the military, became the centerpiece of the Bush administration's war on terror is central to understanding the events of the post-9/11 years, for there three imperatives coalesced. First, Guantanamo could provide detention for the captives who were accumulating in Afghanistan, though its isolation and rudimentary facilities on an unfriendly island made it inferior to other military installations that were available, or could quickly be made so. But those other installations were within the United States or on the territory of governments that would assuredly take a distinct interest in any US plan to bring al Qaeda terrorists to their soil. Working out arrangements would take forever, if it could be done at all.

Guantanamo's second advantage was that, situated in Cuba, it was beyond the jurisdiction of any American court. This was a critical concern to those in the president's inner circle, because they had no intention of creating a conventional prisoner-of-war camp, operated in accordance with international law under the constraints of humane treatment imposed by the Geneva Conventions and monitored by the International Committee of the Red Cross. Gitmo would be a place where terrorists were to be interrogated, and rigorously. No federal judge would hear claims from the lawyers who would surely emerge to argue that detainees were being held unlawfully, or mistreated in violation of Geneva. In that respect, it could not have been better placed had it been on Saturn.

And third, Gitmo could become the tangible demonstration that the United States was winning the war on terrorism. Because it was closed, the Department of Defense could control all access and could determine what the world saw, or did not see. And what DoD wanted the world to see—though not too closely—was an American naval base full of captured terrorists.

These aspects of Guantanamo were crucial to the Bush administration in 2001 because it had no intention of following any rules, and it made no secret of that. Vice President Richard Cheney, to whom President Bush had delegated virtually complete authority to direct the government's war on terror, told a Sunday morning TV audience five days after 9/11, "We have to work the dark side, if you will. Spend time in the shadows of the intelligence world. A lot of what needs to be done here will have to be done quietly, without any discussion." Cofer Black, chief of the CIA's counterterrorism office, told a congressional hearing, "This [anti-terrorism policy] is a very highly classified area. All you need to know is that there was a before 9/11 and there was an after 9/11. After 9/11, the gloves come off."

In the weeks after 9/11, an interagency task force was formed to determine how the United States should treat captured al Qaeda and Taliban operatives. Under the direction of Pierre-Richard Prosper, a State Department lawyer serving as Ambassador at Large for War Crimes Issues, lawyers and policymakers from Cabinet departments and executive agencies met repeatedly for serious discussions on developing rules by which the government could hold and interrogate prisoners. It was focused, it was knowledgeable, it was mindful both of its responsibilities and the limitations imposed by law.

And for that reason it was out of the loop. Its role was usurped by a small and far less visible knot of administration officials that came to be known informally as the "war council." Cheney was its patron, and at its center was his counsel David Addington, little known outside the inner workings of the administration but widely respected and not a little feared within it. Addington was recognized as Cheney's alter ego; when he spoke, he spoke for Cheney. The war council included John Yoo, the thirty-three-year-old deputy assistant attorney general in the Justice Department's Office of Legal Counsel, a former law clerk to Justice Clarence Thomas, on leave from the law faculty at the University of California at Berkeley. Yoo was an influential figure in the Federalist Society, the brain trust of the conservative legal movement, and an avid exponent of robust and untrammeled powers of the president, particularly in time of war.

Also on the war council was the man with direct access to the president, Alberto Gonzales, counsel to the president, a trusted advisor to George W. Bush from Bush's days as governor of Texas. Next to Gonzales was his deputy, Timothy Flanigan, who had from 1990 to 1992 headed the Office of Legal Counsel in the administration of the president's father, George H. W. Bush, and later a key player in *Bush v. Gore*, the Supreme Court case that settled the 2000 presidential election in favor of the younger Bush. John Rizzo, the CIA's general counsel, and William (Jim) Haynes, general counsel at the Department of Defense and Addington's successor and protégé in that role, worked closely in this inner circle with its direct access to the Oval Office. For others with obvious responsibilities but more moderate views—Secretary of State Colin Powell and National Security Adviser Condoleezza Rice chief among them—the self-appointed war council had a simple solution. It ignored them.

This group, with Vice President Cheney, determined the administration's response to 9/11 on matters of presidential authority and the gathering of intelligence. Memos to the president were signed by Gonzales, but they had been drafted by Addington and Yoo, who faced no resistance from the inexperienced and compliant Gonzales. Their animating principle was that the president had complete authority to do what he thought necessary—*whatever* he thought necessary—to protect the country from terrorism. It was an authority that nothing in the Constitution could restrict, an authority that needed no assent, much less could brook any interference, from the Congress or the judiciary.

In this regard, the war council had the benefit of a significant congressional action. A few days after 9/11, anxious to go on record in response to the attacks, Congress had approved, nearly unanimously, a resolution known as the Authorization for the Use of Military Force. The AUMF declared that the president "is authorized to use all necessary and appropriate force against those nations, organizations, or persons he determines planned, authorized, committed, or aided the terrorist attacks that occurred on September 11, 2001, or harbored such organizations or persons, in order to prevent any future acts of international terrorism against the United States by such nations, organizations or persons."

The AUMF was clearly intended to authorize the invasion of Afghanistan in pursuit of Osama bin Laden, his al Qaeda network, the Taliban that had protected it, and anyone else behind the 9/11 attacks or the continued protection of them. But the war council and Cheney did not understand "military" to be a qualification on the president's authority. The president was the commander in chief. Anything he did in the interests of protecting the nation was "military." Nor did it read "the attacks of September 11, 2001" as a qualification. The AUMF was intended to "prevent any future acts" of terrorism against the United States and so anything aimed at countering terrorism was within its scope. Reading the AUMF in this way was not difficult: Addington and Yoo had drafted it. No act of Congress was necessary for presidential action, nor could any act of Congress constrain it, for the war council's unshakeable belief was that presidential authority in war was by definition whatever the president wanted to do, regardless of congressional validation and despite any congressional objection. The AUMF, ostensibly a demonstration of congressional assent, instead underscored the sweeping breadth of the president's authority.

On the other hand, the Geneva Conventions could be a problem. Ratified by the United States and virtually every other country in the world, those four treaties, last revised and updated in 1949, laid out some of the most important international rules of warfare, protecting the sick and wounded on land and sea, prisoners of war, and civilians. The members of the war council, like many of the conservative theoreticians from whom they drew agreement and support, had little patience for international law and in fact openly disdained it. It was, to their way of thinking, a suspicious and threatening imposition of alien notions of what "law" should be that, if taken seriously, would restrict the authority of the United States to act according to its own Constitution.

Particularly problematic was the Third Geneva Convention, which requires that enemy combatants captured during international armed conflict be characterized as prisoners of war and, as such, treated humanely, with adequate food, shelter, clothing, and medical attention, even recreation. POWs can be interrogated, but they are under no obligation to give more than their name, rank, and serial number. If they refuse to give more, the treaty is explicit: "No physical or mental torture, nor any other form of coercion, may be inflicted on prisoners of war to secure from them information of any kind whatever. Prisoners of war who refuse to answer may not be threatened, insulted, or exposed to any unpleasant or disadvantageous treatment of any kind."

That obviously would not do. If the gloves were to come off, no member of al Qaeda, no Taliban operative, no detainee of any stripe could be heard to insist that he was protected from "unpleasant or disadvantageous treatment." For the United States to renounce Geneva, to declare that it was no longer bound by such a universally accepted agreement, would be politically reckless, but the war council devised a way around this problem. Those captured in Afghanistan would simply be deemed to lie outside the protections of Geneva. From the time of the first Geneva Convention in 1864 through the latest revisions in 1949 and some additional protocols in the 1970s, their concern has always been armed conflict between military forces, and in particular the treatment accorded to combatants on the battlefield, combatants taken prisoner, and the civilians impacted by such conflict. The Conventions are not concerned with common criminals, with war's looters and thieves, with freelance marauders and others who fight for their own ends, without state sponsorship.

Excluding members of al Qaeda from Geneva's protections would thus be relatively easy. Al Qaeda was not a party to the Geneva Conventions, nor could it be, because Geneva was an agreement between nation states, which al Qaeda was not. Therefore, to this way of thinking, its members were not prisoners of war entitled to the protections reserved for combatants of the states who were parties to the treaty. The Taliban was a bit trickier, because it was the government of Afghanistan, which was a party to Geneva. But here too the war council had a workaround: Geneva includes within its protections "militias" and "volunteer corps"—somewhat dated terms that refer to what are now more commonly known as partisans, guerrillas, or insurgents who are not members of a nation's actual armed forces but who fight under their supervision. In the Vietnam War, for example, in which the armed forces of the government of North Vietnam fought the forces of the government of South Vietnam, the Viet Cong were South Vietnamese fighters allied with the North against the South. But to claim the POW protections of the Geneva Convention, guerrillas or insurgents must look and act like combatants: they must wear distinctive uniforms or other visible insignia, be organized under a responsible commander, carry arms openly, and obey the laws of war themselves. Geneva thus protects combatants who behave as conventional armed forces and who can be readily identified when they are encountered or captured, while excluding unaffiliated fighters out only for their own gain or to settle personal scores.

Here the Taliban fell short, because they did not wear distinctive uniforms and paid no regard to the laws of war. Therefore, as the Addington-Yoo war council saw it, they were "unlawful" enemy combatants—a term that is not found in the Geneva Conventions but one that could plausibly describe the Taliban.

On February 7, 2002, President Bush, over the objections of Secretary of State Colin Powell, himself a career army officer and former chairman of the Joint Chiefs of Staff, signed a directive, drafted by Addington, declaring that neither the al Qaeda nor the Taliban captives were within the protections of Geneva. The directive did state that as a "matter of policy," the United States "shall continue to treat detainees humanely and, to the extent appropriate and consistent with military necessity, in a manner consistent with the principles of Geneva." But it did not elaborate on what treatment would be "consistent with the principles of Geneva" or the "extent" to which such treatment would be "appropriate" or "consistent with military necessity."

Detainees began to arrive at Guantanamo on January 11, 2002. Staggering off a US Air Force cargo plane in which they had been chained to the fuselage for a fourteen-hour flight from Afghanistan, clad in bright orange jumpsuits, blindfolded and shackled, led stumbling past US Marines with rifles locked and loaded to a fenced holding area, the twenty arrivals hardly seemed like cutthroat terrorists. But Defense Secretary Donald Rumsfeld dispelled that notion in a news conference announcing their arrival. "I mean, these are people that would gnaw hydraulic lines in the back of a C-17 to bring it down. I mean, so this is—these are very, very dangerous people, and that's how they're being treated." In another context, he called them simply "the worst of the worst."

As events were later to reveal, however, those whom the government believed to be truly the worst of the worst were not sent to Guantanamo. They were sent to "black sites" operated by the Central Intelligence Agency in secret locations in Europe and Asia, subjected to years of "enhanced interrogations" that amounted to outright torture. Those sent to Guantanamo were for show. As more and more were sent there—some 537 in 2002, another 92 in the first three months of 2003—it became clear to their captors at Gitmo, and to the Bush administration in Washington, that most were foot soldiers or low-level followers, or travelers unlucky enough to have been scooped up by locals or seized out of personal animosity or family feuds, and turned over for bounty. Few of them had any significant intelligence value. In April 2003, fourteen months after his press conference as the "worst of the worst" were being herded off the plane, Rumsfeld told the chairman of the Joint Chiefs that it was time to "stop populating Guantanamo Bay (GTMO) with low-level enemy combatants." In the rest of that year, there were only 27 new arrivals, and after that almost none at all. Meanwhile, in 2003, 88 were sent home; in 2004, another 102. Except for the transfer of 14 or so true "high-value detainees" from the CIA black sites in 2006, Gitmo ceased receiving detainees fourteen months after it opened.

A great deal has been written about what happened at Guantanamo, which in January 2015 began its fourteenth year as a prison and its sixth year since President Barack Obama, on his first day in office, had ordered it closed within a year. Of the 700 or so who were sent there, its population now has shrunk to about 130, of whom only about a dozen have been charged with crimes—even the crime of supporting terrorism—and fewer still have actually been tried (see chapter 7). But its first and most immediate problem is simply that when it was opened there was no clear understanding of what it was to be. Was it a detention camp? An intelligence-gathering facility? A place to sort out the true terrorists and criminals from its motley population of low-level captives? A venue for trials? A prison for the worst of the worst? Karen Greenberg, in her book *The Least Worst Place: Guantanamo's First 100 Days*, summarized the situation:

What had at first seemed to be a temporary lack of clarification [about its mission] now became standing policy. A sin of omission had become a sin of commission. Rather than a state of limbo being created out of a policy void, administration lawyers had formulated a policy embracing limbo as its primary characteristic. There was to be no policy. That was the policy. Henceforth, the gray areas that had unsettled the lawyers became all-encompassing. There would be no black versus white, legal versus illegal, right versus wrong. It was a policy destined to spawn disaster both from the military and legal perspectives. Rumsfeld had not only circumvented the statutory process of interagency consultation in the legal sphere as in all others.

He had also, intentionally or unintentionally, subverted the elementary premises of military management.

This, then, was the sand on which the Guantanamo operation was precariously built. It was ominously shifting ground on which no person, no code and no precedent could weigh in with authority. It was not just a legal black hole, as it came to be called later. It was also a military black hole, a legally compromised operation whose premise would ultimately come to threaten the integrity of the military and those under its command.

Guantanamo eventually became all of the above: a place for detention, for intelligence, for ill-starred military trials, and for many, a prison in which they were serving indefinite and interminable sentences imposed by no court, not even a military one. Living conditions did not become more tolerable, but less so. Prisoners were isolated, manhandled and abused; harsh interrogations yielded next to nothing but were repeated over and over; prisoners died, some managing to do so by their own devices; communications with families far away were restricted or prohibited; years of unrelieved and endless despair followed one upon the next. Gitmo's purpose, it seemed, was simply to be.

CHAPTER TWO

The First Cases

Rasul v. Bush

This being the United States, the first lawsuit challenging the Guantanamo detentions was filed one day after the detainees arrived. A group
calling itself a "coalition of clergy" went to federal court in Los Angeles,
but the court dismissed the case because the plaintiffs had no standing—
no detainee had authorized them to seek the court's intervention on his
behalf. But a few weeks later, in February 2002, American lawyers representing two British detainees, Shafiq Rasul and Asif Iqbal, and Australian detainee David Hicks, along with twelve Kuwaiti nationals, brought
suit in the federal district court in Washington, D.C. The attorneys had
never spoken to the detainees themselves—the Department of Defense
had prohibited that—but the men's families had authorized them to file
the lawsuit as "next friends," a device that allows a guardian or family
member to initiate litigation when the actual plaintiff is incapable of
giving consent.

All the detainees in the case that came to be known as *Rasul v. Bush*
had been seized in Afghanistan by the Northern Alliance, the local anti-
Taliban forces, or by villagers seeking to collect the prodigious bounties
that the United States was paying for suspected terrorists. They claimed
to have been in Afghanistan for innocent personal reasons or to provide humanitarian aid, and they denied any connection to the Taliban,
terrorism, or anti-American actions. The British and Australian captives sought an order that they be released and allowed to go home; the
Kuwaitis, aiming at a perhaps more attainable outcome, sought permission for their families to visit them at Guantanamo.

The case was assigned by lot to Judge Colleen Kollar-Kotelly, a fifty-eight-year old jurist who had been a lawyer in the Justice Department's Criminal Division and then for thirteen years a judge on the District of Columbia's local trial court before being appointed by President Bill Clinton to the federal bench in 1997. The Department of Justice's litigators had not been part of the war council's formulation of policy, and their initial response, in those early days, was one that would not be heard again in any of the Guantanamo cases. It acknowledged that the detainees "fall within the protections of certain provisions of international law," but that the proper channel for vindicating those protections was diplomatic negotiations between the United States and their home countries, not resort to the courts. Indeed, Australian officials had already been granted access to Hicks. In her eventual order, Judge Kollar-Kotelly reassuringly noted that "the notion that these aliens could be held incommunicado from the rest of the world would appear to be inaccurate." Nonetheless, she put aside considerations of diplomacy and proceeded directly to the question of whether her court had jurisdiction to consider the claims of the detainees and to rule whether they were entitled to be released, or at least have access to their families.

Jurisdiction—in this sense, a court's lawful authority to hear and decide a case brought before it—is a big deal for federal courts. The Constitution limits their jurisdiction to cases "arising under" the Constitution, laws, or treaties of the United States; cases between citizens of different states; cases in which the United States is a party; and a few lesser categories. Even the Supreme Court's appellate jurisdiction is made subject to "such Exceptions, and under such Regulations as the Congress shall make." As to the "inferior Courts," the Constitution, with what may seem a dismissive wave, provides only that "Congress may from time to time ordain and establish" them. These "inferior" courts—the federal district courts that sit in each state to hear cases in the first instance, and the twelve regional courts of appeals that sit over them—must therefore satisfy themselves in each case that Congress has given them authority to hear and decide the type of case that the litigant brings. For example, though the Constitution extends the federal judicial power to suits between citizens of different states, Congress has long specified that there must be a minimum "amount in controversy" (currently $75,000) to qualify; otherwise the litigants are relegated to state courts. The power of Congress to regulate federal court jurisdiction is no small matter. What Congress gives, it believes it can take away, and Congress was to do that, or at least try to, three years later in the contentious Detainee Treatment Act, meant to nullify the authority of federal courts to hear cases like those in Judge Kollar-Kotelly's courtroom.

But for now, Judge Kollar-Kotelly's first order of business was to determine if her court had jurisdiction over the detainees' lawsuit. The detainees brought their suits by filing what are known as petitions for habeas corpus. Habeas, in legal shorthand, is the constitutionally guaranteed right to go before a federal court to seek a ruling that one is being unlawfully confined and must be released. In 2002, the authority of federal courts to summon the petitioner's federal jailer to explain the reason for a petitioner's confinement, and to order his release if the confinement was unlawful, was not in question—at least if the petitioner was being held in the United States. Therein lay a problem for the detainees.

In 1950, in the case of *Johnson v. Eisentrager*, German army officers, convicted after the war of crimes by a US military commission and imprisoned in US-occupied Germany, sought habeas review of their case in the federal court in the District of Columbia. (As more fully described in chapter 5, a military commission is an ad hoc panel of officers convened as needed to conduct a criminal trial, usually of enemy soldiers or civilians in occupied areas, and to render a verdict and punishment.) In an opinion written by Justice Robert H. Jackson, just returned to the Supreme Court after a year as chief US prosecutor of Nazi war criminals at the International Military Tribunal at Nuremberg, the Court denied their petition. It ruled that while aliens in the United States certainly had the protection of US courts, the German enemy aliens, who were not in the United States, did not. "These prisoners," Jackson wrote for the Court, "at no relevant time were within any territory over which the United States is sovereign, and the scenes of their offense, their capture, their trial and their punishment were all beyond the territorial jurisdiction of any court of the United States."

Faced with this precedent, the detainees here pointed out that they were not enemy aliens but British, Australian, and Kuwaiti citizens. Judge Kollar-Kotelly held that distinction irrelevant for jurisdictional purposes. An individual seeking habeas relief must have either "status or situs," she concluded—status as a US citizen or presence in US sovereign territory.

Because the detainees did not have status, Judge Kollar-Kotelly faced the question of what the *Eisentrager* Court had meant by "territory over which the United States is sovereign." The detainees were being held on a US naval base, but the base was in Cuba, which is assuredly not US sovereign territory. The government argued that the petitioners lacked situs as well as status; no courthouse door was open to them, and their habeas case should be dismissed.

But at Gitmo, things were not that simple. In the 1903 lease, Cuba had allowed the United States to build a naval facility there and to operate it for as long as it liked. The lease stated, with studied ambiguity, "While on the one hand the United States recognizes the continuance of the ultimate sovereignty of the Republic of Cuba over [the facility], on the other hand the Republic of Cuba consents that during the period of occupation by the United States of said areas under the terms of this agreement the United States shall exercise complete jurisdiction and control over and within" it. And for a hundred years, and especially for the four decades of Communist rule, the United States had done just that, operating the base as a free-standing American outpost, without any oversight by the host government that was routine in US military bases on foreign soil. Considering that under the still-valid lease the United States did indeed exercise "complete jurisdiction and control," the detainees argued that the base was under the *de facto* sovereignty of the United States and thus its physical location was no bar to the relief they sought. In *Eisentrager*'s words, they had situs.

In international law, "ultimate sovereignty" and "*de facto* sovereignty" are unfamiliar terms, and Kollar-Kotelly resolved this arcane if critical issue in the government's favor; she could find no precedent that would allow her court to exercise jurisdiction on the basis of some imprecise *de facto* sovereignty. She dismissed the case, leaving the detainees' "protections of certain provisions of international law," whatever the Justice Department had meant by that, to be settled through diplomacy. But by the time of her decision—July 30, 2002, some five months after the case had been filed—much had happened at Gitmo, and the Bush administration had no intention of engaging in negotiations with any government over the rights of detainees. Its position had hardened: they had no rights. None whatever. Under the president's February order, they were not even prisoners of war.

The detainees' lawyers appealed their defeat to the US Court of Appeals for the District of Columbia Circuit, the federal appellate court in the nation's capital that is often called the second-most important federal court in the nation, given its jurisdiction over actions of high government officials. Once regarded also as the second-most liberal court in the nation, its decisions on criminal procedure and civil rights had frequently presaged similar rulings from the Supreme Court under Chief Justice Earl Warren in the 1950s and 1960s, but by 2002 the DC Circuit had become a markedly more conservative tribunal. In that court over the ensuing decade, Gitmo detainees were to encounter nearly unbending hostility to their habeas claims.

On March 11, 2003, the three judges of the court of appeals assigned to hear the appeal rejected the detainees' claims for the same reasons Judge Kollar-Kotelly had. Acknowledging that the detainees were not "enemy" aliens, the court nonetheless ruled that no aliens outside the sovereign territory of the United States had any rights under the Constitution. As in *Eisentrager*, the Gitmo detainees "too are aliens, they too were captured during military operations, they were in a foreign country when captured, they are now abroad, they are in the custody of the American military, and they have never had any presence in the United States." Therefore, "we believe that under *Eisentrager* these factors preclude the detainees from seeking habeas relief in the courts of the United States."

The detainees' attorneys could not have been terribly surprised. They began their preparations to ask the Supreme Court to take up the case.

Hamdi v. Rumsfeld

In the meantime, however, a quite different habeas case was working its way through the courts. Yaser Esam Hamdi had been born in Louisiana, the son of two Saudi Arabian nationals in the oil business. The family returned home when Hamdi was a toddler, but the Fourteenth Amendment provides that all persons born in the United States are citizens, and so Hamdi was. In late 2001, he was scooped up like many others in Afghanistan, deemed an enemy combatant by US forces, and soon dispatched to Guantanamo. But Guantanamo was for aliens only, and when Hamdi's birthplace became known in April 2002, he was, alone among all Gitmo detainees, transferred to the United States, to the naval base in Norfolk, Virginia, for further interrogation. When Frank Dunham, the federal public defender in Norfolk, learned of Hamdi's presence, he promptly filed a habeas petition, seeking access to his would-be client.

The Justice Department immediately opposed the action, but it acknowledged, as it had to, that the court had jurisdiction to examine the confinement of this US citizen in Virginia. In *Eisentrager*'s terms, Hamdi had both status and situs, so the issues of sovereignty and alienage that had led Judge Kollar-Kotelly to derail the petitions in *Rasul* were no bar to Hamdi. And federal judge Robert G. Doumar saw the case for what it was. "This case appears to be the first in American jurisprudence where an American citizen has been held incommunicado and subjected to an indefinite detention in the continental United States without charges, without any findings by a military tribunal, and without access to a lawyer," he wrote. On June 11, 2002, he ordered the government to give Dunham unimpeded and unmonitored access to Hamdi in his cell.

It was a startling order from a judge who might have been thought unlikely to be sympathetic to an enemy combatant challenging the Bush administration. The seventy-two-year-old son of Lebanese and Syrian immigrants, Doumar had been born, raised, and educated in Virginia and after a two-year stint in the army had practiced law in Norfolk while running unsuccessfully for state office as a Republican and serving as a Virginia delegate to three national Republican presidential conventions. President Reagan appointed him a federal judge in 1981.

The Justice Department, alarmed at the order of a federal judge allowing an enemy combatant under interrogation to confer with a criminal defense lawyer, quickly obtained a stay of Doumar's order from the US Court of Appeals for the Fourth Circuit in Richmond. With Dunham enjoined, for the time being, from any contact with Hamdi, the court of appeals took the case under advisement, and on July 12, 2002, handed down its decision. The court addressed issues more momentous than the fate of one man in a naval brig: could the president order an American citizen to be confined indefinitely without trial? Must federal courts, in the interests of national security, yield to the president?

This case, the court of appeals began, "arises in the context of foreign relations and national security, where a court's deference to the political branches of our national government is considerable." Quoting a 1936 Supreme Court decision, the court noted "it is the President who wields 'delicate, plenary and exclusive power as the sole organ of the federal government in the field of international relations.'" That power, the court went on, certainly extends to military affairs, where Congress and the president—the "political branches" of the government—share responsibility. In World War II, the Supreme Court had "stated in no uncertain terms that the President's wartime detention decisions are to be accorded great deference from the courts"—true enough, though the court was citing the Supreme Court's since-discredited decision upholding the confinement of Japanese-Americans in fenced and remote "relocation camps." Here, the appeals court said, Judge Doumar had paid little if any attention to these "cardinal principles of constitutional text and practice" and had not given "proper weight to national security concerns."

Nonetheless, the court said, it would not, at least at this stage, grant the government's motion to throw out Hamdi's case. "In dismissing, we ourselves would be summarily embracing a sweeping proposition— namely that, with no meaningful judicial review, any American citizen alleged to be an enemy combatant could be detained indefinitely without charges or counsel on the government's say-so." But any judicial review, the court cautioned, "must reflect a recognition that government has no more profound responsibility than the protection of Americans, both military and civilian, against additional unprovoked attack." The appeals court resolved its uncertainty by giving Judge Doumar another chance, sending the case back to him to hear more evidence and to give more careful deference to Executive authority, as well as a more measured balancing between the government's interests in national security and an American citizen's interests in his liberty.

It was a temperate disposition, the court clearly pained at Judge Doumar's hasty tipping of the scales in Hamdi's favor, and unwilling to let him overturn decisions of the president and Congress without a more thoughtful resolution of the inherent conflict between national security and personal liberty. Yet the court was also careful not to itself rush to reverse Doumar's order, mindful that in a time of national peril courts act dangerously when they act precipitously.

Judge Doumar, duly chastened, did conduct further hearings in August 2002, ordering the government to submit evidence justifying Hamdi's continued detention. In response, Justice Department lawyers produced an affidavit from one Michael Mobbs, identified as "Special Adviser to the Undersecretary of Defense for Policy." Mobbs did not appear at the hearing; his affidavit stated that Hamdi was "affiliated with a Taliban military unit and received weapons training"; that upon capture in Afghanistan he admitted that "he entered Afghanistan the previous summer [2001] to train with and, if necessary, fight for the Taliban"; and that he was found to meet the "criteria" for enemy combatants who should be sent to Guantanamo, though the affidavit did not say what those criteria were.

The statement did not impress Judge Doumar, who by now was openly suspicious of the government's case, despite the higher court's warning. "It leads to more questions than it answers," he wrote. Who was Mobbs? What authority did he have, and where did he get his information? What does "affiliation" with the Taliban mean, since there was no assertion that Hamdi was actually fighting for the Taliban? What are the "criteria" by which he was found to be an enemy combatant, and by which he was sent to Gitmo? The declaration "is little more than the government's 'say-so'" asserting the validity of Hamdi's detention, Judge Doumar said, and accepting it as justification for the government's actions would be "abdicating any semblance of the most minimal level of judicial review. In effect, this Court would be acting as little more than a rubber-stamp."

Beyond his judicial pique at not being given the information he needed to make a decision, Judge Doumar, for the first time in the Guantanamo cases, raised a point that was to prove important not only in Hamdi's case but in others. The Third Geneva Convention, requiring that humane treatment—including freedom from involuntary interrogation and other forms of coercion—be accorded to prisoners of war, specifies that any captive whose entitlement to POW status is unclear "shall enjoy the protection of the present Convention until such time as their status has been determined by a competent tribunal." Captives ineligible for POW status might include, for example, civilians taking up arms, or a freelance fighter beyond military control.

The Convention does not detail what a "competent tribunal" might consist of, but the Department of Defense, to comply with the requirement, had without much fuss set up panels of military officers during the Vietnam War of the 1960s and 1970s to sort out POWs from other captives. In 1997, the DoD had issued detailed regulations for the handling of detainees. Formally known as Army Regulation 190-8, "Enemy Prisoners of War, Retained Personnel, Civilian Internees and Other Detainees," the regulations mandate that a panel of three US military officers hear and consider the matter of any combatant "who asserts that he or she is entitled to treatment as a prisoner of war, or concerning whom any doubt of a like nature exists." It is an impressively formal process, requiring that members of the panel be sworn, that a written record of proceedings be kept, that the captive be allowed to address the panel and call "reasonably available" witnesses on his behalf, and that the panel members, after deliberating in secret, issue a written decision. No such tribunal had been established for Hamdi, or anyone captured in Afghanistan or sent to Guantanamo.

In light of this omission—which would have created a factual record of Hamdi's capture and alleged "affiliation" with the Taliban in a process in which he himself would have participated—Doumar ordered the government to provide him the information he said he needed to engage in the delicate balancing act mandated by the court of appeals. It was quite a list: copies of Hamdi's statements to interrogators upon his capture, their identities and their notes, the "screening criteria" by which Hamdi had been classified as an enemy combatant, the names of US government officials who had ordered his detention, even "statements by members of the Northern Alliance regarding the circumstances" of Hamdi's capture in Afghanistan.

Alarmed anew at this judicial intervention in battlefield matters, the Justice Department went again to the court of appeals for relief. By this time, in the summer of 2002, it was clear that Hamdi's case had become a judicial confrontation between an administration intent on maintaining control over enemy combatants and civil libertarians opposing what they saw as unlawful, indeed unconstitutional, attacks on the rights of

American citizens. Amicus curiae briefs on both sides were filed by activists and interest groups seeking to persuade the court. To signify the importance of the case, Paul Clement, the US deputy solicitor general, who normally appears only before the Supreme Court, came to Richmond to argue the case; Dunham appeared again for Hamdi.

The court of appeals heard oral argument in October 2002 and issued a carefully worded seventeen-page opinion on January 8, 2003, dismissing the case. The court acknowledged the difficulty it faced in wrestling with "complex and serious national security issues" under the Constitution's separation of powers: balancing the demands of national security against the deprivation of a citizen's liberty; measuring the scope of presidential and congressional authority against the limits of judicial authority to review those decisions; appraising the basis and the reasons for the government's actions against this citizen in light of constitutional restraints on imprisonment without due process of law; and, throughout its opinion, trying to set rules on what evidence the government had to produce to justify the detention of a citizen, and how broadly a court could probe that evidence—all this in the context of unprecedented events, in almost wholly uncharted legal territory.

The three-judge panel assigned to hear the case, led by chief judge J. Harvie Wilkinson, did its best to articulate the proper balance of these elusive concerns. It began with a discourse comparing the war powers of the two political branches. Under the Constitution, the president is commander in chief of the armed forces, but that authority is not absolute. The Constitution gives Congress the authority to "provide for the common Defence," to "declare War," to "raise and support Armies," and to "make Rules for the Government and Regulation of the land and naval Forces," including, significantly here, "Rules concerning Captures on Land and Water."

The Constitution says nothing about the role of judges in such matters, and these judges cautioned that "the executive and legislative branches are organized to supervise the conduct of overseas conflict in a way that the judiciary simply is not. The Constitution's allocation of the warmaking powers reflects not only the expertise and experience lodged within the executive, but also the more fundamental truth that those branches most accountable to the people should be the ones to undertake the ultimate protection and to ask the ultimate sacrifice from them."

Thus, courts are to give "great deference to the political branches when called upon to decide cases implicating sensitive matters of foreign policy, national security, or military affairs," not only because this separation of powers is ordained by the Constitution, but because it "promotes a more profound understanding of our rights. For the judicial branch to trespass upon the exercise of the warmaking powers would be an infringement of the right to self-determination and self-governance at a time when the care of the common defense is most critical."

At the same time, the court cautioned, "judicial deference to executive decisions made in the name of war is not unlimited. Drawing on the Bill of Rights' historic guarantees, the judiciary plays its distinctive role in our constitutional structure when it reviews the detention of American citizens by their own government." And this "distinctive role," the court was careful to note, is just as important as the roles of the other two branches. "The Constitution is suffused with concern about how the state will wield its awesome power of forcible restraint. And this preoccupation was not accidental. Our forbears recognized that the power to detain could easily become destructive"—and here the judges turned to the eighteenth-century English jurist William Blackstone—"'if exerted without check or control' by an unrestrained executive free to 'imprison, dispatch, or exile any man that was obnoxious to the government, by an instant declaration that such is their will and pleasure.'" The judicial duty, the judges wrote, is "to protect our individual freedoms," and that duty "does not simply cease whenever our military forces are committed by the political branches to armed conflict."

Because President Bush's designation of Hamdi as an enemy combatant "bears the closest imaginable connection to the President's constitutional responsibility during the actual conduct of hostilities," and because Congress, for its part, had in the Authorization for the Use of Military Force allowed the president to use "all necessary and appropriate force" in response to the 9/11 attacks, the court was framing the conflict before it not so much as between Congress and the president as between the judiciary and the two political branches—a conflict implicating "both the fundamental liberty interest asserted by Hamdi and the extraordinary breadth of warmaking authority conferred by the Constitution and invoked by Congress and the executive branch."

So the issue was joined: how was a court to exercise its undoubted authority to review the legality of the deprivation of an American citizen's liberty—and by executive order, no less—against the broad if sometimes overlapping responsibility of the president and Congress for military affairs, foreign relations, and national security?

The appeals court came down on the side of the political branches, its conclusion decisively influenced by the extraordinarily searching and specific questions that Judge Doumar had ordered the government to answer. That order "could not be more serious," said this court. It would have the government disclose the names of Hamdi's interrogators and the statements he had made to them, the decision-making process that had led to his classification as an enemy combatant and his transfer to Guantanamo and thence to Virginia, and the criteria by which those decisions had been made, and by whom. "The basic question in this case," said the court, was whether such judicial "exploration" would trespass on the powers of the president and Congress. The court had no doubt that it would.

> The risk created by [Judge Doumar's] order is that judicial involvement would proceed, increment by increment, into an area where the political branches have been assigned by law a preeminent role. Litigation cannot be the driving force in effectuating and recording wartime detentions. In demanding such detail the district court would have the United States military instruct not only its own personnel, but also its allies, on precise observations they must make and record during a battlefield capture.

To do so "might require an excavation of facts buried under the rubble of war. The cost of such an inquiry in terms of the efficiency and morale of American forces cannot be disregarded. And these efforts would profoundly unsettle the constitutional balance." The judicial exploration of Hamdi's capture ordered by the district court therefore "cannot stand."

The court had also to meet another argument raised by the public defender: that Hamdi had not been given the "competent tribunal" required by the Third Geneva Convention, and implemented by Army Regulation 190-8 described above, to determine whether he was a prisoner of war and thus entitled by Geneva to be free of unwanted interrogation in the military jail where he had been confined incommunicado for months. Here the calculus changed. Such a tribunal, whose members would presumably inquire into a captive's actions on (or off) the battlefield and the reasons for his detention, and whose decision would determine his treatment as a detainee, would not raise concerns over the separation of powers, because the Convention was a treaty ratified by Congress, specifically authorizing the types of factual inquiries that the court of appeals had held were improper for a federal court to pursue, given its limited constitutional powers and the deference it owed to presidential and congressional warmaking authority. The Geneva Conventions *were* that authority, or more accurately constraints on that authority, constraints that the president and Congress had accepted by ratifying the Convention. The issue thus was straightforward—was the Defense Department in Hamdi's case following the rules that the president and the Congress had imposed? Indeed, was it following its own regulations? In reviewing the actions of government agencies, federal courts routinely decide such questions.

But the court avoided that decision. It ruled that the Geneva Conventions, like many treaties ratified by Congress, were not "self-executing," that is, they did not by themselves confer any rights, even on those whom they were designed to protect. It may seem anomalous that a duly ratified treaty, which under Article VI of the Constitution "shall be the supreme Law of the Land," should be so easily avoided. In many other democracies the question would not even arise. But it is a tenet of American law that a treaty is a binding agreement between or among nations, not a bestowal of rights on individuals. Such rights can only be created if Congress enacts laws that implement the treaty, and Congress had not done so for the Geneva Conventions, at least not for the "competent tribunal" provision at issue here.

The court made no mention of the Defense Department regulations that set forth procedures for such tribunals. Because Defense had issued those regulations in order to fulfill the obligations imposed by the Geneva Convention, the regulations would seem to be the very implementation of Geneva that the court found lacking. The government had summarily dismissed that claim in its brief, arguing that the regulations applied only in cases where the detainee's status was in doubt, and here the president's order of February 7, 2002, had categorically removed any doubt about POW status for the Taliban by denying it to all of them because they were unlawful combatants to begin with. No doubt, no tribunal. By its silence on the point, the appeals court upheld the government's position by default.

More than a year after he had been taken into custody in Afghanistan, Yaser Hamdi remained in his cell in Norfolk. He had communicated with no one outside the walls of his jail, and likely did not even know that his father had initiated the suit on his behalf, and that a public defender had vigorously pursued it, and would continue to do so.

By the spring of 2003, then, the government had prevailed in both of the appellate decisions testing its determination to insulate the detainees from judicial review. The Court of Appeals for the District of Columbia had ruled that aliens outside the United States had no right to go to US courts, and the Court of Appeals for the Fourth Circuit had ruled that courts must defer to presidential authority even for citizens confined as enemy combatants within the United States. But its winning record was not to last.

————

Padilla v. Rumsfeld

As the lawsuits of fifteen detainees at Guantanamo and a single detainee in Virginia made their way through two federal appellate courts, a third case that like the others would eventually reach the Supreme Court was also forming, gathering speed and strength, and heading toward landfall in Washington. Jose Padilla was the eye of what was potentially a cataclysmic storm.

Like Hamdi, Padilla was an American citizen, but not a fortuitous one. Born in New York, he had spent his life in the United States, including a jail term for homicide as a juvenile in Chicago. More significantly, he was no rifle-toting Taliban foot soldier. In 2001, according to the government's allegations, he traveled to Afghanistan and met with Abu Zubaydeh, one of Osama Bin Laden's confidants, and proposed a scheme to steal radioactive material and build a "dirty bomb" to be detonated in the United States. Just how Padilla gained the expertise to make nuclear weapons was not disclosed, but at Abu Zubaydeh's request he met with "al Qaeda officials" in Pakistan to discuss his ideas, and after "extended contacts with senior Al Qaeda members and operatives" was sent to the United States "to conduct reconnaissance and/or conduct other attacks on [al Qaeda's] behalf," according to an affidavit from Michael Mobbs, the same government official who had written up the case against Hamdi. On May 8, 2002, he flew from Pakistan to Chicago. When he got off the plane at O'Hare International Airport, the FBI arrested him.

He was not then charged with being an enemy combatant; his arrest was on a "material witness" warrant in connection with a federal investigation in New York into the 9/11 attacks, the FBI apparently believing that he knew something about those attacks or at least about those who had ordered them. He was flown to New York and put in a holding cell, a lawyer was routinely appointed for him, and he met with her at least twice. But soon thereafter President Bush designated Padilla an enemy combatant. The president's order stated that Padilla had engaged in terrorism against the United States, had intelligence about al Qaeda, and presented "a continuing, present and grave danger" to national security. Defense Department officers immediately took Padilla from Justice Department custody and locked him in the brig at the US naval base in Charleston, South Carolina.

At a press conference a few days later, Secretary Rumsfeld announced Padilla's arrest, describing it as a key step in US efforts to foil a dirty-bomb plot. Padilla, said Rumsfeld, "unambiguously was interested in radiation weapons and terrorist activity, and was in league with al Qaeda." The government had arrested him "to do everything possible" in order to "find out everything he knows so that hopefully we can stop other terrorist acts."

Padilla was not an enemy combatant in any conventional military sense—he was, by the government's reckoning, a conspirator in a terrorist plot—but if his arrest expanded the category of enemy combatants, it also escalated the alarm of those who saw the "global war on terrorism" as a growing and brazen assertion of unchecked and lawless government power. Padilla had not been captured on some Afghanistan battlefield, but in the middle of the United States, and he was being held by the military, with no further resort to a lawyer or to members of his family. For many who had grown apprehensive at the scope of the government's war on terrorism, Padilla's arrest was an ominous escalation of that war. There now seemed to be no barrier to any American being seized anywhere in the country by presidential decree and clapped into a military jail for indefinite detention and interrogation, with no charge, no trial, no lawyer, no judicial oversight, and no communication with the outside world.

Donna Newman, the New York lawyer appointed to represent Padilla in the material-witness matter, could have considered her representation of him over when he was taken away to South Carolina. But she did not. On June 11, 2002, two days after Padilla's departure, Newman, a New York City English teacher who had enrolled in a local law school at age thirty-five and had hung out her shingle as a solo criminal defense lawyer in 1991, filed a habeas corpus petition on Padilla's behalf in federal court in New York. The case was assigned to Chief Judge Michael Mukasey.

At first glance, Mukasey might have appeared to be as unpromising a draw for Padilla as Judge Doumar had appeared to be for Hamdi. The sixty-one-year-old son of Russian immigrants, Mukasey had attended Orthodox Jewish schools in New York City and had graduated from Columbia and Yale Law School; after twenty years of corporate law practice, he became a federal prosecutor in 1976. There he formed an enduring personal and professional relationship with then–US Attorney Rudolph Giuliani, who gained national prominence as the mayor of New York City on 9/11. Mukasey was appointed a federal judge by President Reagan in 1988 and presided over the 1995 prosecution of Omar Abdel Rahman—known as the "Blind Sheik"—and other Islamic terrorists in a plot to blow up the United Nations building and the George Washington Bridge, for which Judge Mukasey sentenced them to life imprisonment. (In 2007, President Bush would choose Mukasey as Attorney General of the United States.)

Like Yaser Hamdi, Jose Padilla clearly had the right, as an American citizen jailed in the United States, to seek habeas relief from a federal court. But the Justice Department vigorously opposed Padilla's habeas petition on jurisdictional grounds—it argued that because Padilla was confined in South Carolina, any habeas case must be heard there, not in New York. But Mukasey disagreed, ruling that his court could properly proceed because it had jurisdiction over Secretary Rumsfeld, who had personally ordered that Padilla be removed from New York, and by whose authority Padilla remained in federal custody. With that out of the way, Mukasey moved to the central issue—whether Padilla was being lawfully detained.

He had little difficulty ruling, first, that the president had authority to order the detention of unlawful enemy combatants, an authority that was undiminished simply because the combatant was an American citizen, even one apprehended on American soil. He relied on the 1942 decision of the Supreme Court in *Ex parte Quirin*, which had upheld the authority of the president to order a military commission trial for a squad of German soldiers, including one born in the United States, after they traveled across the ocean in a German submarine and came ashore on New York's Long Island with intent to disrupt American munitions plants. They were in civilian clothes—a violation of the law of war—and were soon captured when one of them turned himself in to the FBI. So clearly, Mukasey reasoned, American citizenship was no bar to presidential authority over enemy combatants.

But Mukasey went on to rule that, once captured and detained, Padilla was entitled to "challenge the government's naked legal right to hold him as an unlawful combatant on any set of facts whatsoever"— that is, he could come into court to present evidence that he was not in fact an unlawful combatant and thus the president had no lawful authority to summarily capture and detain him. "Quite plainly," said the judge, "Congress intended that a [habeas corpus] petitioner would be able to place facts, and issues of fact, before the reviewing court, and it would frustrate the purpose of [habeas corpus] to prevent him from doing so."

Equally plainly, Mukasey ruled, the "interests of justice" could not be served unless Padilla had legal counsel to present his case that he was no enemy combatant. To the consternation of the government, Mukasey ordered that attorney Newman be allowed to meet her client, in South Carolina, and to represent him at a hearing at which Judge Mukasey could decide whether the evidence justified the government in holding him.

Mukasey had a cautionary note for Padilla and Newman, however. The government would not be required to prove Padilla's unlawful enemy status beyond a reasonable doubt, nor even by the usual preponderance of the evidence standard applicable in other civil proceedings. Rather, giving deference to the president's "controlling political authority" to detain combatants, Mukasey would require the government only to present "some evidence" to prove that Padilla was in fact an enemy combatant, and that, once Padilla's own evidence was considered, the government's "some evidence" might still be enough to justify indefinite detention.

That last point was not particularly welcome news to Padilla—in effect, the judge was saying he might score more points than the government but still lose. And if the government's points were enough, the court would not entertain further argument as to the scope of presidential authority. Padilla had won the first battle—Mukasey had upheld his right to consult his lawyer and have his day in court—but Mukasey's lengthy decision suggests that he probably did not expect Padilla to actually overcome the government's case laid out in the Mobbs affidavit. Padilla would have his hearing because he was entitled to due process of law, but that did not mean that he would win his freedom. Not yet, anyway. That question would await Mukasey's examination of the evidence against him.

But the government had no intention of seeing Padilla in court. The Justice Department asked Mukasey to reconsider his decision, submitting an affidavit from the head of the Defense Intelligence Agency claiming that effective intelligence interrogation required that the interrogators build an atmosphere of trust and confidence with the subject (an ironic assertion, considering how detainees at Guantanamo were then being interrogated), and that meetings with lawyers and hearings in court would frustrate that process. Padilla would stop talking if he thought that help from lawyers and judges might be on the way.

Mukasey didn't buy it; in fact, he turned the argument back against the government, pointing out that Padilla, a veteran of the American criminal process, might even now be holding out hope for a lawyer's intervention, and that a defeat in court, should it come to that after all the evidence was in, might be just the thing that would lead him to give up that hope and cooperate with the government. But Mukasey agreed to stay his order for further proceedings and a visit by attorney Newman, to allow the government to seek review by higher authority.

The Justice Department took an appeal to the US Court of Appeals for the Second Circuit, which oversees the federal courts in New York, the third of the three appeals courts that would rule on the rights of detainees against the powers of the government. It became the first appeals court to hand the president a sharp defeat.

After extensive briefing, including thirteen amicus curiae briefs from academics and former judges, all supporting Padilla's case (and one amicus brief opposing it), the Second Circuit handed down its decision on December 18, 2003, a full year after Mukasey's decision and eighteen months into Padilla's confinement. It began by reminding everyone—and particularly, it would seem, the president whose policies it was about to reject—that it needed no reminder of the seriousness of the issues.

> As this Court sits only a short distance from where the World Trade Center once stood, we are as keenly aware as anyone of the threat al Qaeda poses to our country and of the responsibilities the President and law enforcement officials bear for protecting the nation. But presidential authority does not exist in a vacuum, and this case involves not whether those responsibilities should be aggressively pursued, but whether the President is obligated, in the circumstances presented here, to share them with Congress.

The question of what responsibilities a president might be obligated to "share with Congress" goes to the heart of the separation of powers ordained by the Constitution. The modern statement of that doctrine was articulated by the Supreme Court in 1952, in *Youngstown Sheet & Tube Co. v. Sawyer*, in which the Court had invalidated President Truman's seizure of steel mills during the Korean war to avert a strike and to keep them operating under government control. The Court had rejected the administration's claim that the seizure was a valid exercise of the president's wartime powers as commander in chief, ruling that those powers were not broad enough to seize American businesses, nor was there any other presidential authority to be found in the Constitution. Equally important, no such power had been delegated to the president by Congress in the exercise of its own constitutional powers. Therefore the power to seize the steel mills did not exist, because there is no source of presidential power other than the Constitution and congressional action.

Justice Jackson's opinion in *Youngstown* had laid out the calculus neatly. When the president acts with the authorization of Congress, "his authority is at its maximum, for it includes all that he possesses in his own right plus all that Congress can delegate." When he acts in the face of congressional silence, however, "he can only rely on his own independent powers, but there is a zone of twilight in which he and Congress may have concurrent authority, or in which its distribution is uncertain." But when the president acts in ways that are incompatible with the will of Congress, express or implied, then "his power is at its lowest ebb, for then he can rely only upon his own constitutional powers minus any constitutional powers of Congress over the matter."

The seizure of the mills was in the third category, and so, Justice Jackson wrote, the Supreme Court "can sustain the President only by holding that seizure of such strike-bound industries is within his domain and beyond control by Congress," but those circumstances "leave Presidential power most vulnerable to attack and in the least favorable of possible constitutional postures," and not enough to sustain the seizure.

Guided by *Youngstown*'s calculus, the court of appeals in Padilla's case first rejected the government's argument that the president had authority enough on his own, as commander in chief, to detain Padilla. That might be true in the sphere of foreign policy and actions taken abroad, the court acknowledged, but Justice Jackson's opinion in *Youngstown* had made clear that different concerns are in play when the action takes place at home. "Thus," said the appeals court, "we do not concern ourselves with the Executive's inherent wartime power, generally, to detain enemy combatants on the battlefield. Rather, we are called on to decide whether the Constitution gives the President the power to detain an American citizen seized in this country until the war with al Qaeda ends."

The court concluded that it did not. The Constitution gives Congress, not the president, the authority to define and punish offenses in violation of international law; the authority to suspend the availability of habeas corpus; and—a surprising point here—the authority to legislate exceptions to the Third Amendment's prohibition against quartering troops in private homes. That was enough, said the court, to establish that the president's power by itself was not enough to justify Padilla's detention. The court made clear that its analysis was limited to domestic arrests and had no applicability to detainees captured on a foreign battlefield, for there presidential authority would be paramount.

If the president did not have that authority on his own, then the next question under *Youngstown* was whether Congress delegated any of its power to him—power that would, in Justice Jackson's words, put the president's authority at its maximum. The government had what seemed to be a ready and dispositive answer here: the Authorization for the Use of Military Force, the resolution enacted nearly unanimously by Congress a few days after September 11, authorized the President to use "all necessary force" against those who had brought about, or assisted, the 9/11 attacks, or those who had protected them afterwards.

But the court turned first to another congressional act: a one-sentence law enacted in 1971: "No citizen shall be imprisoned or otherwise detained by the United States except pursuant to an Act of Congress." This Non-Detention Act, as it was known, was meant to prevent a repeat of the shameful executive decision during World War II to remove Japanese-American citizens to detention camps—a significant event in this case, centered on a president's assertion of authority to imprison alleged enemy combatants. The clear statement of congressional authority in the Non-Detention Act, the court said, could be overridden only by "precise and specific language authorizing the detention of American citizens" in the war on terror. But the court found no such language in Congress's Authorization for the Use of Military Force. "While it may be possible to infer a power of detention from the [AUMF] in the battlefield context where detentions are necessary to carry out the war, there is no reason to suspect from the language of the [AUMF] that Congress believed it would be authorizing the detention of an American citizen" who was never on the battlefield against American forces.

Thus, in the *Youngstown* framework, the president had neither the authority from the Constitution to detain Padilla, nor had Congress delegated to him whatever authority it had, and that was the end of the matter. The court ordered Padilla to be released within thirty days, unless in the meantime the government chose to bring criminal charges against him, or hold him on the original material-witness warrant. It could do either, but "in any case, Padilla will be entitled to the constitutional protections extended to other citizens" in those circumstances.

The government's defeat was complete. Under the court of appeals' ruling, there would be no hearing to weigh Padilla's evidence against the government's, because the president simply had no authority to confine him without charges, whatever the evidence. If the government wanted to proceed against him for his alleged activities for al Qaeda, it could charge him with conspiracy, or whatever other crimes he might have committed, and he could stand trial like any other accused criminal in federal court, with all the constitutional protections—presumption of innocence, assistance of counsel, the right against self-incrimination and involuntary confessions, speedy and public jury trial and the rest—that any defendant would receive. Or it could hold him, for a while, as a material witness, with the right to counsel and the right to remain silent. Otherwise, thirty days and he was gone.

The court's decision, though it relieved those who had vigorously protested the seizure of an American citizen in Chicago, rested on a distinctly slim foundation. The court's reliance on the Third Amendment, of all things, to support in part its conclusion that Congress, too, had constitutional responsibilities for the military was a stretch. The prohibition on quartering soldiers in private homes, surely the most obscure provision of the Bill of Rights, and one for which the majority could not even find a judicial precedent, would seem to say nothing at all, even implicitly, about congressional and presidential authority in the *Youngstown* formulation. And while the court was correct that the AUMF did not explicitly authorize the seizure of enemy combatants in the United States, it was setting a high bar in concluding that only by explicitly doing so could Congress give the president the power to confine Padilla. One might as easily conclude that the AUMF's endorsement of "all appropriate force" did not *except* US seizures, because it had implicitly recognized, as the government repeatedly argued, that in the global war on terror, the battlefield was everywhere.

Except, of course, that a Chicago airport is a far cry from an Afghan battlefield. The judges had rejected a sweeping assertion of unprecedented presidential power—that an American citizen, seized in America, could be clapped in a military prison indefinitely without charge, counsel, or outside communication, and subjected to unrelenting interrogation. Other than in number, its breadth exceeded even the internment of Japanese-Americans and far exceeded what the Third Geneva Convention allows for the interrogation of prisoners of war. Perhaps Padilla was an al Qaeda agent, and if so he could be put on trial for conspiracy, or aiding and abetting terrorism, or other crimes, but the specter of any American citizen being arrested in Chicago and confined at the pleasure of the president—for years, maybe even for life—with no lawyer, no trial, no judge and no jury, doubtless unnerved the judges as it unnerved many Americans.

Contemplating its defeat, the government at that point could at least take some consolation that the court of appeals had explicitly confined its decision to domestic seizures, and in fact had noted its agreement with the court of appeals' decision in Hamdi's case upholding presidential authority over combatants captured on foreign battlefields. Hamdi, like Padilla, was an American citizen confined in America, and so the only distinction between the two was the locale of the arrest. Padilla was, at that point, the only American who had been captured in this country and confined as an enemy combatant. So he was the only person affected by the court's ruling, at least as matters then stood. And the Bush administration could always ask Congress to amend its Authorization for the Use of Military Force to specifically include such confinement. That would overturn the court of appeals' rationale and perhaps the ruling itself. But it certainly would also create a contentious and emotional public debate over the powers of the president and the rights of American citizens, a debate the administration had no assurance of winning.

But Congress was not the only resort the government had.

CHAPTER THREE

The Supreme Court

The massive marble home of the Supreme Court of the United States was built between 1932 and 1935. Chief Justice William Howard Taft wanted "a building of dignity and importance," and he got it. (Justice Harlan Fiske Stone was less impressed: "almost bombastically pretentious," he grumbled when it was completed.) With its landscaped grounds, it occupies a city block on Capitol Hill, facing the east entry to the Capitol itself across the street. One approaches the building across a broad marble plaza and up long marble stairs, into the shadows of sixteen Corinthian columns supporting a pediment that proclaims the Constitution's promise of EQUAL JUSTICE UNDER LAW. Tall bronze doors open to more marble inside, as one traverses the Great Hall to the oak doors of the courtroom itself.

At forty-four feet from floor to ceiling, the courtroom at first seems far out of human scale, as any cathedral does. Down the center aisle through rows of pews for visitors, one passes the bar and steps into the arena. The slightly curved mahogany bench sits in front of wine-dark velvet curtains through which, on days of oral argument, the nine justices emerge in their black robes to take their seats in high-backed black leather chairs, several feet higher than the advocates who will come before them. The chief justice sits at the center, the others arranged on either side in order of the seniority of their appointments, the most senior seated at the right hand of the chief, the most junior at the left end of the bench.

In contrast to this imposing grandeur, argument before the Court is often the conversation of earnest discussion. The advocate stands at a lectern with a microphone, but that is for the benefit of visitors; lawyers and justices are close enough to speak to each other without amplification. A long time ago, lawyers could take as much time as they wanted for oral argument, and some went on for a day or more. In 1925, the Court reduced the time to an hour per side; since 1970, each side has been limited to thirty minutes, though the Court sometimes allows more time for complex or multiparty cases. Time limits are firmly enforced. By custom, the Court opens its year on the first Monday in October and concludes it by the end of June.

Notes are allowed, but the Court's rules warn, "Oral argument read from a prepared text is not favored." Indeed, the inexperienced lawyer who comes prepared to deliver an oration will soon be jarred off balance. Supreme Court justices are not a jury but an array of experienced, prepared, and opinionated interrogators. They have read the briefs, the printed 6-by-9-inch pamphlets filed weeks before the argument; their law clerks have written memos analyzing the issues and relevant decisions of the Court, many of which have been written by justices still sitting.

For the lawyers, exhaustive preparation is a given; a thorough knowledge of the proceedings in lower courts and the relevant precedents is essential; and patience is a virtue. The advocate's job is to advance the gist of one's argument while simultaneously fielding the questions tossed, or sometimes thrown high and inside, by the justices. The questions can be pointed, probing, supportive, or skeptical. The experienced advocate will not dodge them, nor put them off with assurances that he or she will get to that point later. The justices can quip to draw laughs from the audience; the advocate had better not dare. Conferring with one's assistants seated at the counsel table is bad form; inept or evasive answers to the justices' questions can be fatal. The questioning can become something of a fencing match among the justices themselves, interrupting the lawyer while precious seconds tick away. It is a truism among Supreme Court advocates that cases are seldom won at oral argument, but they can be lost there.

Nobody, not even the president of the United States, has a right to have the Supreme Court hear a case. Though anyone who is unhappy with a lower court's decision may formally request such review, usually in what is called a petition for a writ of certiorari, the Court grants fewer than 100 of the 10,000 or so cert petitions that it receives every year. It reserves its docket for cases presenting important questions of federal law, such as what the Constitution requires (or forbids), or how an act of Congress is to be applied, or cases in which lower federal courts have given conflicting interpretations of the Constitution or federal statutes.

Securing a decision from the Court is a two-step process: the petition for certiorari tries to convince the justices that the decision of the lower court is both erroneous and important enough for the Court to take up. The opposition filed by the other party tries to convince them that the decision below is correct, or at least not all that important. Review is granted if four members of the Court vote to do so. If that happens, each party in the case (usually two, but sometimes more) submits a written brief (limited to 15,000 words, about 50 pages), more detailed than the cert petition and opposition, urging the Court to take specific action—usually to affirm or reverse the decision of the lower court—and marshaling the precedents and arguments to win the case.

After all the briefs are in, the case is argued orally, always before the full Court of nine, usually two cases a day, two weeks in each month, from October through April. After the week's cases have been argued, the justices meet in "conference"—a justices-only conclave—to discuss them and to vote on each outcome. The chief justice, or if he is in the minority then the senior justice in the majority, assigns a justice, perhaps himself, to draft an opinion setting forth the reasoning of the majority, which becomes the decision of the Court and is binding on all lower courts. Dissenting justices are free to write their own opinions explaining why the majority is mistaken. This process generally takes several months; when it is finished, the Court announces the decision in open court and releases the opinions in the case.

When the United States is a party, as it is in federal criminal cases and others that involve federal officers and agencies, the Justice Department's Office of the Solicitor General represents the government. This relatively small office—the solicitor general, four or five senior lawyers as deputy solicitors general, and fifteen to eighteen staff lawyers as assistants to the solicitor general—writes the petitions and the oppositions to the petitions of others and, if the Court grants review, it briefs and argues the case; in the most significant cases the solicitor general argues. (Elena Kagan, then dean of the Harvard Law School, was the first woman to be appointed SG, by President Obama in 2009, and he appointed her to the Court the following year.)

With the permission of a party or the Court, an amicus curiae—"friend of the court"—may submit a brief and sometimes, though rarely, take part in oral argument. An amicus is not a party to the case, but usually has some special expertise, or some stake in the outcome, that it wishes the Court to consider as it deliberates. In recent years, amicus briefs have proliferated; in some cases there may be a score or more. Some are given little attention by the justices, but others, such as those submitted by the solicitor general in cases where the US government is not itself a party, can carry significant weight. In the Guantanamo cases, dozens of amicus briefs were filed, many by law professors, former military lawyers, and civil liberties groups, all eager to tell the justices just what they should do.

The Petitions for Certiorari

The three cases of the administration's detainees—*Rasul, Hamdi*, and *Padilla*—seemed destined for the Supreme Court from the beginning. They raised fundamental and important questions about individual liberty and government authority; about separation of powers between the president and the judiciary, and between the president and Congress; about due process in war; and about the rights of aliens and citizens. On all these questions three federal courts of appeals had struggled. Still, no experienced Supreme Court advocate takes its review for granted; if the cert petition does not convince the Court that the case is important enough to warrant full consideration, there is no further recourse.

The lawyers for Rasul and Hamdi filed their petitions for certiorari in the fall of 2003, and those for Padilla in January 2004, just a month after the court of appeals' decision in that case. The Rasul case—actually, two cases, one on behalf of an Australian and two citizens of the United Kingdom, the other brought by twelve Kuwaitis—presented the question of whether Guantanamo detainees were barred from seeking habeas relief in federal courts because they were aliens outside the United States and any court's geographic district. Rasul's brief, and the solicitor general's response, laid out each side's distinct perspectives on the case as it had developed to that point. Rasul's lawyers—Joseph Margulies, a Minneapolis human-rights practitioner, and lawyers from the Center for Constitutional Rights in New York—cast the issues in stark terms: "This case presents questions of surpassing importance: whether the United States Government is constrained by the Constitution and international law in its treatment of foreign nationals imprisoned outside the 'ultimate sovereignty' of the United States, and if so, whether foreign nationals may enforce those constraints in a federal court." It went on, in reference to Guantanamo, "The lower court has sanctioned the creation of a prison wholly outside of the law. The Government's disdain for the principles of justice and the rule of law is unprecedented in our history."

The petition did not dwell on the ambiguity of "sovereignty" in the 1903 Cuban lease. Because the court of appeals in the District of Columbia had relied squarely on the Supreme Court's 1950 decision in *Eisentrager*, the petition emphasized the significant distinctions between the two cases: the German soldiers whose appeals for American judicial review had been rejected by the Supreme Court had been convicted of war crimes by an American military commission that had accorded the Germans a full and fair trial, with counsel. But Rasul and the other detainees had been given no trial; they had not been charged with, let alone convicted of, anything. The Germans were enemy aliens; these petitioners were citizens of friendly countries. And Guantanamo Bay, though on Cuban terrain, was not some foreign land but "a fully American enclave under the exclusive jurisdiction and continuous control of the United States Government," in the words of Rasul's petition.

The petition for the Kuwaitis made clear the limited relief they sought:

> Petitioners do not contend that the government lacked power to detain them, nor do they ask for their immediate release. They ask only that, subject to reasonable security measures, they be allowed to meet with their families, consult with counsel, and obtain the judgment of some impartial tribunal as to whether there is cause to detain them. In short, they ask only that the court ensure that adequate procedures are in place so that their detentions are not arbitrary.

This measured request was meant to assure the Supreme Court that, if it took the case, it need not decide whether the Kuwaitis were indeed enemy combatants or how far the president's authority might reach to detain them if they were. They sought only a chance to show some impartial authority, such as the panel of officers contemplated by the army's own regulations, that they were indeed the hapless and innocent charity volunteers they claimed to be. Though they were not seeking immediate release, the procedures that they sought could free them eventually.

The positions of the two groups of petitioners were well coordinated: if the Court did not want to take on the question of whether detainees were entitled to file habeas petitions in federal court, it could grant certiorari to consider the lesser question of whether they were entitled to a status adjudication before a fair authority to whom they could make their case.

The solicitor general, for the government's part, answered both petitions with the arguments that had succeeded so far: *Eisentrager* barred any resort to US courts by aliens abroad; the lower courts correctly applied that ruling to these aliens; Guantanamo was not the "sovereign" territory of the United States; and any interference by the judiciary would breach the separation of powers by impinging on the president's authority to conduct war. The SG's job, not an easy one here, was to characterize the dispute as one that had been properly and correctly resolved through adherence to settled precedent and presented no need of Supreme Court intervention.

There was a poignant personal aspect to the cases, never mentioned in the briefs but known to all. The solicitor general was Theodore B. Olson, whose wife, Barbara, on September 11, 2001, had been a passenger on American Airlines flight 77—the one the hijackers had flown into the Pentagon.

On November 10, 2003, the Court granted both Rasul's petition and that of the Kuwaitis and joined them into a single case under the name of *Rasul v. Bush*. But it ordered the parties to argue a single narrow question: "Whether United States courts lack jurisdiction to consider challenges to the legality of the detention of foreign nationals captured abroad in connection with hostilities and incarcerated at the Guantanamo Naval Base, Cuba." All the Court would decide, in the combined cases, was whether federal courts were open to detainees at Gitmo. It did not disclose how the justices had voted on whether to take the case; it never does.

Representing Yaser Hamdi, Virginia's federal public defender Frank

Dunham presented his case in similarly stark terms: "This case presents fundamental questions about the right of American citizens to be free from indefinite detention by the government without charge or trial, the power of the Executive branch to abbreviate due process of law during wartime, and the role of the federal courts in resolving these issues," the cert petition read. "The appropriate balance between the rights of citizens and the Executive power to defend against threats to national security is an old question, and one that was answered by the Fourth Circuit [court of appeals] in a fundamentally alarming way." The appeals court's ruling "exposes any number of American citizens abroad— from embedded journalists to humanitarian aid workers to unwitting tourists—to indefinite incommunicado detention based on the thinnest of factual grounds."

Dunham's strongest point was also one that was beyond dispute: as an American citizen, Hamdi was inarguably entitled to seek habeas corpus to test the legality of his incarceration, as the Fourth Circuit had acknowledged. Yet that court had simultaneously held that the affidavit of the absent Mr. Mobbs, setting forth the alleged circumstances of Hamdi's capture, had established the lawfulness of that incarceration, a conclusion it had reached without allowing Hamdi any access to a lawyer or to the court itself, even to dispute the account submitted by Mobbs, who, never appearing, could not be questioned. This outcome, said Dunham, "transformed Hamdi's entitlement into a fundamentally hollow exercise" that violated the "constitutional guarantee of access to the courts."

Faced with a case in which it could argue neither the meaning of sovereignty at Guantanamo, nor the rights of enemy aliens, nor the intricacies of habeas corpus jurisdiction, the Justice Department drew a clear line in the sand. Hamdi was entitled to nothing. He was a captured enemy combatant held under the lawful authority of the president to wage war, an authority validated by Congress, which in the AUMF had authorized the president to use "all necessary and appropriate force" to combat al Qaeda and the Taliban. His citizenship ("presumed" to be American, the government characterized it, though citing nothing that would cast doubt on it) was irrelevant. His Virginia confinement was likewise irrelevant, beyond the fact that it entitled him to file a habeas petition. But once in court, the SG argued, he had no rights to anything. Neither his citizenship nor his location "affect the military's settled authority to detain him once *it* has determined that he is an enemy combatant" (the emphasis is mine). Hamdi, Solicitor General Olson's brief argued, was "a classic battlefield detainee—captured in Afghanistan, an area of active combat, with an enemy unit," and so his classification as an enemy combatant "is a quintessentially military judgment." Furthermore, in light of "fundamental separation-of-powers principles," the proper role of a court in a habeas case was limited "to confirm[ing] that there is a factual basis supporting the military's determination that a detainee is indeed an enemy combatant," which is just what the court of appeals had done, relying on the Mobbs declaration that it was so.

Stripped thus of all its jurisdictional arguments, the administration left no doubt that Hamdi's detention was based squarely on the authority of a president backed by Congress. As occasionally happens in important cases, the solicitor general might have conceded that, though the lower court was correct, the case did present an issue so significant that the Supreme Court should grant certiorari and set the case for full briefing, argument, and decision. But SG Olson did not. He was urging the Court to uphold the president's exercise of authority without any need to hear the case.

But there was a surprising footnote in the SG's submission. The Department of Defense, it disclosed, "has determined that Hamdi may be permitted access to counsel subject to appropriate security restrictions." This was news; the decision had been announced only the day before the government's filing. "DoD decided to allow Hamdi access to counsel," the Pentagon's press release had read, "because Hamdi is a U.S. citizen detained by DoD in the United States, because DoD has completed its intelligence collection with Hamdi, and because DoD has determined that the access will not compromise the national security of the United States." It pointedly noted that the decision was "a matter of discretion and military policy; such access is not required by domestic or international law and should not be treated as a precedent." Neither the SG's brief nor the Pentagon's press release elaborated on what "access to counsel" would entail or what "appropriate security restrictions" would be imposed, nor did it suggest that the decision had any relation to the pending decision of the Court on whether to hear the case, though the timing of the decision could hardly have been coincidental.

Others had ideas, however. Viet Dinh, a former law clerk to Justice Sandra Day O'Connor and an assistant attorney general before leaving the Justice Department to teach at Georgetown Law School, told the *New York Times* that the decision was a "significant development" that "moves the government to a more sustainable position" in the Supreme Court—a tactical move "to make its case bulletproof." But the naked assertion of access to counsel seemed unlikely to accomplish so much. As *New York Times* reporter Neil Lewis wrote, allowing Hamdi to see a lawyer "does not necessarily mean anything will come of it." Whether it would have any effect on the Court remained to be seen.

Padilla's case, the third of the big three, was also on the Court's doorstep. This time the petition was filed not by the detainee but by Solicitor General Olson, seeking the Court's review of the decision of the Second Circuit Court of Appeals that had ordered Padilla's release—an order stayed so the government could seek Supreme Court review. Thus, the SG was simultaneously telling the Court that the two cases the administration had won in the lower courts were not worthy of the Court's review, but the case it had lost was. To be sure, this straddle followed from the administration's position that in Rasul and Hamdi's cases, the courts of appeals for the District of Columbia and Fourth Circuits, respectively, had reached the right result in upholding presidential authority over detainees, while the Second Circuit had erroneously reached the opposite result in Padilla's case and should be reversed. Still, at a stage when the question was only whether the administration's detention policies were important enough to deserve the Court's attention, it was an awkward position for the solicitor general, the Justice Department, and the Bush administration to be in.

By the time the solicitor general filed the government's petition in Padilla's case, on January 16, 2004, the Court had already granted cert in *Rasul* (November 10, 2003) and *Hamdi* (January 3, 2004), and there seemed little reason that it would not do so in *Padilla*. But the SG, taking no chances, presented a double-barreled argument. In the first place, the Second Circuit was wrong to distinguish the Fourth Circuit's *Hamdi* decision on grounds that Hamdi had been taken in the combat zone of Afghanistan while Padilla had been taken in Chicago. It matters not, the government argued, where an enemy combatant is found, particularly when al Qaeda, Padilla's ostensible sponsor, had dramatically demonstrated on September 11 its capability to kill Americans in New York, Virginia, and Pennsylvania.

The SG had good grounds for the argument; in its 1942 *Quirin* decision, the Supreme Court had upheld the detention and trial by military commission of seven German saboteurs, one an American-born citizen. To rule, as the court of appeals had here, that presidential authority to detain enemy combatants was somehow less extensive at home than it was abroad "undermines the President's vital authority as Commander in Chief to protect the United States against additional enemy attacks launched within the Nation's borders" and raises "issues of extraordinary national significance."

The government's second argument was that the court of appeals had departed from long-established judicial practice in allowing the case to proceed in New York when Padilla himself was confined in South Carolina, albeit having been brought there by the government. Habeas cases, it argued, must be brought, and traditionally have been, where the petitioner's "immediate custodian" was located, and here that custodian was the navy commander of the brig in Charleston. The government told the Court that the case belonged in the federal court in South Carolina, because upholding jurisdiction in New York would open the door for federal prisoners everywhere to sue the attorney general or the secretary of defense almost anywhere, creating overlapping jurisdiction that would be inefficient and confusing.

But the administration's jurisdiction argument was no doubt also motivated by more pragmatic concerns. By having the Second Circuit's decision vacated on grounds that the case was filed in the wrong court, the administration would avoid a possibly adverse Supreme Court ruling on the scope of presidential authority. Moreover, it had good reason to want the case in South Carolina, within the Fourth Circuit, which in *Hamdi* had shown itself willing to uphold broad presidential power over detainees.

Padilla's lawyers, now including not only Donna Newman but the heavyweight national law firm of Jenner & Block, seemed implicitly to recognize that review was a foregone conclusion. "Under the Government's theory," they told the Court, "the President may declare any citizen within the United States to be an 'enemy combatant,' allowing the military to imprison the individual indefinitely (or until the 'war on terror' is over) and to interrogate him without limit until the Secretary of Defense decides his 'intelligence value' is gone." Although they argued that the decision of the Second Circuit rejecting such authority was correct in every respect, they acknowledged that the government's assertion of a "novel and unchecked power to imprison American citizens as 'enemy combatants' is unarguably of great national significance."

The trio of cases presented the Supreme Court with an almost perfect array. Rasul was an alien captured in the war zone of Afghanistan; Hamdi was a US citizen captured in that war zone; and Padilla was a US citizen arrested in Chicago. *Rasul* was thus clearly the administration's strongest case, though the Court had told the parties to focus only on the question of whether detention at Guantanamo precluded federal jurisdiction. In *Hamdi* the government, although conceding federal jurisdiction, could still argue that the president's authority, at least when backed by the congressional Authorization for the Use of Military Force, was fully sufficient to order war-zone detainees, citizens or not, held and interrogated without judicial oversight and intervention. *Padilla* presented the government with the more formidable challenge of whether that authority was also sufficient to apprehend enemy combatants within the United States and to imprison and interrogate them without lawyers or judicial involvement, practices clearly forbidden in criminal cases.

To no one's surprise, the Supreme Court granted certiorari in *Padilla* on February 20, 2004, and put the case on an expedited schedule so it could catch up to the two cases already granted. The SG was given only a month to file the government's brief, and Padilla's attorneys their brief three weeks after that. *Rasul* would be argued on April 20, and *Hamdi* and *Padilla* on the 28th. This was late in the Court's oral-argument calendar; it would decide the cases without delay.

Briefs and Oral Argument

Rasul v. Bush

In the briefing and argument of *Rasul*, the question posed by the Supreme Court—whether US courts lack jurisdiction to consider challenges to the detention of aliens captured abroad in a war zone and incarcerated at Guantanamo—resolved itself into a nuanced argument: Did *Eisentrager* announce a rule that federal courts have no jurisdiction over the habeas corpus claims of aliens being held in custody abroad, or did it simply hold that under the circumstances of that particular case there was no good reason for the courts to exercise their jurisdiction?

The distinction was critical. Federal courts cannot create jurisdiction—the authority to consider and decide a given case—for themselves. They have only the jurisdiction that the Constitution gives them, and even that jurisdiction is subject to terms and conditions imposed by Congress. If a court does not have jurisdiction, the only thing it can do is dismiss the case without further ado. And to further complicate matters, jurisdiction has three dimensions, all of which must be satisfied before a court can proceed. There is subject-matter jurisdiction, requiring a case to be within the category of disputes federal courts are allowed to decide. The most common types of disputes are those arising under federal law, or between citizens of different states. There is territorial jurisdiction, requiring the case to have sufficient connection to the state in which the court sits, though more than one state might qualify in that respect. And there must be personal jurisdiction over the parties, enabling the court to compel their appearance, through subpoenas if need be.

In *Rasul*, the government and the petitioners agreed that the answer to the Supreme Court's question—whether federal courts had jurisdiction over the claims of detainees held at Gitmo—lay in the habeas corpus statute enacted by Congress. That statute authorizes federal courts, "within their respective [territorial] jurisdictions," to grant release by habeas corpus to "any prisoner . . . in custody under or by color of the authority of the United States" or "in custody in violation of the Constitution or laws or treaties of the United States." ("Under color of law" or "color of authority" means that a government official is asserting that his actions are required by, or justified by, his lawful authority.) Plainly, argued Rasul, the Gitmo detainees were in custody under the authority asserted by the United States. Moreover, their custody was "in violation of the Constitution" and specifically the Fifth Amendment, which provides that "no person shall be . . . deprived of life, liberty, or property, without due process of law."

The first point was obviously true; the government disputed the second. It argued that the Constitution was not being violated, because it didn't protect aliens abroad to begin with, and that the habeas statute, by history and tradition, was never intended to apply to such aliens. The government relied, as it had throughout the litigation, on language in the 1950 *Eisentrager* opinion that did indeed suggest that the Supreme Court was denying judicial review to the German officers because federal courts had no jurisdiction (or "power") to take the case.

In response, the detainees argued that the Court should "examine what the Court [in *Eisentrager*] *did*, not merely what it occasionally said." That case "is best understood not as a limitation on the *power* of the federal judiciary, but as a restraint on the *exercise* of habeas based on the factors present in that case" (emphasis in the brief).

Those factors, Rasul argued, were that the petitioners were enemy aliens who were convicted of war crimes in a trial by a US military commission in which they were accorded full due process of law, including formal charges, the right to counsel, and a trial in which they exercised their right to produce their evidence and question the government's, with a verdict rendered by impartial military officers. In those circumstances, the Supreme Court merely "refused to countenance any further interference with the operation of a lawful and independent system of military justice." Rasul's lawyers were therefore not attacking the Eisentrager decision or asking that it be overruled. They simply contended that the facts in that case were different, and inapplicable to the Guantanamo detainees, who had been accorded no system of justice, military or otherwise, or indeed any process of law at all. They had been convicted of nothing, and as nationals of friendly countries were not even "enemy aliens" to begin with.

The government dismissed all those distinctions as irrelevant, because those factors, it contended, were not what the *Eisentrager* Court had relied on to reach its decision. The meaning of *Eisentrager* was that aliens abroad, and particularly those held in military custody, had no rights to federal judicial review. The government thus was reading the Court's Eisentrager ruling broadly: Aliens abroad? No rights; no jurisdiction. End of discussion. Rasul, by contrast, was reading it narrowly: aliens charged and tried by an impartial panel of military judges, with lawyers and all the attributes of due process, their convictions duly reviewed and upheld by military authority, and now confined in occupied territory? No need for a US court to interfere with the military by exercising its habeas authority in those circumstances. The text of the Eisentrager decision was sublimely ambiguous on what the Supreme Court had actually been deciding, half a century before.

Rasul characterized the government's bottom line starkly: "The Constitution tolerates the creation of a prison beyond the reach of the judiciary, reserved for foreign nationals who may be held on mere Executive fiat." The solicitor general, for the government's part, emphasized the horrific carnage of the 9/11 attacks—"the most deadly and savage foreign attack on civilian lives and property and [US] commercial and government infrastructure in one day in the Nation's history"—and the still-ongoing combat against those responsible for the attacks. For the courts to act here "would thrust the federal courts into the extraordinary role of reviewing the military's conduct of hostilities overseas, second-guessing the military's determination as to which captured aliens pose a threat to the United States or have strategic intelligence value, and, in practical effect, superintending the Executive's conduct of an armed conflict—even while American troops are on the ground in Afghanistan and engaged in daily combat operations."

There were thirty-two amicus briefs filed, twenty-five of them in support of the detainees. A variety of human rights groups came in on the side of the detainees, while groups of retired military officers, former military lawyers, and former government officials, along with a mélange of scholars, academics, and international lawyers, filed briefs, some supporting the detainees, others the government.

The courtroom was crowded for oral argument on April 20, 2004; some spectators had been in line all night. But the argument quickly devolved into a constant series of questions by the justices and responses from the lawyers that brought little clarity to the issues. Several justices remarked that the Eisentrager decision was ambiguous, and its rationale difficult to discern. Representing the detainees, John J. Gibbons, a former federal judge from New Jersey who had left the bench in 1990 to practice with a Newark law firm, made little headway in explaining what *Eisentrager* really meant. For the government, Solicitor General Olson seemed defensive. At one point, in response to a question from Justice John Paul Stevens, Olson conceded that the government would recognize the right of an American citizen detained at Guantanamo to seek habeas in federal court. That suggested the question—not pursued by any of the justices—whether citizen Hamdi (whose case had been briefed but would not be argued until the following week) had been removed to Virginia to avoid putting the government in the uncomfortable position of acknowledging that at least one detainee at Gitmo had a right to habeas corpus. After an hour's argument, there were few clues of where the justices were headed, if indeed they knew themselves.

Hamdi v. Rumsfeld

Hamdi presented the Court with a much cleaner set of facts and a consideration of issues that *Rasul* could not touch. Having been removed from Guantanamo to an American military base in Virginia, Hamdi was a US citizen in the United States, and hence by virtue of both his status and situs was entitled to pursue a habeas corpus ruling on the lawfulness of his confinement. Neither the government nor the judges on the Fourth Circuit disputed that. But what those judges had given him was far less than he had sought: without hearing from him, they had ruled that his confinement was justified on the basis of the affidavit filed by Michael Mobbs, the unseen government official. They had declined to look behind Mobbs's assertions about Hamdi's capture, on grounds that to do so would violate the separation of powers, by inquiring into matters that the Constitution reserved exclusively to the president as commander in chief.

In his Supreme Court brief, public defender Frank Dunham, still representing Hamdi, laid down a clear argument: the appellate court had not upheld the separation of powers and in fact had violated it. Habeas corpus, after all, was enshrined in the Constitution and had been part of Anglo-American common law for centuries before that. Its very purpose was to allow judicial inquiry into the Executive's power to detain. By taking a cramped view of its own powers—accepting the Mobbs affidavit at face value—the court of appeals had in fact inflated the power of the Executive and retreated from the independent review at the heart of the separation of powers doctrine. "Judicial review of executive detention is demanded by, not contrary to, the separation of powers," Dunham argued.

Furthermore, his brief went on, "Hamdi's detention is offensive to the most basic and unimpeachable rule of due process: that no citizen may be incarcerated at the will of the Executive without recourse to a timely proceeding before an independent tribunal to determine whether the Executive's asserted justifications for the detention have a basis in fact and a warrant in law." What Hamdi had received from the court of appeals was a habeas review with nothing in it—"a habeas proceeding in name only"—denying due process of law, which "embraces a requirement of fundamental fairness." In this case, fundamental fairness at the least required that Hamdi be given the assistance of counsel and a "meaningful opportunity to be heard." Indeed, Dunham argued, "Although noting that factual circumstances [as described in the Mobbs declaration] may support the detention of citizens only 'if accurate,'" the Fourth Circuit nonetheless ruled that Hamdi "is not entitled to challenge the facts presented." How could Hamdi prove that Mobbs was wrong if he could not be heard? It was, Dunham wrote, "a quintessential Catch-22."

But Dunham had to tread cautiously here. He could not plausibly claim that an enemy is entitled to a lawyer and a hearing the minute he is captured, disarmed, and moved to the rear. Nor could he plausibly claim that prisoners of war were entitled to lawyers and hearings at any point in their captivity; neither the customary law of war nor the Geneva Conventions suggested that. But POWs are entitled to humane treatment and freedom from unwanted interrogation, and Hamdi was clearly—and under the president's decree of February 7, 2002, explicitly—not being accorded POW status in his Virginia jail. So Dunham emphasized that he was not challenging Hamdi's capture and initial custody, but rather his continuous and interminable stateside detention. He had been held for nearly two years with no end in sight, and the Fourth Circuit had denied him any right to contest the allegation on which his confinement was predicated—that he had been captured in a Taliban unit with a rifle and was thus an enemy combatant. "Once the citizen is removed from the area of actual fighting, the Constitution requires statutory authorization to hold that citizen indefinitely," Dunham's brief argued.

That statutory authorization, he went on, was not to be found in the Authorization for the Use of Military Force or in any other act of Congress. "The AUMF constitutes no greater authorization of power to the President than if Congress had issued a declaration of war," which is basically what the AUMF amounted to. It authorized the president to become a wartime commander in chief, not to put Americans in jail without charge. Combining the separation of powers point with the denial of due process, Dunham had made a cogent argument. The irreducible fact was that Hamdi was a US citizen, he was confined in a US jail, and he had been denied any day in court.

In response, the government's strategy became clear: to minimize any distinction between Yaser Hamdi and the hundreds of other enemy combatants in US custody. In the first place, the solicitor general's brief contended, when it came to enemy combatants, citizenship was irrelevant. The Supreme Court had set that straight in the 1942 *Quirin* case, upholding the right of the government to try German saboteurs, including one born in the United States, for war crimes. And while Hamdi's presence in the United States allowed him to go to federal court to seek habeas corpus, nothing in his situation justified a court to actually grant it. "Once the military makes a determination that an individual is an enemy combatant who should be detained in connection with the conflict, the *place* where the combatant is detained in no way affects the legality of that determination," the brief argued (emphasis in the brief). Nor, furthermore, did his extended incarceration affect that legality. As with all detainees, incommunicado detention was dictated by the critical need to gather intelligence, a process that takes time and would be disrupted by the appointment of a lawyer who would tell his client to say nothing.

"A commander's wartime determination that an individual is an enemy combatant is a quintessentially military judgment, representing a core exercise of the Commander-in-Chief authority," the SG's brief continued. Hamdi had been captured in a war zone. He had been determined to be an enemy combatant by military officers whose job that was. The capture and detention of enemy combatants—citizens or otherwise—was amply supported not only by the president's inherent wartime authority but by the congressional resolution to authorize military force. And because this "classic wartime detention" comes with "the express statutory backing of Congress," the president's constitutional power "is at its apogee" under the *Youngstown* standard: presidential power combined with congressional authorization.

As to Hamdi's separation of powers argument, the government's brief acknowledged the importance of separation principles but rejected any suggestion that the Fourth Circuit had retreated from them. What that court had done, as the government put it, was simply to refuse Hamdi's invitation to "second-guess the factual basis for the exercise of the Commander in Chief's authority to detain a captured enemy combatant in wartime." Guided by its respect for separation, it had correctly ruled that the Mobbs declaration "demonstrated the legality of Hamdi's detention."

So the issues were joined: was Hamdi entitled to any process that was not due to other detainees, and did the Fourth Circuit's summary proceedings abdicate its role as a check on the Executive, or simply refrain from meddling with the authority of the commander in chief? While the Rasul case had presented the question of whether federal courts had jurisdiction to hear the claims of aliens at Guantanamo, this case raised the more nuanced question of what the federal courts should do with the jurisdiction they clearly did have over the claims of those held in the United States. Specifically, was deference to presidential policies and decisions an affirmance of the separation of powers or an abdication of it?

The lawyers assembled for oral argument on April 28, 2004, again in a courtroom with every seat taken. But unlike the Rasul argument, the dialogue between justices and advocates seemed to make progress toward an understanding of the issues.

Dunham, who went first, faced some skeptical questioning from Justice Antonin Scalia on whether he foresaw every captured detainee who might claim American citizenship receiving a hearing in federal court. (Maybe so, Dunham replied, but the possibility of dubious claims should not justify denying rights to a citizen.) But other justices, particularly Sandra Day O'Connor, asked Dunham to elaborate on whether there might be some way, some process other than a full-fledged habeas hearing in federal court, to give his client a fair and meaningful hearing in which he could participate. Though it had barely been mentioned in his brief, Dunham immediately cited the US military's process in Regulation 190-8 that provided for a three-officer tribunal to rule on claims that a captive was entitled to be treated as a POW or, possibly, set free because he was not an enemy combatant at all.

Justice O'Connor: "Would those military proceedings satisfy your claim?"

Dunham: "He has never had an opportunity to assert a claim of innocence. Those proceedings would go a long way toward satisfying the process part of our claim. Those regulations, if they had been followed in this case, would certainly have given him that opportunity."

Justice David Souter: "At this stage of the game, I take it, you have no *per se* objection to some form of military process, so long as he could be heard?"

Dunham: "The military has refused to give this process to him."

Justice Souter: "I realize that, but if I understand your argument, if ultimately your client was found [by this Court] to be entitled to some process, it might be that military process with an opportunity to be heard in response would satisfy your demand."

Dunham: "Yes. That's correct, Your Honor."

Dunham went on to explain that, even with that "military process," his client would still be entitled, as any citizen would, to file a habeas corpus petition afterwards to determine if the process had been fair, but clearly the implications of O'Connor's and Souter's questions had opened a door for the Court to decouple due process of law from formal habeas corpus and to conclude that due process could be satisfied by something less than a full habeas hearing in a federal court, such as participation in the military's three-officer panel. Whether the Court would go through that door would have to await its decision.

When Deputy SG Paul Clement took the podium for the government, he immediately faced a barrage of pointed questions.

Justice Ruth Bader Ginsburg: "Does the government have any rhyme or rationale" as to why some detainees are referred for trial in federal court, and Hamdi and others are "just being held indefinitely?"

Clement answered that the decision "reflects the sound exercise of prosecutorial and executive discretion." In any event, individuals with "paramount intelligence value" should not be provided with counsel "whose first advice would certainly be to not talk to the Government."

Justice Anthony Kennedy: "Can you give me any ideas of the outer bounds of how long the detention would take in order to get the value from the interrogation that you want? And then we could begin to get some understanding of this process?"

Each case is different, Clement replied. "There is a unique interest, especially in the course of this conflict, where intelligence is at unprecedented value, to have some ability with some detainees to deal with them in a way that allows us to get intelligence to prevent future terrorist attacks, and not be limited just to going after them retrospectively for past terrorist attacks." He cited the Authorization for the Use of Military Force as the justification for prolonged interrogation, but Justice Souter interrupted.

Justice Souter: "But it doesn't follow that the President's authority to do that is indefinite for all time. Doesn't Congress at some point have a responsibility to do more than pass that resolution? It's two and a half years later."

Congress has not seen fit to revisit that resolution, Clement noted.

Souter again: "Is it not reasonable to at least consider whether that resolution needs, at this point, to be supplemented and made more specific to authorize what you are doing?"

Clement: "But Justice Souter, they have authorized the use of force."

Souter: "Without any specific reference to keeping American citizens detained indefinitely. I mean, that's the problem."

Justice Stephen Breyer intervened, revisiting the tribunal contempled by the military regulations. "Is there any reason why you could not have that kind of proceeding, the kind of proceeding that the military itself has given over and over and over" in the 1990–1991 Gulf War and in the ongoing Iraq war?

Clement: "These individuals have gotten military process." But Clement was referring to the initial screening by field officers in Afghanistan that led to the classification of Hamdi and others as enemy combatants, and Breyer wasn't buying that. "That wasn't the question I asked. Is there any reason why the Army itself could not give a comparable basic proceeding where you have a neutral decision maker, and a practical but fair opportunity to present proofs and arguments? I want a practical answer."

Clement acknowledged that the regulations did provide for that kind of proceeding. But those regulations were based on the Geneva Conventions, he went on, and thus were inapplicable here, given the president's decision that none of the combatants in Afghanistan were protected by those conventions. "He did receive military process," Clement said again. "It may not seem what you think of as traditional due process in an Article III [of the Constitution, the judicial part] sense, but the interrogation process itself provides an opportunity for an individual to explain that this has all been a mistake."

Clement's equation of the battlefield screening interrogation to an actual opportunity for a captive to make his case in a structured hearing before impartial decision makers fell flat.

Justice Ginsburg: "I take it your position is that [in a habeas proceeding] the Government has to come forward with something, and the something they came forward with is the Mobbs affidavit, which is hearsay, because Mobbs doesn't know what happened on the battlefield either. There is no statement at any point from Hamdi."

The Mobbs affidavit summarizes what Hamdi said, Clement replied.

Ginsburg: "The person who is locked up, doesn't he have a right to bring before some tribunal himself his own words, rather than have a government agent say what was told to him that somebody else said?"

Justice O'Connor: "How about a neutral decision maker of some kind, perhaps in the military? Is that so extreme that it should not be required?"

Clement was on the spot. "No, Justice O'Connor," he answered. He suggested that the field interrogator might be considered a "neutral decision maker" in the sense that the army had no interest in holding people who were not enemy combatants. That answer did not take into account the natural tendency of even conscientious soldiers in the field to resolve any doubts in favor of internment, and in any event it clearly fell quite short of the impartial tribunal that the army's regulations had long prescribed.

Several justices returned to the matter of the indefinite length of detention, limited apparently only by the government's decision as to when the detainee's intelligence value expired. "Let's say it's the Hundred Years War," Justice Breyer said. "Is there no opportunity for a court to say that this violates, for an American citizen, the elementary due process that the Constitution guarantees?"

Clement: "There certainly is a challenge that can be brought to the length of the detention at some point."

Souter: "The concern about Afghanistan will go on as long as there is concern about al Qaeda, and there is no endpoint that we can see at this point to that. So it seems to me your answer boils down to saying, don't worry about the timing question, we'll tell you when it's over."

Clement: "I continue to think that there may be a role for the courts in dealing with the timing question at some point." But not yet. "It makes no sense whatsoever to release an individual detained as an enemy combatant in Afghanistan while the troops are still on the ground in Afghanistan."

It had been a long half hour for the government. Clement looked at the justices with his final statement. "Everything provided to date is more than sufficient," he concluded. But it was readily apparent that at least four justices had serious questions about that.

Rumsfeld v. Padilla

Padilla and Hamdi were both US citizens in US military jails, but because Hamdi had been initially seized in a combat zone in Afghanistan, while Padilla was arrested at an airport in Chicago, Hamdi gave the government a stronger case to support presidential authority. If the government lost its presidential-authority argument in Hamdi's case— and after oral argument that position was looking none too solid—it would surely lose it in Padilla's as well. But Padilla's case offered an independent route to victory, and the government embraced it. If it could persuade the court that Padilla should have filed his habeas petition in South Carolina instead of New York, it could win outright without putting presidential authority to the test. A ruling from the Supreme Court that the New York court had lacked jurisdiction would vacate the Second Circuit's decision, wiping the government's defeat off the books and, in the bargain, forcing Padilla to start all over again in military-friendly South Carolina. Winning the case on procedural grounds that only lawyers and judges would care much about would avoid the politically explosive issue of whether the president could arrest US citizens at home and jail them indefinitely without recourse to the courts.

The SG's argument in its brief was straightforward: the habeas statute gave federal courts the authority to issue writs of habeas corpus "within their respective jurisdictions," and so the "settled rule" in a habeas case was that the petitioner had to sue his "immediate custodian"—the warden of the jail. The SG called "seriously flawed" the reasoning of Judge Mukasey and the Second Circuit that Secretary of Defense Rumsfeld was a proper defendant because he had the ultimate authority to determine Padilla's fate and that, moreover, he could be sued in New York because he had sent military police there to escort Padilla to South Carolina.

There was an impressive line of cases supporting the government's argument, and the solicitor general devoted nearly a third of his fifty-page brief to the point. In addition to precedent, he urged the Court to consider the reasons that the rule was as settled as it was. In 1867, Congress had imposed the territorial limits because otherwise, as one senator had put it then, "a judge of a United States court in one part of the Union would be authorized to issue a writ of habeas corpus to bring before him a person confined in another and a remote part of the Union." In 1961, the Supreme Court had explained that it would be "inconvenient, potentially embarrassing, certainly expensive and on the whole quite unnecessary to provide any judge anywhere with authority to issue the Great Writ [of habeas corpus] on behalf of applicants far distantly removed from the courts whereon they sat."

Still, it was not a foregone conclusion. In the 1970s both Congress and the Court had loosened the jurisdictional strictures somewhat in some cases—for example, to allow a prisoner to seek habeas from the court that had sentenced him, even if it was in a district other than the prisoner's jail. But the SG argued that those exceptions did not apply to the "classic habeas challenge" now before the Court. Padilla was simply contesting his present physical incarceration, as thousands of prisoners do every year. There was nothing special about his case.

But this argument had a significant vulnerability, and Justice John Paul Stevens raised it in the first minute of oral argument. He asked Clement, "Supposing this petition had been filed while he was still in New York, and then he was removed to South Carolina, would the petition be okay, then?" Clement readily acknowledged that it would be. He was right to do so: not only had the Court so ruled in a 1944 case, but any different rule would let the government foil a habeas petition simply by transferring the prisoner out of the jurisdiction and foil any subsequent petition by transferring him again. So the government's argument rested on a narrow ledge: habeas in New York would be appropriate if Padilla's lawyer had filed the petition the day before, instead of two days after, her client was moved to South Carolina. Given the importance of the case, the Court might well be disposed to create another exception to the immediate-custodian rule, and then proceed apace to rule on the jackpot issue: whether the president could order the arrest of a US citizen, in the United States, and imprison him indefinitely without any legal process at all.

Its jurisdictional argument completed, the government's brief turned to that issue. The solicitor general emphasized, as he had in the other detainee cases, that the president's commander-in-chief powers in wartime were vast, but that the Court need not decide whether that authority alone was sufficient to confine enemy combatants, only whether that authority and the powers of Congress, taken together, were sufficient to do so, an argument directly tied to the landmark Youngstown steel mill decision.

Here, the SG argued, congressional assent was clearly given in the Authorization for the Use of Military Force. The president's determination that Padilla was an enemy combatant therefore "lies at the heart of his constitutional powers as Commander in Chief, and it is fully supported by Congress's broad grant of authority to the President." The president certainly had authority to order that enemy combatants be taken into custody and held, as armies had been doing for centuries, not only to keep them from returning to the battlefield, but to gather intelligence. The latter need was particularly imperative when the enemy was a shadowy and dispersed network of terrorists fully capable of infiltrating the United States to attack civilians.

For the first time in any of the litigation to date, the administration disclosed the decision-making process for determining whether a US citizen was an enemy combatant who should be confined—a disclosure perhaps motivated by news reports that field officers in Afghanistan, acting on fragmentary and unreliable information, had made hasty and poorly considered decisions on who should be sent to Guantanamo.

Not so, said the government, at least for US citizens such as Padilla (who had never been at Guantanamo). The information available on a captured citizen was initially reviewed by the Office of Legal Counsel in the Department of Justice to determine if he was "associated" with the enemy's military and bent on "hostile acts" against the United States.

That determination was then reviewed by the CIA, whose director sent it to the secretary of defense, who added his views and forwarded the package to the attorney general for legal review, whence it went to the White House for review by the counsel to the president and a decision by the president, personally. The brief did not disclose when this "careful, thorough and deliberative process" had been put into place, nor did it disclose what evidence, or how much, sufficed to label a citizen as an enemy fighter. Nor, for that matter, did it disclose whether any of the reviewing authorities in Washington had any information that the front-line soldiers in Afghanistan did not.

But however the decision was made, and however many government offices reviewed it, did the president's power, even when backed by Congress, allow him to seize Americans in this country and put them in jail without any process of law? Here the government relied heavily, as it had in its cert petition, on the 1942 case of German saboteurs in *Quirin*. The Court in that case had held that President Roosevelt had authority to try the saboteurs, including the one who was a US citizen, and since they were arrested in New York, the SG argued, a president certainly has authority to detain suspected enemy combatants, citizens or not, seized here or abroad. "Indeed," the SG urged, "the factual parallels between *Quirin* and this case are striking." In short, the government was arguing that because citizenship provides no immunity or protection to Americans who take up arms with the enemy, and because al Qaeda operates throughout the world, demonstrably including the United States, an al Qaeda operative who happens to be in Chicago is as subject to capture and detention as any other operative, whatever his citizenship, in any other place in the world.

The government's brief, however, downplayed the obvious distinctions between the Quirin defendants and Padilla's situation. Those combatants had been captured in the course of military action, charged with committing war crimes, and held to await a trial that was soon to follow. Padilla had been arrested as he walked through an airport, with no military designs evident, he had been charged with no crime, and he was being held indefinitely with no prospect of any tribunal to judge him. The solicitor general did not address the question of why, if Padilla intended to go about planting a bomb in an American city, the government could not arrest him, charge him with conspiracy to commit murder, and put him on trial in Chicago's federal court. Its likely answer to that question would have been, as it was to say in answer to Justice O'Connor in the Hamdi oral argument, that the presidential decision "reflects the sound exercise of prosecutorial and executive discretion."

Padilla's lawyers, for their part, left the entire matter of New York or South Carolina habeas jurisdiction for the last few pages of their brief, clearly determined to keep the Court focused on the president's actions. If the justices could be persuaded that the president was acting unlawfully, they might well be disposed to tweak the technical rules of habeas jurisdiction and uphold the course that the case had taken to reach them.

"The Executive today seeks to validate an unprecedented new system of extrajudicial military imprisonment of citizens," the brief argued. "It seeks to do so absent any authorization of Congress defining the permissible scope and duration of such imprisonments, absent any meaningful review by the courts, and absent any charge or trial or procedural protections of any kind." Whatever the levels of review at Justice, the CIA, Defense, and the White House, "in our constitutional system, it is not enough to trust that our leaders act in good faith, for 'ours is a government of laws, not of men,'" quoting Chief Justice John Marshall's famous words in the 1803 case of *Marbury v. Madison.*

But to get to that sweeping proposition, Padilla had to undercut two supports of the government's position. First, they argued, the Authorization for Use of Military Force could not be read as a congressional assent to what the president was doing, because that resolution did not explicitly—nor, they argued, implicitly—contemplate or permit the arrest of American citizens on American soil to be held without charge. It was an authorization to use military force, not a free pass for the president to do whatever he wished. If Congress is to authorize the "unbounded and extensive curtailment of individual liberties" inherent in imprisonment without trial, they argued, it must at the very least do so in unmistakable language, leaving no doubt as to its intent. "There is nothing in the AUMF," they argued, "to suggest that Congress intended to displace the criminal laws (and protections associated with those laws) with a wholly new, unbounded scheme of preventive military detention by executive fiat." This required them to acknowledge that Padilla, in allegedly consorting with al Qaeda and embarking on a dirty-bomb plot, would have violated American criminal laws, but they readily did so. Moving Padilla from his military brig to an orthodox criminal trial in federal court would have been total victory.

Second, Padilla's brief argued, *Quirin* provided no valid precedent, because contrary to the government's argument, "the power to detain without trial is not *lesser* than the power to put on trial, for detention without trial carries a greater risk of error and abuse" (emphasis in the brief). The German saboteurs, it pointed out, were given a formal accusation of crime, the assistance of counsel, the presumption of innocence, and a trial, with at least a possibility of acquittal. Padilla had sat for two years in a military prison with no resort to any legal process, no lawyer, and not even the theoretical prospect of release except at such time, if it ever came, as the president decided to release him. "Indefinite detention—especially in solitary confinement, incommunicado, and subject to coercive interrogation—plainly raises unique constitutional problems not presented by the adversarial trial of [the *Quirin*] defendants represented by counsel." Moreover, "the *Quirin* Court reached its decision in the context of a traditional war between nation-states and simply had no occasion to address the questions that would be raised in the circumstances of a 'war' with a secret, non-state terrorist organization."

The argument thus did not go so far as to say that someone in Padilla's shoes could never under any circumstances be imprisoned as he had been, only that it could not be done by the president, with or without the 2001 AUMF. "Within our constitutional framework, it is for Congress to define, in the first instance, what an 'enemy combatant' *is*; the *process* by which a citizen may be subjected to military detention as such a combatant; and the *length of time* a citizen may be so imprisoned" (emphasis in the brief).

It was a careful argument, going only as far as it needed to in order to win the case, accepting that Congress might authorize the president to detain citizens arrested in this country, but that such extraordinary powers must be granted so explicitly that the AUMF as voted by Congress in 2001 plainly fell short. But it was also a risky argument, because it depended on persuading the Court that the AUMF's approval of "all necessary and appropriate force" indeed did not authorize the seizure of enemy combatants in the United States. No one needed to be reminded that the 9/11 attacks had been carried out by just such men.

So Padilla's argument suggested a troubling question: had one of the airplane hijackers happened to be an American citizen who somehow survived the crash, could he not be confined indefinitely for interrogation, given the president's commander in chief authority and the congressional resolution? Would the government's only recourse be to arrest him, give him *Miranda* warnings, charge him with his crimes, appoint a lawyer for him, and bind him over for trial in a federal court, interrogating him only to the extent he consented to be interrogated? The government had not raised the point quite like that, but its argument that neither citizenship nor national boundaries diminished the reach of the president's power over enemy combatants seemed to suggest that Padilla's argument would require the president and the Department of Justice to proceed in just that way.

On April 28, 2004, Deputy SG Clement barely had time to sit down after his argument in *Hamdi* than he rose again to argue the government's case in *Padilla*. Acknowledging that "there are many aspects of this case that raise issues that are really extraordinary," Clement immediately assured the Court that it could dispose of the case without having to decide those issues. There followed a long and not terribly productive discourse between Clement and the justices on the jurisdictional issue: whether Padilla was properly before the Court to begin with, given that his habeas petition was filed in New York while he was held in South Carolina. Clement and the justices spent much of the government's half hour on the details of the Court's sporadic exceptions to the rule that the petition had to be filed where the petitioner's "immediate custodian" was to be found, and whether those exceptions applied, or could be expanded, for the circumstances of this case.

When attention turned to the merits of Padilla's claim, Justice Souter asked Clement point blank whether, the Authorization for the Use of Military Force aside, the president himself had the authority to order Padilla confined at length without trial. Clement answered that he did have that authority, as commander in chief. That brought a question from Justice Scalia: "How does he get that just from being Commander in Chief? I understand the commander-in-chief power to be a power over the military forces, when they're being used as military forces. It doesn't mean that he has power to do whatever it takes to win the war. The steel seizure case illustrates that well enough."

Not whatever it takes, perhaps, Clement answered, but certainly the power to detain enemy combatants. But he quickly dismissed that as "hypothetical" because the president was not acting on his power alone but with the approval of Congress in the AUMF. Given the time spent on the jurisdictional question, Clement had little opportunity to pursue that train of thought with the Court.

Arguing for Padilla, Stanford Law School professor Jenny Martinez went straight to her point.

> We ask this Court for a narrow ruling that leaves for another day the grave constitutional question of whether our system would permit the indefinite imprisonment without trial of American citizens on American soil based on suspicion that they have associated with terrorism. We simply ask this Court to hold that at a minimum Congress would have to clearly and unequivocally authorize such a departure from our nation's traditions. And since Congress has not done so, Mr. Padilla is entitled to be charged with a crime and have his day in court.

The AUMF, she urged, was not that authorization, because "there is no reference in the text to any power to detain American citizens on American soil based on suspicion."

Her argument was buttressed by the Non-Detention Act, the statute enacted by Congress in 1971, providing that no citizen could be detained without an "act of Congress." Where the government had claimed that AUMF was that act, Martinez argued that it simply was not broad enough to cover what was being done to Padilla. But then she allowed that, if the president had sought an authorization as broad as she envisioned, "I have no doubt that Congress would step into the breach very quickly to provide whatever authorization the executive branch deemed necessary." That admission seemed to demote the confrontation from a balance of powers question in which Congress had an important and substantive role to one in which Congress simply had not yet been asked to do what it would surely and quickly do if it were asked.

Martinez argued that the Court did not have to decide the mega-question of whether the president alone could order Padilla detained indefinitely, only that he could not do so without more explicit authority from Congress. "We've had war on our soil before and never before in our nation's history has this Court granted the President a blank check to do whatever he wants to American citizens," she concluded.

Neither the justices nor counsel had raised the question that had so occupied them just the hour before, in the *Hamdi* argument: would Padilla have received his due process as a citizen if an impartial panel of military officers were convened to determine his status as an enemy combatant? To be sure, military tribunals seemed ill-suited for a man who had been arrested by the FBI in Chicago. A military tribunal in a combat zone was one thing; such a tribunal in a large American city would seem to be another. Padilla's case had almost entirely demilitarized the context of presidential authority, leaving the government to argue that in the shadowy terrorist war of the twenty-first century, combatants could turn up in Chicago as well as in Afghan mountains, and the president was as much the commander in chief in one place as the other.

When the advocates gathered up their papers and the Supreme Court turned to the next case on its docket, *Hamdi* and *Padilla* joined *Rasul* behind the Court's red curtains and the justices' closed doors. The justices convened a few days later, voted on the outcomes, and began to draft their opinions. Given the late date of the arguments, the assumption was that the decisions would come down together, on the last day of the Court's term in late June. They did.

CHAPTER FOUR

The Decisions of 2004: *Rasul,* *Hamdi,* and *Padilla*

On June 28, 2004, two months after the arguments, and on its last day of business, the Supreme Court issued its decisions in the three cases. It was not a good day for the president, for in none of them did the Court vindicate the authority he had asserted.

In *Rasul,* it ruled 6-3 in favor of the detainees. The opinion, written by Justice John Paul Stevens, traced a history of habeas corpus in order to unravel what the Eisentrager decision really meant. To understand *Eisentrager,* and the Court's decision in *Rasul,* it helps to have an understanding of the distinction between habeas corpus as it is preserved in the Constitution and what has become known as "statutory habeas corpus."

The Constitution's somewhat indirect language—"The privilege of the Writ of Habeas Corpus shall not be suspended, unless when in Cases of Rebellion or Invasion the public Safety may require it"—has traditionally been taken to preserve habeas corpus as it had existed when the Constitution was ratified in 1788. That constitutional guarantee is inviolate, although the scope of habeas corpus in the mists of 1788 has always been a subject of debate. In any event, Congress has occasionally enacted statutes that regulate the administration of habeas, beginning in 1789 when the first Congress gave federal courts explicit jurisdiction over such cases. Over the years both Congress and the Supreme Court had loosened the strictures a bit here and there, yet one of the requirements that remained was that courts could issue the writ only "within their respective jurisdictions."

By 1950, when *Eisentrager* was decided, the Court had long interpreted that limitation to mean that federal courts could grant the writ only to a petitioner whose immediate custodian was physically in the court's district—its territorial jurisdiction, which followed state boundaries. If the prisoner was in Alabama, for example, only the federal court in Alabama could consider his petition. That left unanswered the question of what if any rule applied to a prisoner who was not in the jurisdiction of any federal court, and the Court in *Eisentrager*, faced with just such a situation, had seemed to simply assume that German soldiers in Germany, being in no federal court's jurisdiction, had no right to seek habeas at all—or so the government had insisted in the Rasul litigation.

But *Eisentrager*, decided in 1950, was no longer the last word. In a 1973 case, the Court had loosened its interpretation, ruling that the requirement of territorial jurisdiction could also be satisfied if the court had within its district the official who had ordered the confinement, not necessarily the prisoner's present custodian. So if the prisoner in Alabama had been sent there after having been sentenced by a judge in Tennessee, he could file his habeas petition in either place.

The federal court in the District of Columbia, where the detainees had filed their habeas suit, certainly had jurisdiction over the president and the secretary of defense, by whose authority they were being held at Gitmo. And since the habeas statute, as Justice Stevens wrote for the majority, "draws no distinction between Americans and aliens held in federal custody, there is little reason to think that Congress intended the geographical coverage of the statute to vary depending on the detainee's citizenship." Recalling Solicitor General Olson's concession at oral argument that federal courts would have jurisdiction in the case of an American at Gitmo seeking habeas, Stevens therefore concluded, "Aliens held at the base, no less than American citizens, are entitled to invoke the federal courts' authority" under the habeas statute by filing their petitions in the federal court in Washington.

By basing its decision on relatively recent interpretations of the habeas statute, the Court avoided wading into the thicket of interpreting what was meant by the unique and ambiguous language in the 1903 lease that gave Cuba "ultimate sovereignty" but the United States "complete jurisdiction and control" (what had come to be dubbed "*de facto* sovereignty") over the installation on Guantanamo Bay. That point had been a contentious issue throughout the litigation, but now it simply no longer mattered; aliens detained outside the country by presidential authority could present their habeas petitions to the court in Washington, to invoke its jurisdiction over the president. The Court also avoided the need to deconstruct the ambiguity in *Eisentrager*: did the Court there mean to bar all aliens abroad from habeas relief, or did it simply rule that under the circumstances the German petitioners, having been duly charged, tried, and convicted in a military tribunal, were not entitled to further review by a federal court? The Court now disposed of that matter by relegating *Eisentrager* to history: it became just another decision applying a now-obsolete interpretation of statutory habeas corpus, and so its rationale, muddy as it was, was no longer a matter of any importance—or so the majority's opinion seemed to treat it.

Justice Anthony Kennedy, writing a concurring opinion (that is, voting for the outcome but not necessarily the reasoning the majority followed to get there), agreed that federal courts had jurisdiction over the Gitmo detainees, but he walked a narrower path to that conclusion. Rather than "creating automatic statutory authority to adjudicate the claims of persons located outside the United States," he would have confined the decision to Guantanamo's boundaries, ruling that its unique status qualified it as US territory and so detainees there could petition for habeas corpus just as if they were being held within US borders.

Justice Scalia, writing for himself, Justice Clarence Thomas, and Chief Justice William Rehnquist, dissented, and he did so with the customary exuberance—some would say hyperbole—that often marks his dissents. "This is an irresponsible overturning of settled law in a matter of extreme importance to our forces currently in the field," he wrote. "Today's carefree Court," Scalia warned, "springs a trap on the Executive, subjecting Guantanamo Bay to the oversight of the federal courts even though it has never before been thought to be within their jurisdiction—and thus making it a foolish place to have housed alien wartime detainees." Though the majority would not acknowledge doing so, Scalia said, it had overturned *Eisentrager* and given alien enemies—enemies!—broad rights in US courts. "It would be difficult to devise more effective fettering of a field commander," Scalia wrote, quoting *Eisentrager*, "than to allow the very enemies he is ordered to reduce to submission to call him to account in his own civil courts and divert his efforts and attention from the military offensive abroad to the legal defensive at home." Here, Scalia concluded, the Court had created "a wrenching departure from precedent," a "monstrous scheme in time of war," and "judicial adventurism of the worst sort."

Scalia's angry rhetoric was at the least premature, for the Court had said only that Guantanamo's location was no bar to the courthouse door. It had not ruled that their detention was illegal, or that they had an actual right to be released on habeas corpus, or, once through the courthouse door, what they might have to prove there about their detention in order to secure such a right. In fact, Stevens's opinion for the majority had said nothing about what might happen once they filed their petitions, and certainly nothing about whether "field commanders" must leave their combat outposts to come home and testify in court. It had simply left for another day any consideration of what rights the detainees might have or what obligations the government must meet. That was no oversight; when announcing interpretations of law, the Supreme Court is generally careful not to say too much, leaving to the lower courts the task of applying those interpretations to the specific facts of cases that come before them. What the Court might not have foreseen here, however, was that, once the detainees got inside the courthouse door, the question of what rights they had—indeed, whether they had any rights at all—would roil the federal courts in Washington for the next four years.

Padilla also turned on the question of where alleged enemy combatants, this time in the United States, could file a habeas petition, but this time the shoe was on the other foot. The Court ruled 5-4 against Padilla. Justices O'Connor and Kennedy, who had voted in *Rasul* to uphold jurisdiction in the District of Columbia for the Gitmo detainees, voted this time, with the three *Rasul* dissenters, to disallow jurisdiction for Padilla in New York. Chief Justice Rehnquist wrote the opinion for the majority, making clear that the decision had nothing to do with Guantanamo or with Padilla's designation as an enemy combatant. "While Padilla's detention is undeniably unique in many respects," the Chief Justice wrote, it "is not unique in any way that would provide [an] arguable basis for a departure from the immediate custodian rule." It was just another case of a prisoner in the United States who was challenging his present physical confinement. Padilla had been taken into custody in New York, but by the time his lawyer filed the habeas petition Padilla was in South Carolina. His immediate custodian was the commander of the brig there, and there the case should have been brought. Thus resolved, there was no occasion for the Court to address whether the president had authority to order his detention. That matter could be litigated if and when Padilla filed a petition for habeas—in South Carolina.

Justice Stevens, joined by Justices Ginsburg, Breyer, and Souter, wrote a sharp dissent. The immediate-custodian rule, he pointed out, was "riddled with exceptions"—a fact the majority had more or less acknowledged—in cases where the petitioner was out on bail, or confined overseas (as in *Rasul* and some earlier cases of Americans abroad), or had been transferred after filing the petition. Such an exception should be drawn here as well, Stevens wrote, particularly because the government did not tell Padilla's lawyer that it was taking him away; she learned of it only the next day, in a DoD press release, and she filed the habeas petition the day after that. That circumstance, Stevens wrote for his dissenting colleagues, was more than enough justification to make another exception in the much-riddled rule.

Though Stevens did not actually accuse the majority of rejuvenating a tattered rule in order to avoid a decision on presidential authority, that implication was hard to miss. In language as strident as Scalia's had been that day in *Rasul*—and influenced perhaps by shocking revelations only a few weeks earlier of abusive mistreatment of captives by American soldiers at the Abu Ghraib prison in Iraq—Stevens wrote, "At stake in this case is nothing less than the essence of a free society. Even more important than the method of selecting the people's rulers and their successors is the character of the constraints imposed on the Executive by the rule of law. Unconstrained Executive detention for the purpose of investigating and preventing subversive activity is the hallmark of the Star Chamber." Such detention, he went on, may not

> be justified by the naked interest in using unlawful procedures to extract information. Incommunicado detention for months on end is such a procedure. Whether the information so procured is more or less reliable than that acquired by more extreme forms of torture is of no consequence. For if this Nation is to remain true to the ideals symbolized by its flag, it must not wield the tools of tyrants even to resist an assault by the forces of tyranny.

Had the four dissenters picked up one more vote—most logically, from O'Connor or Kennedy—then Padilla's habeas petition would have been ruled in order and the Court would have faced the substantive question of whether his detention was lawful. That would have put the Court in direct confrontation with the president, for Stevens's "tools of tyrants" opinion left little doubt how he and his three dissenting colleagues would have come out on detention. One might surmise that O'Connor and Kennedy joined with Rehnquist (and Scalia and Thomas) to dispose of the case on procedural grounds in order to avoid that showdown.

If that is so, one may also infer that they were not ready to deliver a rebuke to the president on such a fundamental question of his authority, less than three years after the 9/11 attacks. But while that might have been true, the Court was not that day reluctant to deliver a defeat to the president on the procedures by which he was exercising his acknowledged authority over military detainees, and in particular Yaser Hamdi.

In *Hamdi*, the Court handed down a stinging rejection of the government's assertion of presidential authority to confine enemy combatants without interference by the courts. They ruled 8-1 in favor of Hamdi, with only Justice Clarence Thomas voting to uphold the government. The eight justices wrote three separate opinions, each one firmly unsympathetic to the president's claims.

Justice Sandra Day O'Connor wrote for herself and Justices Breyer and Kennedy and, perhaps surprisingly, Chief Justice Rehnquist as well. It was a lengthy and meticulously documented treatise that addressed the issue of detention with the most probing analysis of due process of law in nearly thirty years of Supreme Court jurisprudence.

"At this difficult time in our Nation's history," she began,

> we are called upon to consider the legality of the Government's detention of a United States citizen on United States soil as an 'enemy combatant' and to address the process that is constitutionally owed to one who seeks to challenge his classification as such. We hold that although Congress authorized the detention of combatants in the narrow circumstances alleged here, due process demands that a citizen held in the United States as an enemy combatant be given a meaningful opportunity to contest the factual basis for that detention before a neutral decisionmaker.

For reasons that were to become clear (but that the four other justices who also voted against the government—Breyer, Souter, Stevens, and Scalia—did not fully share), Justice O'Connor's analysis depended upon a conclusion that Hamdi's detention was lawful at its outset. She traced the traditional authority of armies, upheld by centuries-old laws of war, to capture and detain enemies seized in combat to prevent them "from returning to the field of battle and taking up arms once again," and she dismissed any thought that US citizenship somehow provided immunity to Americans fighting on the enemy side. Given the long history of war, therefore, when Congress in the post-9/11 Authorization for the Use of Military Force authorized the president to use "necessary and appropriate force," it "clearly and unmistakably authorized detention" of enemy combatants even without specifically referring to it.

But that authority allows detention only when it is, in O'Connor's words, "sufficiently clear that the individual is, in fact, an enemy combatant." Moreover, the "clearly established principle of the law of war [is] that detention may last no longer than active hostilities." Here, she wrote, Hamdi had a well-grounded fear of "the substantial prospect of perpetual detention." Indeed, the government's position "throughout the litigation of this case suggests that Hamdi's detention could last for the rest of his life." The Fifth Amendment of the US Constitution provides that no person shall be deprived of liberty without due process of law. So the question facing the Court, O'Connor wrote, was, "what process is constitutionally due to a citizen who disputes his enemy-combatant status."

The government's answer had been clear. Because of the constitutional separation of powers, and the judiciary's traditional reluctance to overturn a president's wartime military decisions, a court's role is at an end when it ascertains that the detention practices *as a whole* are legal, and detention of enemy combatants was surely a legal practice. Individual detainees are entitled to nothing beyond that—or at most simply a statement, such as the Mobbs declaration, explaining the circumstances that led to the detainee's designation as an enemy combatant.

Justice O'Connor did not agree, and she was direct about it. Hamdi was being deprived of his liberty, and "this Court has consistently recognized that an individual challenging his detention may not be held at the will of the Executive without recourse to some proceeding before a neutral tribunal to determine whether the Executive's asserted justifications for that detention have basis in fact and warrant in law."

To determine whether there is such a basis, and such a law, courts must examine what is at stake both for the government and for the prisoner. Their interests—individual liberty versus national security—necessarily conflict, yet both interests, O'Connor wrote, are based on valid and important concerns. They exemplify the tension between, on the one hand, "the autonomy that the Government asserts is necessary in order to pursue effectively a particular goal" and, on the other, "the process that a citizen contends he is due before he is deprived of a constitutional right." To determine what the due process of law requires, therefore, courts have traditionally sought to strike a balance, weighing "the private interest that will be affected by the official action"—here, Hamdi's interest in securing his liberty—"against the Government's asserted interest" in protecting national security, "including the function involved and the burdens the Government would face in providing greater process" to the petitioner. To reach a fair balance, courts weigh "the risk of an erroneous deprivation of the private interest if the process were reduced and the probable value, if any, of additional or substitute procedural safeguards."

To use more concrete terms for Justice O'Connor's explication: the greater the importance of the citizen's right, the more process he is due, and so the more he is entitled to participate in the decision, up to a full and even adversarial examination of whether the government's interest is sufficient to deprive him of that right. One who is accused of crime and is on trial for his life or liberty is entitled to the highest level of process—a full-blown trial before a judge, with the assistance of counsel and the presumption of innocence, with the burden on the government to prove guilt to a jury beyond a reasonable doubt according to formal rules of evidence. When lesser interests are at stake, less process may be due, taking into account the government's interest and the cost and burden of providing ascending levels of process. The government need not provide a full-blown trial before a federal judge and a jury, for example, to one who claims that his Social Security benefits have been miscalculated. That matter can be handled in a relatively informal proceeding before an administrative hearing examiner whose duty is to decide such disputes impartially, based on the evidence as a whole, not necessarily beyond a reasonable doubt.

In this case, as no one needed to be reminded, the interests on both sides were extraordinarily high. Hamdi was facing the possibility of a prolonged, even lifetime, deprivation of his liberty, while the government was fighting an enemy threatening the security of the nation. It was, as Justice O'Connor wrote, "the most elemental of liberty interests—the interest in being free from physical detention by one's own government" weighed against the significant government interest in "ensuring that those who have in fact fought with the enemy during a war do not return to battle against the United States." The government also had a legitimate interest in seeing that "military officers who are engaged in the serious work of waging battle" not be "unnecessarily and dangerously distracted by litigation half a world away," as well as an interest in avoiding judicial scrutiny of military operations that "would both intrude on the sensitive secrets of national defense and result in a futile search for evidence buried under the rubble of war"—outcomes the government feared should the Court uphold the searching habeas hearing that Judge Doumar in Virginia had ordered in Hamdi's case. (Notably, throughout her opinion Justice O'Connor did not include as a governmental interest the need to gather intelligence from captured combatants.)

With the interests of each side in the due process analysis thus identified and contrasted, Justice O'Connor paused for a cautionary observation that suggested where she was headed.

Striking the proper constitutional balance here is of great importance to the nation during this period of ongoing combat. But it is equally vital that our calculus not give short shrift to the values that this country holds dear or to the privilege that is American citizenship. It is during our most challenging and uncertain moments that our nation's commitment to due process is most severely tested; and it is in those times that we must preserve our commitment at home to the principles for which we fight abroad.

She rejected the processes urged by the government and Hamdi both. Neither the government's once-over Mobbs affidavit nor a federal court's probing examination of military operations properly balanced the conflicting interests she had identified. The requirements of due process landed somewhere in between. But where?

O'Connor answered: "A citizen-detainee seeking to challenge his classification as an enemy combatant must receive notice of the factual basis for his classification, and a fair opportunity to rebut the Government's factual assertions before a neutral decisionmaker," she wrote. "These essential constitutional promises"—fair notice, fair hearing, fair decision—"may not be eroded."

But they could be flexed. Notice of the government's reasons for detention, a fair opportunity to be heard in reply, and a "neutral decisionmaker" did not necessarily equate to, or require, an adversarial hearing before a federal judge in a US court applying formal rules of evidence, which is what a habeas case amounts to. Some less formal proceeding would suffice. Hearsay evidence might be allowed. The government's evidence of enemy combatancy, even if it left some doubts that might doom a criminal case, might be enough to justify detention, provided the detainee had sufficient opportunity to rebut it. And the process would be triggered not at the time of capture but when the government determined to continue the detention beyond the combat zone. Thus moderated, some "threats to military operations posed by a basic system of independent review" might remain, but they would be "not so weighty as to trump a citizen's core rights to challenge meaningfully the government's case and to be heard by an impartial adjudicator." Under that standard, the government's treatment of Hamdi was clearly defective, for he had received no notice, no fair chance to tell his side of the story, and certainly no impartial adjudicator of his fate.

O'Connor was particularly careful to address the government's argument that by imposing due process requirements on the military's detainee practices, her Court would be infringing on the prerogatives of the Executive. She spoke firmly about what separation of powers means. "The [government's] position that the courts must forego any examination of the individual case and focus exclusively on the legality of the broader detention scheme cannot be mandated by any reasonable view of separation of powers, as this approach serves only to *condense* power into a single branch of government" (emphasis by O'Connor). "We have long since made clear," she wrote, "that a state of war is not a blank check for the President when it comes to the rights of the Nation's citizens"—a reference to the Court's 1952 Youngstown decision invalidating the presidential seizure of steel mills. "The Great Writ of habeas corpus allows the Judicial Branch to play a necessary role in maintaining this delicate balance of governance, serving as an important judicial check on the Executive's discretion in the realm of detentions."

When examined in that light, the "military process" cited by the solicitor general at oral argument—the field interrogation of detainees in Afghanistan that had classified them once and for all as enemy combatants—plainly did not amount to due process of law. "Hamdi has received no process," O'Connor wrote. "An interrogation by one's captor, however effective an intelligence-gathering tool, hardly constitutes a constitutionally adequate factfinding before a neutral decisionmaker." But that decision maker did not need to be a federal judge. In fact, O'Connor pointed out, the military's Vietnam-era regulations for military proceedings, which provided three impartial military officers to separate POWs from civilians, would likely suffice, but with an important addition: Hamdi "unquestionably" had the right to a lawyer in any further proceedings on his status.

O'Connor closed with a tacit recognition of the delicacy of the balance between liberty and security: "We have no reason to doubt that courts faced with these sensitive matters will pay proper heed both to the matters of national security that might arise in an individual case and to the constitutional limitations safeguarding essential liberties that remain vibrant even in times of security concerns."

O'Connor's opinion, however, was signed only by herself and three other justices—not a majority of the Court. Justice Scalia wrote a dissenting opinion, joined by Justice Stevens, a distinctly unusual pair of justices to be in agreement. Scalia's argument was not that O'Connor had gone too far, but that she had not gone far enough. In an opinion redolent with the words of Blackstone, Alexander Hamilton, and Thomas Jefferson, tracing the history of habeas corpus from 1350 to 1789—territory that Scalia knew well and invoked often—he concluded that, unless the writ of habeas corpus were suspended, which it had not been since the Civil War, then the government's only options were to put Hamdi on trial for treason or some other applicable crime, or to release him. Holding him without trial, even if providing him with O'Connor's idea of an impartial decision maker in the form of a military tribunal, was simply unconstitutional.

Justice Souter also wrote a separate opinion, joined by Justice Ginsburg, in which they parted company with O'Connor, but in a different direction from that taken by Scalia and Stevens. They concluded that the Authorization for the Use of Military Force did not in fact authorize Hamdi's detention, at least not on the basis of the facts adduced by the government in the Mobbs affidavit, and that unless the government could produce further evidence on his alleged status as an enemy combatant, Hamdi was entitled to be released under the Non-Detention Act, which required that no citizen be detained except pursuant to an act of Congress. For Souter and Ginsburg, the AUMF did not authorize detention clearly enough to satisfy the Non-Detention Act. "Its focus is clear," wrote Souter of the AUMF, "and that is on the use of military power. It never so much as uses the word detention," nor for that matter was there any reason for Congress to consider detention in the United States, given the plentitude of laws criminalizing terrorism, its support, and its conspiracies.

By this reasoning, Souter wrote, there is no occasion for further proceedings of the type described by Justice O'Connor. Hamdi deserved to be freed unless the government was prepared to treat him as a prisoner of war under the Geneva Conventions, which plainly it was not, or to put him into the criminal process, which it showed no signs of doing. Souter and Ginsburg did not address the question of whether there was a third option—for Congress to revise the AUMF to authorize detention.

This juxtaposition of opinions put the Court in a real fix. There was only one vote (Thomas) for upholding what the government was doing; four votes (Scalia and Stevens; Souter and Ginsburg) for freeing Hamdi unless he was to be criminally charged and tried; and four votes (O'Connor, Rehnquist, Kennedy, and Breyer) for holding him pending the outcome of some new process left to the military to devise. There was no majority for any outcome.

Souter and Ginsburg alleviated the situation by formally concurring with O'Connor, thereby giving her a majority of six, even though they made clear they thought she had not gone far enough. Souter was reluctant but resigned. Since his preferred outcome of releasing Hamdi absent criminal charges or a specific act of Congress justifying his continued detention "does not command a majority of the Court," he wrote in his opinion for himself and Ginsburg, "the need to give practical effect to the conclusions of eight members of the Court rejecting the Government's position calls for me to join with the [O'Connor] plurality in ordering remand on terms closest to those I would impose." He made clear that he did not "adopt the plurality's resolution" of the due process issues because by his lights there was no need even to address those issues. But there had to be a majority for something, and so Souter and Ginsburg cast their votes with O'Connor's result, distancing themselves from her reasoning.

So it was clear that the government had been handed a thumping defeat, even though Hamdi had not been given the victory of freedom that he wanted. But the Court had created a path that might lead him there—someday.

The someday came sooner than he had no doubt imagined, and not on the path the Court had created. Almost immediately after the decision, the Department of Defense began negotiations with the Saudis to return Hamdi home, provided only that he renounce his American citizenship and refrain from any anti-American actions once he got there. On October 12, 2004, less than three months after the Court had spoken, he was put on a plane to Riyadh. "As we have repeatedly stated," the DoD press release read, "the United States has no interest in detaining enemy combatants beyond the point that they pose a threat to the U.S. and our allies." There was no indication of just what led the authorities to conclude that Hamdi was no longer a threat. Professor David Cole of Georgetown Law School commented, "It's quite something for the government to declare this person one of the worst of the worst, hold him for almost three years and then, when they're told by the Supreme Court to give him a fair hearing, turn around and give up." A *Washington Post* editorial was succinct. "A blithe 'never mind,'" it said of DoD's action.

It is one of the ironies of Hamdi's case that, although he was the centerpiece of one of the Supreme Court's most important decisions on the due process rights of citizens, he never really thought of himself as a US citizen at all. He may not even have known until the litigation was well under way that his birth in Louisiana twenty-four years earlier had made him one. "He has always thought of himself as a Saudi citizen," his lawyer Frank Dunham explained when his client's release was imminent. So agreeing to renounce his American citizenship was no big deal. "He wasn't willing to spend an extra day in jail over it." But Hamdi had evidently picked up some Americanisms during his two and a half years at Gitmo. "That's what I'm talking about!" he declared when he learned of his imminent release. "Awesome!"

One aspect of the Hamdi litigation deserves notice. Because the government had never treated its captives as prisoners of war—indeed, had explicitly denied that they were POWs, pursuant to President Bush's declaration on February 7, 2002—it sacrificed a strategy that might have made a critical difference in the case. The Third Geneva Convention allows captives to be held as prisoners of war until the "cessation of active hostilities," provided that they are given access to a "competent tribunal" if they claim that they were never combatants at all and should be released. But the Convention goes no further, so captives have no resort to a court. As noted earlier, the Defense Department had regulations in place for such tribunals: Army Regulation 190-8 provided for three military officers to hear and decide such claims. Had the Bush administration followed that course, it might have been able to defeat Hamdi's suit by arguing that its compliance with the Geneva Conventions fulfilled its obligations and obviated any need for US courts to determine whether he had a Constitution-based right to something more. But there was no room for that argument in the government's case and the Supreme Court did not address it.

Meanwhile, even before the Hamdi decision was announced, the military lawyers in the Department of Defense, who had never embraced the hard line on due process for detainees put forth by the Justice Department and the White House, were preparing for the possibility that the administration would lose the case. Directed by the Court to provide due process to detainees, DoD announced only a few weeks afterwards that it would give everyone at Guantanamo a hearing, in a novel process known as Combatant Status Review Tribunals.

These CSRTs were not courts. They were boards that would bear some resemblance to the tribunals established by military regulations in Vietnam to sort out enemy combatants from civilians. The tribunals would consist of a panel of three US military officers who would review the file on each detainee, call him before them under secure conditions at Gitmo to tell his side of the story if he wished to do so, allow him to call witnesses who were "reasonably available," and then render a decision on whether he was an enemy combatant.

Each detainee would be given a US officer to act as a "personal representative" to assist him in preparing for the tribunal's hearing, but, despite Justice O'Connor's point that detainees were "unquestionably" entitled to legal counsel, these officers were not lawyers and hence whatever a detainee might say to his representative would not be in confidence. Unlike the Vietnam-era tribunals, no detainee would be given prisoner-of-war status. President Bush's decree in February 2002 that neither the Taliban nor al Qaeda were lawful combatants had closed off that avenue. Instead, those who were found to be enemy combatants would be retained at Gitmo as most of them had been for two years or more. Those found not to have been enemy combatants would be released and sent home—but only if the reviewing authorities in the Pentagon agreed with the panel's verdict.

The CSRTs are not to be confused with military commissions, whose function, as will be seen in the next chapter, is to put detainees on trial for crimes and to jail them, even execute them, if the commissions find them guilty. The CSRTs were ostensibly intended only to sort out true enemy combatants from unlucky bystanders who did not need to be detained at Guantanamo. Except for the absence of defense lawyers, they did resemble, if somewhat superficially, what Justice O'Connor had sketched as due process for detainees. The three tribunal officers were to be "neutral decisionmakers," and the detainee would be allowed to be present and to be heard, and even to submit evidence. On the other hand, the government would be allowed to rely on written affidavits to make its case, not unlike the Mobbs declaration that had summarized the circumstances of Hamdi's capture, and any classified information in those submissions would be blacked out, concealed from the detainee. The burden would be on him to overcome the government's case: once the government submitted its evidence that the detainee was a combatant—evidence which might or might not be disclosed to him—he would be presumed so unless he could satisfy the tribunal officers that he was not.

Over the following two years, from 2004 to 2006, CSRTs were convened for every detainee at Guantanamo, some 558 in all. Judged by any standard of "neutral decisionmaking," they proved to be an empty promise for nearly every one. Evidence was routinely denied to them, particularly the names of persons who had allegedly fingered them as enemy combatants or "terrorists," which put the detainees in the position of having to answer a case that was largely secret.

This excerpt of one detainee's CSRT hearing was included in a later Supreme Court brief. Mustafa Ait Idir was being held at Gitmo for "associating" with an unnamed person said to have been an al Qaeda operative. Idir, an Algerian-born citizen of Bosnia and reportedly a martial arts champion, was asked to respond.

Idir: Give me his name.

Tribunal President: I do not know.

Idir: How can I respond to this?

President: Did you know anybody that was a member of Al Qaida?

Idir: No, no. This is something the interrogators told me a long while ago. I asked the interrogators to tell me who this person was. Then I could tell you if I might have known this person, but not if this person is a terrorist. Maybe I knew this person as a friend. Maybe it was a person that worked with me. Maybe it was a person that was on my team. But I do not know if this person is Bosnian, Indian or whatever. If you tell me the name, then I can respond and defend myself against this accusation.

President: We are asking you the questions and we need you to respond to what is on the unclassified summary.

Idir: Why? Because these are accusations that I can't even answer. I am not able to answer them. You tell me I am from Al Qaida, but I am not an Al Qaida. I don't have any proof to give you except to ask you to catch Bin Laden and ask him if I am a part of Al Qaida. To tell me that I thought, I'll just tell you that I did not. I don't have proof regarding this. What should be done is you should give me evidence regarding these accusations because I am not able to give you any evidence. I can just tell you no, and that is it.

The CSRT ruled that Idir remain confined as an enemy combatant.

In addition to the anonymous accusations, few if any witnesses requested by detainees were found to be "reasonably available," even though some were themselves being held at Gitmo. Moreover, evidence of enemy combatancy was often based on highly attenuated circumstances. In many cases, such as Idir's, it was enough that a detainee had been identified as having "associated" with al Qaeda. In other cases, it was enough that a detainee had traveled to Afghanistan and stayed in a rooming house known to be frequented by al Qaeda or Taliban operatives, or was captured while fleeing an American attack—the apparent premise being that only an enemy fighter would run away from American forces. And when a panel did, on occasion, rule that evidence of combatancy was insufficient and that the detainee should be released, the Pentagon frequently sent the case back for further findings—a less than subtle signal that the panel should reverse its decision. In the end, some 93 percent of detainees were found to have been "enemy combatants." Their detention continued, with no end in sight; indeed, with no assurance that it would ever end.

The case of Jose Padilla deserves an epilogue. On July 2, 2004, four days after the Supreme Court dismissed his habeas petition because it should have been filed in South Carolina, Padilla's lawyers, including Donna Newman and now Jenny Martinez, who had argued his case in the Supreme Court, did just that. The reloaded case was assigned to Judge Henry F. Floyd in Charleston, who had taken his seat on the federal court ten months earlier, having served six years in the South Carolina legislature and ten years as a state court trial judge.

If the Bush administration thought it would have an easier time in a conservative southern court, its hopes were quickly dashed. On February 28, 2005, Judge Floyd emphatically rejected the government's contention that the president, with or without the Authorization for the Use of Military Force, had authority to confine Padilla without charge or trial. Floyd ruled that the Supreme Court's decision allowing the detention of Yaser Hamdi was not controlling; Padilla had been arrested in the United States, not on a foreign battlefield. Moreover, the AUMF's permission for the president to use "all necessary and appropriate force" to detain enemy combatants did not apply, because Padilla was in the custody of federal officials on suspicion of complicity in a terrorist plot. "There [are] no impediments whatsoever to the Government bringing charges against him for any or all of the array of heinous crimes that he has been effectively accused of committing," Floyd noted. His alleged plot having been "thwarted when he was arrested on the material witness warrant, the Court finds that the President's subsequent decision to detain [Padilla] as an enemy combatant was neither necessary nor appropriate." This being so, Padilla's confinement was in "direct contradiction" to the Non-Detention Act, the statute that prohibits the imprisonment or detention of a US citizen "except pursuant to an Act of Congress." To uphold government authority to detain Padilla, Floyd ruled, "would not only offend the rule of law and violate this country's constitutional tradition, but it would also be a betrayal of this Nation's commitment to the separation of powers that safeguards our democratic values and individual liberties."

He ordered Padilla released from detention within forty-five days, making clear that the government was perfectly free to hold him on the original material witness warrant, or to bring criminal charges against him, just as it would any other accused criminal. He did not need to add that, in either event, Padilla would have the right to a lawyer, the right to remain silent, and other aspects of due process of law, just as any other material witness or accused criminal.

The government appealed the ruling to the Court of Appeals for the Fourth Circuit, and the big guns came out again. The government's case was presented by the solicitor general's office and argued by SG Paul Clement himself; Padilla was represented by Andrew Patel, a veteran New York criminal defense lawyer, supported by a dozen amicus briefs urging the court of appeals to uphold the habeas decision, including a brief filed by Janet Reno, who had been attorney general under President Clinton, and Eric Holder, who three and a half years later would become attorney general under President Obama—and would in that capacity resolutely oppose Guantanamo detainees seeking their release on habeas corpus.

Given the magnitude of the issues, the court expedited the appeal, and after oral argument it handed down its decision on September 9, 2005, reversing Judge Floyd and ruling firmly in favor of the government, all three judges on the panel in agreement on what they called the "exceedingly important question" of the president's authority to seize and detain an enemy combatant in the United States. The crux of the decision was the court's reading of the Authorization for the Use of Military Force. It overturned Judge Floyd's conclusion that, given the availability of criminal proceedings, detention was neither "necessary" nor "appropriate." Padilla had been duly designated an enemy combatant, and neither his citizenship nor his apprehension in the United States undercut the president's authority to detain him. The court relied on the Supreme Court's decision in *Hamdi*, upholding detention of a citizen combatant, and went on to conclude that the place where Padilla had been taken into custody—O'Hare airport in Chicago—was legally irrelevant: neither the law of war nor the AUMF precluded the government from apprehending enemy combatants who happened to be in the United States.

"We can discern no difference in principle between Hamdi and Padilla," the court wrote. "Because, like Hamdi, Padilla is an enemy combatant, and because his detention is no less necessary than was Hamdi's in order to prevent his return to the battlefield, the President is authorized by the AUMF to detain Padilla as a fundamental incident to the conduct of war." The availability of criminal prosecution was beside the point, the court ruled. Without the power to detain enemy combatants, whatever their place of arrest and whatever the prospect of subsequent prosecution, "the President could well be unable to protect American citizens from the very kind of savage attack that occurred four years ago, almost to the day" of its decision.

Padilla's lawyers of course filed a petition for certiorari in the Supreme Court. Few cases ever seemed as certain of the Court's review as this one. After all, the Court had taken this very case, raising this very issue, just the year before, and the jurisdictional problem that had led the Court to dispose of it without reaching the question of presidential authority had now been cured. The Court hardly needed to be reminded that the case presented, in the court of appeals' words, an "exceedingly important question."

But a curious thing happened. In November 2005, two days before the government's answer to Padilla's cert petition was due in the Supreme Court, the Justice Department announced that a grand jury in Florida had indicted Padilla on criminal charges of conspiracy—considerably less momentous charges than plotting to detonate al Qaeda's "dirty bomb" in an American city, which the indictment did not even mention. On the same day, the Justice Department applied to the court of appeals for permission to transfer Padilla to civilian custody, to withdraw the habeas case altogether from the federal courts, and to have the court of appeals vacate its decision upholding the president's authority to deal with Padilla as an enemy combatant.

Normally, the government would need no judicial permission

to move a prisoner from military to civilian custody to face criminal charges, but a Supreme Court rule provided that no petitioner whose habeas case was before the Court could be transferred without judicial approval, a rule designed to preclude the government from moving a prisoner hither and yon, playing jurisdictional games to evade Supreme Court review. There seemed little reason for the court of appeals to deny the application; indeed, Padilla's lawyers themselves told the court of appeals to grant the transfer. No doubt they were disappointed at losing the opportunity to argue and win a historic victory in the nation's highest court, but they had been arguing all along that Padilla should be released from military detention to face whatever criminal charges the government might bring in a conventional federal trial, and now the government was seeking to do exactly that. In the interests of their client, they could do nothing else but go along with what the government proposed to do.

But on December 21, 2005, the court of appeals denied the application, and did so with a barely concealed anger seldom seen in appellate opinions. Though the government had given the court no explanation for why it wanted to move Padilla, the three judges who had decided the case two months earlier left little doubt that they believed the purpose "may be to avoid consideration of our decision by the Supreme Court." That, they said, is not a "legitimate justification." The government "cannot be seen as conducting litigation with the enormous implications of this litigation—litigation imbued with significant public interest—in such a way as to select by which forum as between the Supreme Court of the United States and an inferior appellate court it wishes to be bound."

Moreover, they wrote, the government's actions "have left not only the impression that Padilla may have been held for these years, even if justifiably, by mistake" but also the impression that the principle of presidential authority "can, in the end, yield to expediency with little or no cost to its conduct of the war against terror." These impressions

> have been left, we fear, at what may ultimately prove to be substantial cost to the government's credibility before the courts, to whom it will one day need to argue again in support of a principle of assertedly like importance and necessity to the one that it seems to abandon today. While there could be an objective that could command

such a price as all of this, it is difficult to imagine what that objective would be.

Undaunted by the court's hostility, the government went to the Supreme Court and renewed its application for permission, and the Supreme Court, in a brief and unexplained order on January 4, 2006, granted it. Three months later, on April 3, it also denied—by the narrowest of margins—Padilla's petition for certiorari to review the court of appeals' underlying decision on his habeas case, with an explanation by Justice Kennedy that the government had made the habeas case moot by releasing him from military custody. But Justices Souter, Ginsburg, and Breyer noted that they would have granted the petition; Justice Ginsburg wrote in a brief statement that the issue of presidential authority remained one of "profound importance," notwithstanding Padilla's release. One more vote and the Court would have taken the case. But for the second time in as many years, Padilla's lawyers were ushered out of the Supreme Court without a decision on the constitutionality of their client's imprisonment. The extent of presidential authority would have to await another case, on another day.

Padilla was eventually tried and convicted in federal court in Florida of providing material support for terrorism, apparently on the basis of his application to al Qaeda for training in Afghanistan. Whether that training ever took place is unclear. He was sentenced to twenty-one years in prison. The government did not charge or prove that he had conspired to bring a bomb to the United States, or indeed that he had done anything on al Qaeda's behalf.

There is a sequel to the epilogue: in 2003, President Bush designated one Ali al-Marri, a citizen of Qatar living in Illinois on a student visa, an enemy combatant, reportedly because he had come to the United States at the direction of Khalid Sheikh Mohammed, a senior al Qaeda operative (see chapter 7), to await further instructions on how to carry out al Qaeda's work here. Like Padilla, al-Marri was brought to the US Navy brig in Charleston, South Carolina, and held incommunicado there. Through a lawyer, he sought habeas corpus, essentially on the same grounds that Padilla had raised—that the president had no lawful authority to order the indefinite military detention of a person living in the United States. In 2008, three years after the Supreme Court had put an end to Padilla's case, the US Court of Appeals for the Fourth Circuit—the court that had upheld Padilla's continued confinement—declined al-Marri's request for release, but it ordered that he be given a hearing in the district court at which he could contest his imprisonment and perhaps win release then. The Supreme Court granted al-Marri's cert petition, to consider—once again—the extent of the president's authority to hold US residents in confinement as enemy combatants. And again—this time in the presidency of Barack Obama, five weeks after his inauguration—the United States transferred a petitioner to civilian custody to stand trial on terrorism charges, and asked the Supreme Court to dismiss the case as moot. On March 6, 2009, the Court did so.

In 2009, al-Marri pleaded guilty to one count of conspiracy to provide material support to terrorism; the remaining charges were dropped, and he was sentenced to eight years in the federal "supermax" prison in Colorado.

Twice, then, the Supreme Court had taken a case to address the scope of presidential authority to detain US residents, and twice it had declined to address it.

CHAPTER FIVE

Hamdan

As the imprisonment at Guantanamo continued—the Supreme Court's three cases were decided some two and a half years after the first detainees arrived in January 2002—life at the once-backwater naval base for those held captive fluctuated between tedium and despair. At the beginning of 2004, there were some 570 men imprisoned there; some number of them had taken up arms against the invading American and coalition forces, others had been swept up and turned over for bounty.

In all, they were a pretty motley crew of captives. Men thought to have important al Qaeda ties, including several who were close to Osama bin Laden and the attacks of September 11, were not at Guantanamo at all, but at secret "black sites" set up by the Central Intelligence Agency in Poland, Thailand, and elsewhere. They were being interrogated harshly—as became clear later, they were being tortured—for whatever intelligence could be extracted from them, on the location of bin Laden, on the planning and execution of the attacks, on what al Qaeda might be planning next. By the beginning of 2004, whatever low-grade information the Gitmo detainees might once have known had grown stale and useless after two years. Guantanamo itself was all but closed to new arrivals; only 10 arrived in 2004, another 15 in 2005. More than 100 were sent home during that time. Those who remained were no longer worth interrogating, and so the worst practices had gradually receded, but conditions in the primitive and isolated camp remained harsh.

In his speech to a joint session of Congress nine days after the 9/11 attacks, President Bush made a promise: "Whether we bring our enemies to justice or bring justice to our enemies, justice will be done." He promised imminent military action—presumably the bringing of justice to our enemies—but said nothing more then about how he planned to bring our enemies to justice.

The events that culminated on September 11, 2001, were capital crimes—kidnapping, aircraft hijacking, and mass murders, to name just the most obvious—and while those who had carried them out that day were killed with their victims, there was never any doubt that others who had instigated, planned, conspired, and assisted in their commission—leaders and operatives of al Qaeda, in short—could be tried in America's federal courts. Although the acts of bin Laden and other conspirators had taken place in foreign lands, the devastation struck in the United States, and so under international law the United States inarguably could exercise its jurisdiction. All that was needed was to capture them and bring them here, to be held without bail, charged with their crimes, and put on trial before a federal judge and jury, and convictions would surely follow.

Indeed, al Qaeda was no stranger to America's courts. On February 26, 1993, its operatives had detonated a truck bomb in the World Trade Center that now lay in smoking rubble as President Bush addressed the Congress. It had been a failed attempt to bring down both towers, but the bomb killed 6 people and injured 1,000 more. Six men were convicted and sentenced to life without parole, and the investigation led also to the conviction of Omar Abdel-Rahman, known as the "blind sheikh," convicted of conspiracy and sentenced to life in a federal prison, where he remains.

But President Bush did not look to the federal courts to bring the nation's enemies to justice. It was an article of faith in his administration—among those the president listened to—that civilian trials would be too good for al Qaeda's thugs and those who had helped or sheltered them. In federal court, they would be entitled to lawyers, to a presumption of innocence that could be overcome only by proof beyond a reasonable doubt, to a unanimous verdict of a jury, and to a life-tenured federal judge obliged to conduct trials under the same rules that applied to bank robbers, drug dealers, and swindlers. Confessions or other incriminating statements obtained under duress would be excluded from evidence. Their silence could not be held against them. They could appeal their convictions; some might even, conceivably, be acquitted. The courthouses where trials were held would be obvious targets for al Qaeda attacks.

Those who had the president's ear were the members of the self-appointed "war council" that had devised the plan to bring those captured in Afghanistan to Guantanamo Bay (see chapter 1)—Vice President Cheney and White House counsel Alberto Gonzales; Cheney's counsel David Addington, a skilled lawyer and bureaucratic infighter; John Yoo of the Department of Justice's Office of Legal Counsel; and Tim Flanigan, a former deputy assistant attorney general in that office. They were committed to the belief that the president's authority as a wartime commander in chief was limitless and unconditional. He could do whatever he wanted to do.

The war council was resolutely opposed to acknowledging any rights of accused terrorists, and they had no faith in the ability of federal courts to deliver swift and sure justice. They devised a plan that cut those civilian courts out of the picture, a plan to place America's enemies before military officers who would sit in judgment and determine their fate. The plan was for military commissions.

Military commissions were not exactly unknown in American history—the first ones had been held in the Mexican war of the 1840s, and they were common in the Civil War—but the United States had not convened one in the half century since the end of World War II, when German and Japanese captives had been brought before commissions to be tried for war crimes. They were not actually courts, though they had a judicial function—they received evidence for and against an accused and handed down a verdict and punishment. But they had always been decidedly ad hoc proceedings, with few restrictions on the evidence they could consider. Hearsay was routine, and the commissioners (military officers, not trained judges, often not even lawyers) were free to consider whatever evidence they found "probative," without regard to the rules of evidence that prevailed in civilian criminal trials and, since congressional enactment of the Uniform Code of Military Justice in 1951, in courts-martial as well. Ad hoc proceedings were the norm because, unlike civilian trials and courts-martial, there were almost no laws on the books to regulate military commissions. They were convened as needed by military commanders (occasionally even the president as commander in chief) for those not normally subject to US laws, most often enemy combatants charged with war crimes, and when their work was done they were dissolved.

The International Military Tribunal at Nuremberg that tried twenty-two Nazis on charges of war crimes and crimes against humanity, convicting most of them, was a military commission, albeit with prominent civilian lawyers from four victorious nations as the judges. But lesser-known commissions were convened as well. In the 1942 Quirin case, the Supreme Court had affirmed the authority of President Roosevelt to appoint a military commission to try German saboteurs who had landed on Long Island. In 1946 the Supreme Court had upheld the conviction of Tomoyuki Yamashita, a Japanese general tried by a US military commission in Manila for having failed to prevent troops nominally under his control from committing ferocious war crimes in the Philippines during the last year of the war. Commissions had made their last appearance in Supreme Court jurisprudence in the 1950 Eisentrager decision, when the Court had refused to review a commission's conviction of German officers for war crimes. But by 2001 there was no one in the US military or elsewhere in the government who had ever seen a commission, and few other than military lawyers—and not many of those—even knew what they were.

Because there are no standing rules to govern commission trials, such trials are not inherently unfair; if they follow the rules laid down in the Uniform Code of Military Justice for the court-martial of American service members they could be fair, even by civilian standards, in many important respects. Indeed, in 1951 the Uniform Code of Military Justice enacted by Congress reformed courts-martial to bring them significantly closer to standards of fairness and due process recognized by federal courts, and in doing so it also directed that military commissions, if and when convened, follow federal court rules or court-martial rules to the extent "practicable." But that was an untested standard, because no commissions had been convened in the fifty years since then.

In any event, trials with federal criminal rules, even court-martial rules, were certainly not what the war council wanted. The president should write his own rules, and so they plucked the malleable military commission from its dusty history. Its advantages for quick and summary convictions were apparent. Trials would be conducted on charges written by military prosecutors and decided by military officers, all of whom were subordinates of the president. Evidence gained by duress could be admitted and weighed. Classified information need not be disclosed. The press could be excluded. Trials could be held not in federal courthouses but at Guantanamo, which the war council was then bring-ing to the fore as a suitable detention center, to avoid judicial review. Appeals of those convicted would go up a chain of command that led only to the president. No federal judge would be involved.

And so, on November 13, 2001, a month after the invasion of Afghani-stan, the president issued an order, drafted by Addington, authorizing the secretary of defense to operate a detainee facility at Guantanamo and to place on trial before a military commission any noncitizen of the United States who was a member of al Qaeda; or had engaged in international terrorism against the United States; or had aided, abet-ted, conspired with, or harbored those who had committed such acts. The commissions were to have jurisdiction over "all offenses triable by military commission" under historical standards, and those convicted could be jailed for life or executed. The order specified few procedures for commissions, other than providing that verdicts could be rendered by a two-thirds vote (rather than the unanimity of a jury required in federal criminal trials), and that only the president or the secretary of defense could review a conviction. As for courts, the order was explicit: the accused "shall not be privileged to seek any remedy or maintain any proceeding, directly or indirectly, or to have any such remedy or proceeding sought on [his] behalf, in any court of the United States, or any State thereof."

The public reaction to the president's announcement was puzzle-ment and, for some, apprehension. Few people had even heard of mil-itary commissions, and the president's order, scant on specifics, shed little light on what they were or how they would operate. It was up to the Department of Defense to fill in the blanks. Four months later, on March 21, 2002, Secretary of Defense Rumsfeld did so, signing off on Military Commission Order No. 1, drafted by a task force of judge ad-vocates—the uniformed military lawyers. (A "judge advocate" is not a judge, but a lawyer serving in uniform as a prosecutor or defense coun-sel, or a staff attorney.) Many outside the administration who had been disquieted by the president's order were at least somewhat relieved to see that nearly all of the blanks had been filled in with familiar forms of due process. The accused was to receive notice of the charges, military defense counsel (and civilian counsel if desired, at his own expense), sufficient time before trial to prepare a defense and, subject to some restrictions, the right to see before trial the prosecution's evidence as well as any evidence in the prosecution's hands that would tend to cast doubt on his guilt. He had the right to a public trial except when classified information was being presented, and the right to remain silent, to present evidence, and call witnesses and cross-examine those called by the prosecution. A guilty verdict required proof beyond a reasonable doubt, although, as the president had decreed, not unanimity; it could be rendered if two-thirds of the commission members (at least three, and as many as seven) so voted. A death sentence could be pronounced only by a commission of seven members, and only if they were unanimous.

But the restrictions were certainly significant. The presiding officer could not only close the trial to the public when necessary to avoid disclosure of classified information or intelligence sources, methods, or activities, but could exclude the accused himself from the courtroom during such occasions. The accused's military defense counsel could not be excluded for such reasons (or any other), but neither could he disclose to his client any protected information from a closed session.

Moreover, the rules of evidence that applied in civil trials and in courts-martial were ignored. Commissions could consider any evidence they believed to have "probative value to a reasonable person"—again, as the president's order had decreed. This was a noticeably vague standard, stripping proffered evidence of nearly all requirements of reliability by allowing testimony from other trials at which the accused and his lawyer would not have been present, as well as "sworn or unsworn written statements" impervious to cross-examination, and "scientific or other reports"—including, presumably, reports from undisclosed persons such as intelligence officers, interrogators or bureaucrats like the affidavit-writing Mr. Mobbs of the Hamdi case.

Despite the procedural guarantees, therefore, it was entirely possible, indeed foreseeable, that an accused could be convicted and sentenced, even executed, on the basis of evidence that was kept secret from him, submitted by persons not identified to him, and presented to the commission in his absence—evidence which he would be unable to explain or rebut. And his defense counsel, who would know of the evidence, could not tell the accused what it was and thus would be handicapped in framing a response. Counsel could not even refer to it in court while the accused was present.

One has the impression that the military lawyers who drafted the regulations made them as fair as their authority allowed—there are several references to the obligation of the presiding officer and the commission members to conduct a "full and fair trial"—but they could not countermand the president's order allowing any "probative" evidence and prohibiting the disclosure of classified material to the man on trial. Nor could they provide for judicial review that the president had prohibited; guilty verdicts and sentences were to be reviewed only by the secretary of defense and the president, although the regulations did authorize the secretary to appoint a panel of three military or civilian lawyers to review the record of trial and make recommendations as to how he should rule on verdicts and sentences.

What the war council had devised, and what President Bush had signed, was in every respect a complete, self-contained, alternative judicial system, designed to bring "our enemies to justice" by displacing America's judicial system.

It took two years of preparation for the government to bring the first detainee to trial before a military commission. He was Salim Ahmed Hamdan, a thirty-four-year-old Yemeni citizen. Because the significant al Qaeda figures were being held in secret isolation by the CIA and off limits to military prosecutors, Hamdan personified the government's self-imposed difficulty in finding any terrorist of importance at Guantanamo. Hamdan was, depending on one's perspective, either an industrious cog in Osama Bin Laden's terror network, or an unassuming gofer whose role was to drive people around bin Laden's Afghan outpost and to perform other errands as needed. He was apparently chosen as the first defendant because, unlike nearly everyone else at Guantanamo, his trial would allow prosecutors to refer often to bin Laden himself. On July 9, 2004, the government charged Hamdan with conspiracy to attack civilians, with conspiracy to murder by an unlawful combatant, the combatant presumably being bin Laden, since there was no contention that Hamdan himself engaged in murder, and with terrorism. Hamdan's military counsel, US Navy lieutenant commander Charles Swift, lost no time in challenging the government's right to try Hamdan, filing a petition for habeas corpus in federal court, aided by Neal Katyal, a Georgetown University law professor.

Swift and Katyal did not take on what might have appeared to be the government's biggest weakness: that conspiracy and terrorism were not war crimes and had never been tried by military commissions, and thus were outside the president's directive giving commissions jurisdiction over "offenses triable by military commission." But on November 8, 2004, Judge James Robertson in the US District Court in Washington nevertheless struck down the entire military commission structure as a violation of US law.

The grounds for Robertson's decision were several, and not simple. Rejecting the government's assertion that the president "has untrammeled power to establish military tribunals" in his role as commander in chief of the armed forces, Robertson ruled that the president needed congressional authority to establish such tribunals, and the president did not have that authority because he had never asked Congress for it. Curiously, Robertson did not mention the Authorization for the Use of Military Force, by which Congress had authorized the president to "use all necessary and appropriate force" against those responsible for the attacks on the United States. Whether such "force" could be construed to authorize military tribunals was thus left unanswered by his decision.

Robertson also ruled that Hamdan had never had the benefit of US military regulation 190-8, the one drawn up in 1997 to replace similar Vietnam-era practices and to implement the Geneva Convention on prisoners of war. That regulation required that any person whose entitlement to POW status was unclear was to have his status determined by a panel of three officers. Robertson rejected the government's contention that such a tribunal was unnecessary in light of the presidential decree in 2002 that al Qaeda operatives were categorically disqualified from prisoner-of-war status to begin with. He ruled that the Geneva POW Convention "applies to all persons detained in Afghanistan during the hostilities there," regardless of any al Qaeda affiliation.

The lack of a POW-determining tribunal was important, Robertson explained, because the Geneva Convention on POWs, like the US regulation itself, requires that a detainee be treated as a prisoner of war unless and until such a tribunal determines that he is not entitled to such status—for example, if he was not affiliated with a military unit, or did not wear the uniform or other "distinctive insignia" required of lawful combatants. With no tribunal having ruled otherwise, Hamdan was therefore entitled to be treated as a POW.

The reason that POW status was a critical issue in Hamdan's case was not so much that it would entitle him to humane treatment and relief from involuntary interrogation. That would be nice, but the real importance of the Geneva POW Convention for Hamdan was its ban on kangaroo courts. It required that POWs be convicted of crimes only "by the same courts according to the same procedure as in the case of members of the armed forces" of the detaining country. For the United States, that meant a court-martial convened under the Uniform Code of Military Justice, or at least arguably by a commission that followed the UCMJ's court-martial rules and procedures. The commissions established by the president and DoD fell well short of that standard, Judge Robertson ruled, because a "substantial number of rights and procedures conferred by the UCMJ are missing" in the commission structure. The most serious absence was the right of the accused to be present throughout his trial. Because "*the accused himself may be excluded from proceedings,*" Robertson wrote, "evidence may be adduced that he will never see (because his lawyer will be forbidden to disclose it to him)" (the emphasis is Robertson's). This "dramatic deviation" from the right to confront and rebut the evidence "could not be countenanced in any American court," including a court-martial. Excluding the accused from his own trial "is indeed directly contrary to the UCMJ's right to be present," Robertson ruled, and therefore "so long as it operates under such a rule, the Military Commission cannot try Hamdan." Robertson enjoined any further commission proceedings against Hamdan—and by implication everyone else at Guantanamo.

Coming only a few months after its twin losses in *Rasul* and *Hamdi*, this was another bitter defeat for the administration. Three full years after the president's order, it brought the entire military commission process to a halt in its first case, without a witness being called.

The government took its appeal to the US Court of Appeals for the District of Columbia Circuit, and on July 15, 2005, a three-judge panel—including Judge John Roberts, a former law clerk to Chief Justice Rehnquist and a former deputy solicitor general and associate White House counsel, just starting his third year on the bench—put things back in place for the administration. The court reversed Judge Robertson on every point and held that Hamdan could indeed be tried by military commission under the president's order and the Defense Department's regulations. If the president needs congressional authorization to establish such tribunals, the court of appeals ruled, the Authorization for the Use of Military Force had provided it. The appeals court relied on the Supreme Court's 1946 decision in the Yamashita case, in which the Court had ruled that the conduct of war was broader than combat alone and included the power "to seize and subject to disciplinary measures those enemies who, in their attempt to thwart or impede our military effort, have violated the law of war." Hamdan had not been directly involved in impeding the US military in Afghanistan and had not been accused of violating the law of war, but for the court of appeals Yamashita's case was close enough; it brought commissions within the "force" authorized by Congress in the AUMF.

As to the Geneva Conventions, Roberts and his two colleagues ruled that, whatever they meant, they could not be enforced in court: they were agreements between nations and did not confer any actual rights on individual prisoners. This was the same rationale that the US Court of Appeals for the Fourth Circuit had relied upon when it had denied Yaser Hamdi the protection of Geneva in his case, two years before, an aspect of that case that the Supreme Court had not mentioned when it reversed the court's decision.

The provision that prisoners of war could not be convicted in proceedings that departed from a nation's rules for its own troops thus availed Hamdan nothing. Such a right, if it was to be created at all, would have to be conferred by Congress, enacting laws to implement the Geneva Convention. In any event, the court of appeals ruled, Hamdan was not qualified to be a POW—he had not conformed to the requirements of a lawful combatant because he didn't wear a uniform and al Qaeda did not conduct its operations according to the laws of war.

In so ruling, the court of appeals was making its own determination that Hamdan was not a POW protected by the Geneva Conventions—a decision that the military's regulations had entrusted to the tribunal of military officers that had never been convened for Hamdan, or anyone else at Guantanamo. That conclusion, and the others reversing each of Judge Robertson's rulings, suggest that the court of appeals was determined to find a way to uphold the validity of the president's military commissions. In this first case to consider such commissions in nearly sixty years, it had found that way.

Four days after the decision was handed down, President Bush nominated Judge Roberts to be the next chief justice of the United States.

Hamdan's lawyers, now raising the argument that conspiracy was beyond the jurisdiction of military commissions, turned to the Supreme Court. They filed a petition for certiorari that "challenges (1) a commission without explicit Congressional authorization, (2) in a place far removed from hostilities, (3) to try an offense [i.e., conspiracy] unknown to the laws of war, (4) under procedures that flout basic tenets of military justice, (5) against a civilian who contests his unlawful combatancy." In response, Solicitor General Paul Clement, who had succeeded Ted Olson shortly after the Rasul and Hamdi decisions a year earlier, acknowledged that the case presented "questions implicating the most sensitive national security concerns" but told the Court that taking up such questions now would be premature, because Hamdan might be acquitted at his trial, or might have no classified information introduced against him, thereby mooting his claim that he might be unconstitutionally excluded.

Four years after the president's military commission order, the SG also urged that the Court not "compound the delay" already plaguing commission trials, pointing out that the "district court's ill-considered and unprecedented injunction has already resulted in delaying military commission proceedings for nearly a year." Implicit in the SG's opposition was the recognition that if Hamdan were to be convicted, particularly if he were to be excluded in the process, the Supreme Court would have opportunity enough then to review the entire proceeding.

Unpersuaded by the government's reasoning, the Court on November 7, 2005, took *Hamdan v. Rumsfeld*, and the lawyers turned to the task of writing their briefs and preparing oral argument. Representing Hamdan, Georgetown Law's Neal Katyal, a former law clerk to Justice Breyer, followed a strategy familiar to Supreme Court litigators: win only what you have to win. He made clear in his brief that he was not challenging the authority of the United States to try Hamdan, even by military commission. He was challenging *this* military commission (and thus the administration's entire commission strategy), on several grounds. The president had established it unilaterally, without the assent of Congress, a violation of the separation of powers that made the Executive the convenor, the prosecutor, the trial judge, the jury, and the appeals judge. Second, the commission violated the Uniform Code of Military Justice, which required commissions to adhere "insofar as practicable" to the procedures for courts-martial, and those procedures did not allow the exclusion of the accused from his own trial. It also violated Geneva's requirement that any trial be conducted by a "regularly constituted court" of the captor, which this commission clearly was not, because it was not independent of the Executive; indeed, it was an Executive production from start to finish.

And third, argued Katyal, the crime of conspiracy was not one that could be tried by military commissions in any event. Katyal's point was that conspiracy was a crime like, for example, drug dealing or forgery or perjury. It might be committed while a war is being fought, but it is not the sort of conflict-specific crime with which the law of war concerns itself. And because conspiracy is not a war crime, it is not within the jurisdiction of military commissions. All in all, Katyal wrote, here "the President seeks not to revive, but to invent, a new form of military jurisdiction." And that he could not do in this way and could not do by himself.

Katyal left open the possibility that Congress might amend the Uniform Code of Military Justice to accommodate the president's commissions, or it might expand the bounds of military-commission jurisdiction to include conspiracy, but he was giving little away in that acknowledgment, since it looked to a possible future, and Katyal was intent on winning his case in the present. "Our fundamental principles of separation of powers have survived many dire threats to this nation's security," he wrote, "from capture of the nation's capital by enemy forces [in the War of 1812], to Civil War, to the threat of nuclear annihilation during the Cold War—and those principles must not be abandoned now."

For the government, Solicitor General Clement yielded no ground. The president as commander in chief has inherent authority to convene and define military commissions, Clement argued; congressional approval is not necessary, because "trying unlawful combatants for violating the law of war is a fundamental part of the conduct of the war itself," as the Court had recognized sixty years earlier in General Yamashita's case. And in any event, Congress had given the president any authority he might need when it approved the Authorization for the Use of Military Force, and it had implicitly reinforced its permission by not raising any objection to what the president had done here. To refute Hamdan's claim that conspiracy was not properly within the universe of war crimes triable by commission, the SG pointed to several Civil War–era cases in which conspiracy had been charged. And whatever the Geneva Conventions might say, he argued, they did not help Hamdan because, as the court of appeals had ruled, they did not create rights for individual detainees and, furthermore, the president had declared them inoperative in the wars against the Taliban and al Qaeda.

On December 30, 2005, seven weeks after the Supreme Court agreed to hear the case, Congress injected a new issue into it: the Detainee Treatment Act of 2005. In addition to outlawing the "enhanced interrogation" techniques that by then had become public knowledge, the DTA stripped the federal courts—all of them, including the Supreme Court, and immediately—of all jurisdiction to "hear or consider" any habeas corpus case brought by any Guantanamo detainee. The solicitor general quickly filed a motion urging the Supreme Court to dismiss the case, which would have left standing the court of appeals' decision in the government's favor. The Court put off any ruling until the entire case could be argued as scheduled, on March 28, 2006.

The Court allocated each side forty-five minutes for argument—fifteen minutes longer than usual—in recognition of the importance and complexity of the case, but when argument began, the middle seat on the Court's bench was empty. Chief Justice Roberts, who had taken his seat in September 2005, had recused himself from hearing the case that he had decided eight months earlier on the court of appeals. There are no formal rules for when a Supreme Court justice must recuse himself and, as customary, Roberts provided no explanation. But the reason was obvious—he would have been sitting in judgment of his own decision.

Roberts's absence, and with it his certain vote to uphold the military commission structure, was not as severe a blow to the government's position as might have appeared. The case would be decided by eight justices, raising the distinct possibility of a tie vote on whether the court of appeals' ruling would stand. In such cases, the Court issues no opinion at all, merely a one-sentence order that the judgment below is "affirmed by an equally divided Court." That nondecision has no precedential value and leaves the court of appeals' decision as the final word on the case—a result that would leave the military commission structure standing, and which the government would be quite content to have.

The argument was presented by two of the nation's ablest appellate litigators. Neal Katyal, the son of Indian immigrants, had been a champion debater at Dartmouth College and after Yale Law School and his clerkship for Justice Breyer he had been a junior colleague of John Roberts at the Washington law firm of Hogan and Hartson. (He was to serve as acting solicitor general of the United States in 2010–2011.) Paul Clement, the solicitor general, had clerked for Justice Scalia and was a seasoned advocate in the Supreme Court; as deputy SG he had argued a score of cases before the Court, including *Hamdi* two years earlier.

Like many Supreme Court arguments, the Hamdan case was less a stage for eloquent oratory than a detailed, sometimes plodding, examination of the issues and arguments by the justices and the lawyers. And in this difficult case, there were no fewer than four primary issues. First, could the Court decide the case at all, given the recent jurisdiction-stripping provisions of the Detainee Treatment Act? Second, did the president have authority to establish military commissions in the way he had, with or without the Authorization for the Use of Military Force? Third, was conspiracy a crime that could be tried by military commissions? Fourth, did the Geneva Conventions provide any rights to Hamdan, and if so what were they, and did the military commission procedures violate the requirement of "regularly constituted courts"?

These technical issues, however important, could be subsumed into a larger perspective: was the presidential commission regime simply a resumption after fifty years of the procedures that had passed constitutional muster in the Supreme Court's World War II cases of Quirin and Yamashita? Or was it a dangerous arrogation of power by the president, in violation of a detainee's rights under the Geneva Conventions, in violation of the Uniform Code of Military Justice and other laws enacted by Congress, and in violation of the very separation of powers that was the foundation of the Constitution? The current Geneva Conventions, as well as the UCMJ, were not yet on the books when those World War II cases had been decided. And did Congress act within its powers in sweeping all these questions off the table by revoking habeas jurisdiction from federal courts, including the Supreme Court, in Guantanamo cases—while this very case was pending before it? The Constitution specifies that "The privilege of the writ of Habeas Corpus shall not be suspended" except in cases of "Rebellion or Invasion." Had Congress impermissibly "suspended" habeas by revoking the jurisdiction of the courts to grant it to Guantanamo's detainees?

The latter point, especially, concerned the justices. "Isn't there a pretty good argument," Justice David Souter asked Clement at one point during oral argument, "that a suspension of [habeas corpus] is just about the most stupendously significant act that the Congress of the United States can take? And therefore we ought to be at least a little slow to accept your argument that it can be done" by the expedient of altering a court's jurisdiction? And Justice Ginsburg: The Detainee Treatment Act "was proposed and enacted some weeks after this Court granted cert in this very case. It is an extraordinary act, I think, to withdraw jurisdiction from this Court in a pending case. So why should we assume that Congress" meant to do that, as Clement had argued it did?

This judicial skepticism was not surprising; courts, especially the Supreme Court, do not lightly accept the contention that they have no business deciding a case. Certainly this case, in which the president, with the active acquiescence of Congress, was trying to displace the Supreme Court from its role as the arbiter of what the Constitution means, on a matter as important as habeas, presented that question.

The Court handed down its decision in the Hamdan case on June 29, 2006, two years almost to the day after its decisions in *Rasul*, *Hamdi*, and *Padilla*. There was no tie vote. For the third time in the Supreme Court, the government lost, this time by a vote of 5-3. The majority concluded, with something of a stretch, that the wording of the Detainee Treatment Act justified an inference that Congress did not mean it to apply to pending cases. That resolution of the matter allowed the Court to avoid the serious constitutional question of whether the Congress, purposely or not, had suspended habeas. But it no doubt dismayed those in Congress who had voted for it precisely to preclude the Supreme Court from deciding this case.

Moving to the merits of the case, John Paul Stevens, the senior justice in the absence of the Chief Justice, writing for the five-justice majority, ruled that the military commission "lacks power to proceed because its structure and procedures violate both the [Uniform Code of Military Justice] and the Geneva Conventions." As to the first point, Stevens's opinion retraced the sporadic history of military commissions from their beginnings in the 1840's Mexican War as a makeshift device to fill in the gaps that then existed in court-martial jurisdiction. It concluded that, whatever might have been the authority of the president to convene commissions in World War II, the enactment of the UCMJ in 1951 had altered that authority by requiring that commissions adhere to the procedures for courts-martial "insofar as practicable." Here, said the majority, two attributes of commissions—excluding the accused from his own trial, and allowing evidence of all kinds to be considered, "dispens[ing] with virtually all evidentiary rules applicable in courts-martial"—clearly departed from explicit court-martial rules. The president had made no "official determination that it is impracticable to apply" those rules, nor could the Court discern anything in the record that "demonstrates that it would be impracticable to apply court-martial rules in this case."

That absence of impractability was "particularly disturbing," Stevens wrote, when one considered that the accused was denied the right to be present. The Court summarily dismissed the government's contention that to do otherwise would place an "undue burden" on commissions. That assertion, Stevens wrote, not only ignores the plain meaning of the UCMJ but the purpose and history of commissions. "The military commission was not born of a desire to dispense a more summary form of justice than is afforded by courts-martial: it developed, rather, as a tribunal of necessity" to fill in the historical gaps in court-martial jurisdiction by providing a forum for the trial of aliens, including accused war criminals.

Though he refrained from saying so explicitly, Justice Stevens had identified the exact reason that President Bush and his war council had devised the commission regime. It was indeed to "dispense a more summary form of justice" than could be expected under UCMJ rules, particularly rules that prohibited statements obtained under duress and evidence introduced without the accused's knowledge. Whatever "burdens" might be imposed by such rules, Stevens wrote, were therefore irrelevant to the question of whether the rules could be dispensed with as somehow not "practicable." Those rules were important. They protected the accused from summary convictions based on arbitrary government actions.

Having concluded that the commission's procedures violated US law, the majority went on to rule that they violated the Geneva Conventions as well. The rationale was novel, and somewhat surprising. Generally speaking, the Geneva Conventions apply to international armed conflict—"armed conflict which may arise between two or more" nation states. Insurrections, civil wars, and domestic riots had been traditionally outside their scope. But Article 3 in all four of those Conventions (thus known as "Common Article 3") was an exception. It provided, in quite brief terms, that in "armed conflict not of an international character" certain rules nonetheless applied: humane treatment of noncombatants, care of the wounded and sick, and this: "the passing of sentences and the carrying out of executions without previous judgment pronounced by a regularly constituted court, affording all the judicial guarantees which are recognized as indispensable by civilized peoples."

The government had devoted only a couple of paragraphs in its fifty-page brief to Common Article 3, dismissing it as inapplicable because the conflict between the United States and al Qaeda "has taken place and is ongoing in several countries" and thus *is* "of an international character." But the Court now ruled that the government's reading was too narrow. Because al Qaeda is not a nation, the conflict between it and the United States is not between nations. It is therefore not "international" (or, "inter-national") and Common Article 3 therefore applies.

From that point, the Court went on to conclude that military commissions are not the "regularly constituted courts" that Common Article 3 requires. As created by the president, they are unique, ad hoc tribunals whose rules depart significantly from courts-marital, which *are* the United States' regularly constituted military courts. The requirements of Common Article 3, the Court acknowledged, are flexible and general, "crafted to accommodate a wide variety of legal systems. But *requirements* they are nonetheless. The commission that the President has convened to try Hamdan does not meet those requirements" (emphasis by the Court). The majority thus bypassed the question of whether the Geneva Conventions, as international treaties, conferred "rights" on individuals. That question was irrelevant, because Common Article 3 was a restraint on the government, a restraint that the United States had imposed on itself by ratifying the Conventions.

Five of the eight justices joined in all of the foregoing. But for reasons of his own, Justice Kennedy did not join two other sections of Justice Stevens's opinion. With only four justices on board, therefore, those sections lacked a majority and did not constitute rulings of the Court itself. In the first such section Justices Stevens, Breyer, Ginsburg, and Souter concluded that conspiracy was not a crime that was triable by military commission. In the second section the same four concluded that the commissions were not "regularly constituted courts" not only because they were ad hoc creations (a conclusion Kennedy agreed with) but also because defects in their procedures—in particular, the exclusion of the accused and the concealment of classified evidence—further disqualified them as "regularly constituted courts."

The loss of a majority on these two points was not fatal to anything; they were just additional reasons for conclusions that the five justices (including Kennedy) agreed invalidated the commissions. Kennedy simply said he saw no need to address those points in order to dispose of the case, which was true enough: they were cumulative. But his refusal to join left unresolved the significant issue of whether military commissions could try people for conspiracy.

Justices Scalia, Thomas, and Samuel Alito dissented, each of them writing lengthy explanations of why the court of appeals and the government were correct and criticizing the Court's majority for not allowing the commissions to proceed unimpeded as the president had intended. The decision will "sorely hamper the President's ability to confront and defeat a new and deadly enemy," Justice Thomas wrote in his dissent.

In a brief concurring opinion, Justice Breyer, answering the dissenters, pointed out that nothing in the decision would prevent the president from going to Congress to seek the authority that Breyer and the others in the majority found was missing, in order to create proper military commissions. Such consultation, Breyer wrote in implicit response to Thomas, "does not weaken our Nation's ability to deal with danger. To the contrary, that insistence strengthens the Nation's ability to determine—through democratic means—how best to do so. The Constitution places its faith in those democratic means. Our Court today simply does the same."

The president and Congress would very soon take up Breyer's invitation.

Why did the president's plan for military commissions fail? The Supreme Court was scrupulously focused on the law: the traditional role of military commissions, the enactment of the Uniform Code of Military Justice, the meaning of the Geneva Conventions, the procedural requirements of courts-martial. But the reason that military commissions fell short by these measures reflects a larger reality: they were a legal process created to advance an overtly political objective. Like Gitmo itself, commissions could give the Bush administration something to display as tangible evidence of its aggressiveness in the war on terror. It could have done so in the time-tested procedures of American criminal procedure: indicting the bad guys in federal court on conspiring to commit capital crimes as members of a terrorist group, proving the case against them before a judge and jury, and urging stiff sentences, even execution. Indeed, as shown in chapter 7, the Department of Justice had been doing just that, and succeeding, long before Guantanamo was opened, and it continued to do so for terrorists, including some Americans, who were never sent to Guantanamo and thus were exempt from military commissions.

President Bush's commissions were founded on the erroneous belief that the US system of justice and due process of law was not up to the crimes of 9/11, that it would accord "rights" to those who had savagely attacked and killed nearly 3,000 civilians, that it would hamstring prosecutors with technical rules and place the fate of the defendants in the hands of ordinary citizens who might set terrorists free. Military commissions, with their sporadic history and their ad hoc procedures, could be whatever the president wanted them to be, and so could dispense with rules and rights and adopt procedures that would virtually guarantee convictions.

They failed for a simple reason: as the self-styled war council had designed them, and despite the efforts of military lawyers to bring them closer to due process, they were against the law. In a sense, they were *supposed* to be against the law, at least the law that had always applied to the trial of accused criminals. The war council thought they had found a wormhole in the legal universe, a humble military procedure that had been occasionally used in distant theaters of war that could now deliver the United States into an alternate legal universe in which constitutional gravity was absent.

Given the political objectives of the commissions, the administration could reach this alternative universe only if it ignored and excluded anyone who did not buy into the political agenda, and that meant just about anyone outside the little war council. That was a second reason for the failure of the commissions plan: it was exempted from review and analysis by others in the government who knew better, whose experience and perspectives ranged far more broadly than the small and secret knot of Addington, Yoo, and Gonzales—none of whom had any experience in the military, in criminal law, or in trial courtrooms of any kind. Gonzales was a corporate lawyer in a Texas law firm before joining Governor Bush's staff; Bush later appointed him to the Texas Supreme Court (which does not decide criminal cases), which he left after two years to serve as Bush's White House counsel. Yoo went from his Supreme Court clerkship into academia at Berkeley. Addington spent a few months at the US Naval Academy before transferring to Georgetown; his legal career spanned a number of positions in the CIA and other federal agencies and political appointments on congressional staffs, with a brief interval in law firm practice during the Clinton administration. Cheney himself had avoided military service and went on to spend his whole career as a political staffer and elected representative, with a few years as CEO of Halliburton Company, a multinational defense contractor.

They also lacked historical perspective. They assumed that what the Supreme Court had upheld in *Quirin*—the 1942 case in which German saboteurs captured in New York were tried by military commission—it and lower courts would uphold again. They paid little attention and showed little interest in the significant postwar changes in the law that made *Quirin* dangerously treacherous ground: the US ratification of the 1949 Geneva Conventions, enactment of the Uniform Code of Military Justice, the Supreme Court's expansion of habeas corpus rules, and a considerable body of commentary by lawyers and historians that with the benefit of hindsight had been able to place *Quirin* in a historical context—one of several discredited World War II cases (the Japanese-American "relocation" case was another) in which the Supreme Court had shown undue deference to the president because the United States was in the middle of a war. That deference had ended after the war and subsequent cases had not revived it.

By not subjecting their theories to any searching analysis—from the military's judge advocates general, from the State Department, the National Security Council or anyone beyond Yoo in the Justice Department—they failed to see weaknesses in the facts and the law that to an experienced eye would have demanded greater scrutiny. They dismissed procedural protections because enemies had no "constitutional rights," subordinating any thought that these safeguards were the infrastructure of due process of law that gives prosecutions and convictions credibility abroad and at home and a legitimacy to stand the test of history. They adopted the probative-evidence test and the exclusion of defendants with no real understanding of how it would work or how the prosecutors sent in to try the cases, or the military officers charged with deciding them, would navigate their uncharted legal waters. They apparently believed that courts would accept the president's dictate that those subject to trial by military commission were barred from any recourse to the courts—a restriction that even the Quirin and Yamashita cases had dismissed out of hand. In short, they gave little thought, much less did they have any coherent response, to the judicial challenges that any experienced litigator, or even any lawyer conversant in legal history, would have realized were inevitable.

In place of searching analysis, they relied on Yoo's theory of an all-powerful president in wartime—the so-called "unitary executive"—which was little more than a contention, of which Yoo was the leading exponent, that the commander in chief's authority transcended the constitutional separation of powers and was immune from checks and balances, that it was limitless, muscular, and impregnable, beyond the power of courts to review or curtail. Few lawyers outside the Federalist Society placed much credence in such sweeping assertions that so minimized the Constitution's role for the other branches of government.

In proceeding on Yoo's theory, the war council paid little attention to the constitutional war powers entrusted to Congress, including the authority to make "Rules for the Government and Regulation of the land and naval Forces." They showed no particular recognition of judicial reluctance to uphold sweeping executive powers, even wartime powers, as the Court had vividly demonstrated in striking down President Truman's seizure of the steel mills. No "unitary executive" theory of presidential power can be reconciled with the ruling of the Supreme Court in that case, but in a lengthy memorandum that Yoo wrote for Gonzales on August 1, 2002, on the president's commander-in-chief powers, he did not so much as mention it.

Without trial or appellate experience, they also lacked any informed sense of how far a court could or would go, how far a favorable precedent could be relied on, or how to answer unfavorable precedents, of which the steel-seizure case was but one. Nor did they give any evident thought to how courts might react to being told they had no business reviewing presidential action: a red-flag argument of which any experienced federal appellate litigator would have been wary. They appear to have given little thought at all to how federal courts in the twenty-first century—including the Supreme Court—would assess issues of military jurisdiction that had not been examined in half a century.

Not only were outsiders excluded, at no point did President Bush himself press the war council on their plan or the theory on which it was based. Bush listened to the hapless Gonzales, who did little more than channel the theories of the more capable, credentialed, and determined Addington, Yoo, and Cheney himself. He called in no other lawyers, from the Department of Justice, the State Department, or anywhere else, to vet the war council's thinking. The presidential order establishing military commissions was not even staffed to those, or any other, government offices. According to Jess Bravin of the *Wall Street Journal*, the several-page order was placed in Bush's hands as he was hurriedly departing for Texas. "Bush flipped to the last page, signed his name, and left." No one close to the president was heard to express any doubts about the astonishing breadth of the commission plan or its disregard for any constitutional provision that might check presidential dictates. By the time experienced government litigators became involved—only when the commission plan faced its inevitable challenge in civilian courts before federal judges—the die had been cast and the litigators were forced to defend what the war council had ordained and the president had approved unread.

Given their lack of forensic legal experience, the exclusion of review beyond their tight circle, their reliance on assertion over analysis, their inattention to foreseeable judicial reaction, their ignorance or disregard of postwar developments in the law, and the president's unquestioning adoption of their work, failure of the plan was inevitable.

Within weeks of the Supreme Court's Hamdan decision, the Republican-controlled Congress set about doing what Justice Breyer had acknowledged it could do. It proceeded to undo the Court's invalidation of the military commission structure by passing the Military Commissions Act of 2006. The MCA addressed every defect the Court had identified and rejected every conclusion the Court had reached. It authorized the president to establish commissions, which Congress clearly had authority to do and surely would have done earlier had it been given the opportunity. But everything after that was a patch job. The act decreed the UCMJ largely inapplicable to commissions. It prohibited any commission defendant from invoking the Geneva Conventions as a "source of rights," and then went on to prohibit any person of any category from invoking Geneva against the United States in any US court, a provision aimed at noncommission detainees seeking the intervention of federal courts. It deemed military commissions to be "regularly constituted courts" for purposes of Geneva's Common Article 3.

Beyond plugging the gaps that had led the Court to strike down the commission structure, Congress also reenacted the jurisdiction-stripping provisions of its Detainee Treatment Act of the year before, this time making explicit that the ban applied "to all cases, without exception" pending on the date of passage.

In addition, the Military Commissions Act set out in considerable detail rules and regulations to govern military commissions, in place of the ones that had been written in the Pentagon. It addressed their jurisdiction, their composition and rules of evidence and procedure, the persons they could try—"alien unlawful enemy combatants"—and the offenses they could try, now including conspiracy, terrorism, and "material support for terrorism." Although conspiracy arguably had been a crime properly within the jurisdiction of military commissions—an argument that survived because Justice Stevens in *Hamdan* could muster only four votes to reject it—terrorism and material support of terrorism had never in the past been charged or tried before any commission.

Congress preserved the ability of commissions to receive evidence of almost any nature. It allowed the admission of hearsay if the presiding judge found that such statements were otherwise reliable and "probative." And it went further, allowing the consideration of even statements obtained by coercion, provided that the judge found them reliable and probative and concluded that "the interests of justice would best be served" by considering them. If the statements had been obtained through "cruel, inhuman or degrading treatment," they would be categorically excluded from evidence only if they had been given after enactment of the Detainee Treatment Act on December 30, 2005 (which had prohibited such treatment in interrogations); otherwise such treatment, much of which did indeed predate the DTA's enactment—would not necessarily bar their consideration.

In some respects, the MCA did bring commissions more into line with courts-martial. It required the presiding officer of military commissions to be a certified military judge. Commissions were to have a minimum of five members (jurors), rather than the president's three, and twelve members in capital cases. The MCA retained the two-thirds majority for conviction in noncapital cases but required unanimity of twelve in capital cases. It also created a right of appeal of any commission conviction to a newly created Court of Military Commission Review (in fact, not a court but an administrative board of lawyers) and then to the US Court of Appeals for the District of Columbia, thus bringing the judiciary officially into the process for the first time. Significantly, however, the MCA retained two of the most controversial aspects of the commissions: exclusion of the defendant from portions of the trial and the concealment of classified evidence used against him.

In passing the Military Commissions Act, Congress strengthened the legal standing of those tribunals: they were no longer based on a presidential dictate but on a law duly enacted by Congress. As Justice Jackson had said in the Youngstown case long before, the president's authority is strongest when he acts with the assent of Congress. Now he had that assent. But in giving it to him, and in giving commissions a congressional seal of approval, Congress also moved front and center the question of whether these new and improved commissions were consistent with the Constitution.

That question was unavoidable because in *Hamdan*, the Supreme Court had gone only so far: it had ruled that the commissions as the president and the Department of Defense had implemented them were in conflict with the statutes and treaties of the United States—namely, the Uniform Code of Military Justice and the Geneva Conventions. Moreover, the Court had managed to work around the jurisdiction-stripping provision by concluding, dubiously, that Congress did not mean it to apply to pending cases. It thus had invalidated the commission structure without implicating the Constitution.

Congress had now written a new statute to fill the statutory and treaty gaps that had been fatal in *Hamdan*. But it had not changed the aspects that had troubled at least four of the justices—the military judge's authority to exclude the accused and to conceal classified evidence used against him. Lawyers for the detainees would now have a clear avenue to argue that the congressional fixes did not cure the problem—that the plan for military commissions, even as Congress had revised it, was still in violation of the Constitution itself.

But that day would have to wait.

On April 5, 2007, ten months after the Supreme Court's decision and some five months after enactment of the Military Commissions Act, Hamdan was charged again, under the new law—this time, on two counts: the original charge of conspiracy, which now alleged that Hamdan conspired with Osama bin Laden and others to carry out the 1998 attack against the US embassies in Kenya and Tanzania and the 2000 attack against the *Cole* in Yemen, as well as the 9/11 attacks. The second count was material support of terrorism, alleging that Hamdan gave such support to al Qaeda.

Conspiracy was clearly the more significant charge, implicating Hamdan in the planning of murderous acts. The material-support charge rested only on the allegation that Hamdan was a driver and general helper for bin Laden and other al Qaeda operatives, facts that Hamdan had more or less admitted in his defense, to show that he was just a handyman around the camps, a grade-school dropout earning a living doing the menial chores he was given. The conspiracy charge would require much more: proof that, in doing these things, he was willfully and knowingly joining a criminal enterprise with the intent and purpose of killing innocent civilians, and that he had intentionally worked with his terrorist colleagues to accomplish that objective by carrying out his responsibilities in the al Qaeda organization, however low in the hierarchy he might have been. The critical difference between the two charges was Hamdan's state of mind: was he a committed terrorist, willfully and knowingly working to kill civilians, or just a tire-changer for those who were?

Hamdan's trial began at Guantanamo in mid-July 2008, before six military officers on the commission and a navy captain as the military judge. It was, at long last, the first commission trial to actually take place in the nearly seven years since President Bush established them, and in fact the first commission trial since the World War II era. It lasted two weeks. Hamdan was excluded from portions of the trial and some evidence was introduced without his knowledge.

After eight hours of deliberation over three days, the commission acquitted him of conspiracy and convicted him only of material support of terrorism. The *New York Times* account characterized the conspiracy acquittal as a "stinging setback for the military prosecutors" but also a "long-sought, if somewhat qualified victory for the Bush administration" because acquittal on one charge and conviction on the other arguably demonstrated that military trials were not kangaroo courts but orderly judicial proceedings that could reach considered verdicts, "a vindication of sorts" for the system.

The commission sentenced Hamdan to sixty-six months' imprisonment on the material-support conviction. The military judge deducted from that the sixty-one months Hamdan had been confined at Guantanamo after being designated for trial in 2003, leaving him with only five months to serve. Three months later, in November 2008, the Defense Department put him on a plane back to Yemen.

But his case was not over. His attorneys appealed his material-support conviction to the US Court of Appeals for the District of Columbia Circuit, which on October 16, 2012, reversed it.

The court of appeals' decision was a surprise to many. The three-judge panel assigned to the case included the veteran circuit judge David Sentelle (appointed by President Reagan in 1987) and Brett Kavanaugh (appointed by President Bush in 2006), a former law clerk to Justice Anthony Kennedy and later the chief assistant to Kenneth Starr, whose 1998 report led the House of Representatives to impeach President Clinton. Both judges were dependably rooted in the conservative wing of that court. The third judge, Douglas Ginsburg (no relation to Ruth Bader Ginsburg), a former law clerk to Justice Thurgood Marshall, had been appointed to the court in 1986 by President Reagan, but tended to centrist positions.

The issue facing the court was a new one, which did not call into question the wartime powers of the president or the procedures of military commissions. Could the United States lawfully charge and convict Hamdan of the crime of material support for terrorism that had taken place between 1996 and 2001, considering that Congress had not given military commissions jurisdiction over that crime until 2006? The Ex Post Facto Clause of the Constitution forbids a criminal conviction for conduct that was not a crime when the defendant did it. Congress first criminalized material support for terrorism in 1994, but specified that the crime consisted of support given "in the United States." That condition was deleted in the USA PATRIOT Act, enacted on October 26, 2001, shortly before Hamdan was captured in Afghanistan. So Hamdan's material support for terrorism, whatever it consisted of, was not a crime under US law when he did it.

Federal courts generally try to avoid deciding constitutional questions if the case can be resolved without doing so, and the court did avoid the question, by the expedient of ruling that Congress had not intended the Military Commissions Act to apply retroactively in the first place, a conclusion similar to the Supreme Court's avoidance of the question in *Hamdan*. But then the Court had been construing the 2005 Detainee Treatment Act, not the post-*Hamdan* Military Commissions Act that was now before the court of appeals, and the MCA specified that it "does not establish new crimes that did not exist before its enactment, but rather codifies those crimes for trial by military commission." That seemed to be a congressional determination that the MCA applied to crimes committed "before its enactment." But, in a contorted analysis, the court of appeals first dismissed this premise as "incorrect:" the MCA *had* established a new crime, as far as military commissions were concerned. But the court then had to face an unambiguous provision in the MCA, that the act did not "preclude trial for crimes that occurred before the date" of its enactment. Congress plainly intended retroactive application. But rather than deal with the question of whether retroactive application would violate the Ex Post Facto Clause, the court simply ruled that, had Congress correctly understood that it *was* establishing new crimes, it would not have intended the act to apply retroactively. Thus there was no need to decide whether it was ex post facto.

With that out of the way, the court of appeals took up the question of whether any pre-2006 law on the books would have allowed Hamdan's prosecution for material support of terrorism. The government contended that there was: the Uniform Code of Military Justice specifically preserved the jurisdiction of military commissions to try offenses under the "law of war." But the court of appeals ruled that this referred to the *international* law of war, and it went on to demonstrate that nothing in that body of law—not the Hague or Geneva Conventions, not Nuremberg, not the 1998 treaty establishing the International Criminal Court, not the "customary law of war" as it had grown in the past two centuries—prohibited material support for terrorism. Rather, said the court, "International law leaves it to individual nations to proscribe material support for terrorism under their domestic laws if they so choose"; there is "no international-law proscription of material support for terrorism."

In short, no provision of law—not the MCA's 2006 criminalization of material support, not the international law of war prior to that time—could support Hamdan's conviction for support allegedly given when Hamdan was with bin Laden from 1995 to 2001. His conviction was vacated: taken off the books.

It probably made little difference to Hamdan, who had returned to Yemen four years earlier, but it was another blow to the battered military commissions: they could not try any al Qaeda functionary for the relatively easy to prove crime of material support for terrorism. They were limited to war crimes recognized by international law, or material support given after the MCA's 2006 enactment, a date that would eliminate every one of the long-confined Guantanamo detainees. (The decision proved to be short-lived; the full court was to overturn it in the al-Bahlul case, discussed in chapter 7.)

Hamdan, never charged with being more than a driver in al Qaeda's motor pool, had compiled quite a record in American courts. His lawyers had won dismissal of the first military commission trial ordered by President Bush and had won again when the Supreme Court invalidated the whole commission structure. Tried under a new structure, he had been acquitted of the serious conspiracy charge and convicted on facts he had readily admitted, serving only three more months at Guantanamo before he was sent back home. And even that conviction was now deleted. Eleven years after the self-centered war council had reinvented military commissions as a quick and sure route to consign detainees to life imprisonment or death, Salim Hamdan had all but obliterated them.

CHAPTER SIX

Boumediene

While military commissions were making their way to the Supreme Court, what fate awaited the general population at Guantanamo? Of the several hundred detainees, only a couple dozen had been singled out for prosecution before the commissions. For the rest, their lawyers had won two victories in the Supreme Court, but they were still imprisoned, their lawsuits continuing, their release a distant mirage.

In 2004, the Supreme Court in *Rasul* had ruled that the detainees' Guantanamo emplacement was no bar to their seeking release by habeas corpus in federal courts, but it had said nothing about what they would have to prove in order to gain their release or even whether the courts actually had authority to order that they be released. The Court had opened the courthouse door to these aliens but had left them standing there, letting the trial and appeals courts, as is often the Court's practice, hear and rule on individual cases, wrestle with the issues, and develop the law through their decisions. The justices could later revisit the issues, if they chose, with the benefit of full factual records and the reasoned legal analysis of federal judges, or so it was assumed.

On the same day, in *Hamdi*, the Court had provided a second win for the Gitmo detainees, ruling that, though lawfully captured and initially interned, they were entitled to due process of law to test the legality of their ongoing imprisonment. In this context, due process required some fair opportunity to test the government's basis for holding them, to present their side of the story, and to have an impartial decider rule on whether they were being lawfully held. But the Court had refrained from any suggestion that this process must take place in a federal court or that it must adhere to judicial standards, and had in fact invited the military to create its own structure to carry out this responsibility.

The military had gone through the motions of complying, by creating the Combatant Status Review Tribunals, each detainee appearing before a panel of three officers to hear the facts supporting his designation as an enemy combatant. But he would hear only the facts—the assertions, really—deemed safe to disclose to him, which would exclude such things as the identities of informants. They could then—again in form—explain themselves and call "reasonably available" witnesses to support them, and await the decision of the formally impartial officers as to whether the information, considered as a whole, justified their continued detention.

However seemly all this may have appeared on paper, the detainees' lawyers were having none of it. Their clients' fate would be decided by the same military bureaucracy that had cast them into Gitmo in the first place; they would be presumed to be enemy combatants unless they could prove they were not; they were barred from having legal counsel appear and present their case; they would be given only limited access to the information their captors had, with no access at all to whatever the military deemed too secret to disclose; they would be unable to confront and question anyone with actual knowledge of the facts underlying the allegations; and they could call on their own behalf only those witnesses that the authorities permitted.

As the CSRT proceedings got under way in 2004 and continued into 2005, these restrictions proved overwhelming. The evidence against the detainees was for the most part both conclusory and anonymous. They couldn't confront their accusers because they weren't told who they were. Few of the witnesses they asked for were found to be "reasonably available," even those who were detainees themselves. Few detainees were able to explain or refute information allegedly establishing that they were enemy combatants when they were not told who had accused them or what was said or in what circumstances.

The government's statistics told the story: 93 percent of the detainees were found to be enemy combatants and were returned to their cells for continued imprisonment. Those rulings were subject to review by military superiors, but, as far as the records show, that review did not result in the exoneration or release of any detainee.

Meanwhile, in the wake of the Rasul decision, lawyers for sixty detainees were filing petitions for habeas corpus in the US District Court for the District of Columbia. Their contention was that the "due process" the detainees were receiving in the CSRTs was grossly inadequate and that the detainees were entitled to full-fledged habeas hearings before federal judges, where they would be represented by counsel, be fully informed of the basis for the government's decision to hold them, and be able to cross-examine live witnesses and compel the attendance of their own witnesses with federal subpoenas.

The federal trial court in Washington had a dozen judges, but all of the habeas petitions ended up with two of them: Joyce Hens Green and Richard Leon. The issue facing the judges was straightforward: what actual rights, if any, do aliens confined outside the United States have when courts review their confinement by habeas corpus? The Supreme Court had never squarely answered that question; indeed, it was only in the 1950s that the Court had ruled that *Americans* confined abroad by the US government had a right to proceed by habeas corpus to vindicate constitutional rights. (In that case, *Toth v. Quarles*, the Court vacated the court-martial conviction of a former US serviceman in Korea on grounds that at the time of his trial he was a civilian and no longer subject to court-martial jurisdiction.) Confronted with the issue of aliens' rights to habeas corpus, Judges Green and Leon in their respective courtrooms reached two diametrically opposed conclusions.

Judge Green ruled that aliens at Guantanamo did have a right to a full-fledged review of their confinement, and that the CSRTs did not provide the due process of law that *Hamdi* required. But she based her decision in large part on a single ambiguous sentence in a footnote in the Rasul decision, in which the majority had noted that the detainees' allegations about their confinement "unquestionably describe 'custody in violation of the Constitution or laws or treaties of the United States'"— the basis for habeas corpus relief. But it seemed quite unlikely that the Court had intended to decide such a momentous issue so tersely, especially considering that the substantive rights of detainees had not been briefed or argued in the case.

Judge Leon had the better view, that the Supreme Court had never in any case, including *Rasul* and *Hamdi*, recognized substantive legal rights, much less any rights derived from the Constitution, for "aliens outside sovereign United States territory with no connection to the United States." He dismissed the Rasul footnote as "unpersuasive," especially in light of the Court's observation that "further proceedings" in lower courts such as Leon's would be necessary to consider "the merits of petitioners' claims" that they had the right to full habeas review.

Not surprisingly, the government appealed Judge Green's decision and the detainees' lawyers appealed Judge Leon's. But they were to wait over two years for the US Court of Appeals for the District of Columbia to resolve matters: two years of sharp conflict between the Congress and the judiciary.

The conflict arose because the Republican majorities in both houses of Congress, dismayed at the government's losses in *Rasul* and *Hamdi*, feared that more was to come if Judge Green's view of the law prevailed. They were determined to keep the federal courts out of the business of adjudicating the rights of Gitmo detainees, or at least to minimize their role as much as possible. So in the Detainee Treatment Act of 2005, Congress stripped the federal courts of jurisdiction to "hear or consider" any habeas corpus petition from any Guantanamo detainee, or for that matter any lawsuit "relating to any aspect" of their detention. (That was the provision that the government invoked in its attempt to preclude the Supreme Court's review of military commissions in *Hamdan*, but the Court had avoided entangling itself in it, concluding that the law did not apply to then-pending cases.)

In place of habeas proceedings, the Detainee Treatment Act provided only a limited right to have the determination of a CSRT reviewed by the court of appeals in Washington. That was a deeply unsatisfactory alternative from the detainees' perspective, for two reasons. The CSRTs were not the fair and impartial review of their disputed status as "enemy combatants" that the Court in *Hamdi* had required. Furthermore, Congress had limited the court of appeals, in effect, to ruling only on whether the CSRTs had followed the procedures the Defense Department had written for them. Whether the CSRTs unconstitutionally displaced the right to habeas corpus, or even whether such a right existed at all for Gitmo detainees, was off limits.

The Detainee Treatment Act tested the very meaning of the separation of powers in the US government. The Constitution allocates the "judicial Power of the United States" to the Supreme Court and to "such inferior Courts as the Congress may from time to time ordain and establish." Given this congressional authority, the district courts and courts of appeals decide only cases in categories that Congress defines—for example, cases arising under federal law, including prosecutions for federal crimes; certain civil disputes between citizens of different states; and appeals from decisions of federal administrative agencies. The scope of federal courts' jurisdiction is thus broad but not unbounded. When Congress in the DTA told the federal judiciary that it had no jurisdiction to consider habeas petitions from Guantanamo detainees, or in fact any matter arising from Gitmo, saving only a narrow exception for the court of appeals in Washington to review CSRT proceedings, it was relying on its constitutional authority to define jurisdiction, with the aim of excluding from habeas corpus review a specific category of troublesome cases brought by a specific category of disfavored petitioners.

But the Constitution also provides that "the privilege of the Writ of Habeas Corpus shall not be suspended, unless when in Cases of Rebellion or Invasion the public Safety may require it." This provision, known as the Suspension Clause (though a better name would be the Non-Suspension Clause, or the Habeas Protection Clause), was understood to be the Constitution's preservation and protection of the right of habeas corpus as it existed in 1788, when the Constitution was adopted. At that time, habeas was largely the product of a century of adjudication in British courts, which the framers knew well. In passing the Detainee Treatment Act, Congress had not explicitly suspended habeas, and no one was contending that a rebellion or invasion was at hand, so the DTA provision brought two constitutional provisions face to face: in habeas cases, did the Suspension Clause restrict the authority of Congress to restrict the authority of federal courts?

One starts from the fact that the Suspension Clause does not mean that habeas corpus is untouchable by Congress. Over the years, Congress had occasionally legislated rules for the judicial administration of habeas cases, generally on such procedural matters as which court a petition should be filed in. The Supreme Court had upheld such congressional housekeeping, but only after first satisfying itself that Congress had not restricted an applicant's rights to a full and fair determination of his case before some federal court. This jurisprudence had created, somewhat confusingly, two classes of habeas protection. There was "constitutional habeas"—the rights that the

Constitution protects, habeas as it existed in 1788. Constitutional habeas cannot be altered save by amendment of the Constitution (unless suspended in times of rebellion or invasion). And there is "statutory habeas," the additional rights conferred by Congress since 1788 in various statutes, largely regulating how, when, and where habeas petitions are to be filed and decided. Rights created by statute can be altered or withdrawn by statute, so long as doing so does not impinge on the scope of constitutional habeas.

Had the DTA limited itself to providing that Gitmo detainees must file their habeas petitions only in the federal district court in Washington, it would have been an unexceptional adjustment of statutory habeas. But the DTA was far more restrictive than that. It was the first time Congress had actually revoked habeas jurisdiction altogether from federal courts in a defined category of cases. Was that a "suspension" of the writ? If so, it was unconstitutional, given the absence of any invasion or rebellion.

In 2006, a year after Congress enacted this jurisdiction-stripping, the Supreme Court had in *Hamdan* side-stepped the constitutional question by concluding that the DTA did not apply to that pending case, but Congress was not to be put off. In the Military Commissions Act of 2006, enacted a few months after—and in direct response to—*Hamdan*, it again stripped habeas jurisdiction from the federal courts in cases brought by Gitmo detainees (and for good measure, any habeas case brought by any alien held anywhere abroad in US military custody), making clear that pending cases were most definitely included.

The Military Commissions Act, superseding the Detainee Treatment Act in this respect, thus squarely raised a conflict between constitutional habeas, protected by the Suspension Clause, and congressional authority to define federal courts' jurisdiction. Judges Leon and Green had not had to deal with the issue because they had decided their cases in January 2005, before the DTA was enacted. But the court of appeals had put the detainees' and the government's appeals from those decisions on hold while it waited to see what Congress would do about habeas jurisdiction. The Supreme Court's decision in *Hamdan* was no help, because the Leon-Green cases, like Hamdan's, had been pending when the DTA was enacted. Only after the MCA was passed in 2006 did the court of appeals have a clear statement from Congress that no court had jurisdiction over Gitmo habeas petitions, period, end of discussion.

Congress having spoken, the court of appeals had to resolve matters one way or the other: could Congress constitutionally revoke habeas jurisdiction from the federal courts in Gitmo cases? Did Gitmo detainees have a right to have US courts hear and rule on their habeas corpus petitions and order their release if the detentions were unlawful, or did they not? Whatever the court of appeals decided would in due course likely be reviewed by the Supreme Court, but that did not make its job any easier or any less important. The government and the detainees each wanted to go to the Supreme Court with a victory to defend, not a defeat to overturn.

The accumulation of appeals from the decisions of Judges Green and Leon were consolidated in the court of appeals under the name of Lakhdar Boumediene, an Algerian detainee. The case was assigned (by lot, as cases are) to a three-judge panel consisting of Judges Raymond Randolph and David Sentelle, reliable conservatives—Randolph had written the court's Hamdan decision upholding military commissions—and Judith Rogers, appointed by President Clinton in 1994 to fill the seat vacated by Clarence Thomas three years earlier. *Boumediene* was a protracted appeal. The court held two rounds of oral argument and four rounds of briefing to accommodate the shifting questions of what effect the Detainee Treatment Act of 2005, the Supreme Court's Hamdan decision, and the Military Commissions Act of 2006 had on the court of appeals' jurisdiction to rule on habeas petitions.

On February 20, 2007, two years after the decisions of Leon and Green in the district court, the court of appeals in a split decision dismissed the detainees' cases. In an opinion by Judge Randolph, joined by Judge Sentelle, it ruled that the Military Commissions Act had lawfully divested federal courts of jurisdiction. In disposing of the detainees' argument that not even the MCA applied to pending cases (an argument their lawyers could not realistically have expected to win), the majority was scornful. "Everyone who has followed the interaction between Congress and the Supreme Court knows full well that one of the primary purposes of the MCA was to overrule *Hamdan*," Randolph wrote. "Everyone, that is, except the detainees. Their cases, they argue, are not covered. Their arguments are creative but not cogent. To accept them would be to defy the will of Congress. [The MCA] could not be clearer. . . . It is almost as if the [congressional] proponents of these words were slamming their fists on the table[,] shouting 'When we say "all," we mean all—without exception.'" The detainees' argument was "nonsense," Randolph wrote. It "goes nowhere."

That argument trashed, the majority took up the more challenging question of whether ousting federal courts from habeas jurisdiction for detainees was an unconstitutional suspension of the writ. To determine the scope of the constitutional preservation of habeas corpus, it is accepted that eighteenth-century English cases are instructive, because they demonstrate what the drafters of the Constitution understood habeas to be. The majority thus delved deeply into obscure English and early American cases and found no case in which aliens abroad were granted the writ. From this they concluded that when the Constitution was ratified the writ was not available to aliens held outside the territorial sovereignty of the United States. With no right to begin with, there was nothing for the MCA to suspend, therefore no violation of the Suspension Clause. The revocation of habeas jurisdiction was constitutional.

But as Judge Rogers pointed out in her dissent, the historical cases cited by the majority were no models of clarity, and they did not actually rule that aliens abroad were ineligible for the writ; they showed only that, for a variety of reasons, no court had actually granted it. But Judge Randolph's majority opinion went beyond that, to make a larger point: "Precedent in this court and the Supreme Court holds that the Constitution does not confer rights"—*any* rights, not just the right to habeas—"on aliens without property or presence within the United States." Rogers's dissent to the contrary was dismissed as "filled with holes." Federal courts, the majority concluded, therefore "have no jurisdiction in these cases." It was an unequivocal defeat for the detainees, leaving them no hope for any review of their status save in the detested CSRTs—unless the Supreme Court could redeem them, again.

To bring the case to the Court, Washington attorney Seth P. Waxman, in private practice after serving as solicitor general in President Clinton's second term, took over the representation of Lakhdar Boumediene. Given the gravity of the separation of powers issue, a grant of certiorari seemed a sure thing, but the Supreme Court confounded those expectations and denied Waxman's petition. It takes only four justices to grant certiorari, and Breyer, Souter, and Ginsburg filed a written dissent—an uncommon occurrence when cert is denied—noting that the jurisdictional questions "deserve this Court's immediate attention." Stevens and Kennedy, in a joint opinion, explained why they had not voted to take the case. "Despite the obvious importance of the issues raised," their statement said, "we are persuaded that traditional rules governing our decision of constitutional questions"—a reference to the Court's practice of deciding such questions only when necessary, and on the fullest possible record from lower courts—"and our practice of requiring the exhaustion of available remedies as a precondition to accepting jurisdiction over applications for the writ of habeas corpus"—a reference to the availability of judicial review of the CSRT decisions—"make it appropriate to deny these petitions at this time." They went on to note, however, that review in the future would be possible, even likely, "to ensure that the office and purpose of the writ of habeas corpus are not compromised." (One of the authorities quoted by Stevens and Kennedy on the exhaustion point was the concurring opinion of Justice Wiley Rutledge in *Marino v. Ragen*, a little-known 1947 case. Justice Stevens was the law clerk for Justice Rutledge in 1947–1948. Thus he and Kennedy were citing, perhaps slyly, an opinion Stevens himself likely had a hand in drafting, sixty years earlier.)

What Stevens and Kennedy were saying, somewhat obliquely, was that the petitioners should appeal the CSRT decisions (decisions they had lost, like nearly all detainees) in the appeals court as the Detainee Treatment Act and then the Military Commissions Act had ordained, and then seek Supreme Court review again if and when that process had been exhausted to their detriment. But that wait-and-see position did not satisfy Breyer: "Ordinarily, habeas petitioners need not exhaust a remedy that is inadequate to vindicate the asserted right," he wrote. Here a CSRT appeal would consign the detainees back to the same appeals court that had just ruled in their habeas case that they had "*no constitutional rights* (not merely the right to habeas)" (emphasis by Justice Breyer). But he and Souter and Ginsburg were a vote short of granting review.

There is no appeal from a Supreme Court decision, but Waxman persisted. Twenty-five days after the Court turned down the case, he filed a petition for reconsideration of its denial, a request the Court seldom sees and almost never grants. Waxman put forth a lengthy and intricate procedural argument that the Court should withdraw its denial of certiorari and simply keep Boumediene's case on hold until the court of appeals handed down its anticipated rulings in two other cases already pending before that court that were expected to flesh out the scope of review of CSRT proceedings. That course of action, Waxman argued in an obvious appeal to Stevens and Kennedy, would allow the Supreme Court then to grant cert to his client, informed by what the court of appeals would rule on the scope of CSRT review, rather than requiring Boumediene himself to go through a lengthy CSRT appeal and have to argue both the CSRT and habeas questions in the same case, in some future year, languishing all the while at Gitmo. It was a resourceful argument, earnestly seeking to preserve the opportunity to argue the habeas case to the Supreme Court cleanly, without the baggage of having to argue the CSRT issues, too, and to give Boumediene his chance before the Court without having to return to the demonstrably unfriendly court of appeals and endure more months, even years, of litigation.

Waxman's lawyerly presentation was soon joined and perhaps overshadowed by another petition for reconsideration filed by Thomas Wilner, also a prominent Washington lawyer and *pro bono* advocate for detainees, who was representing other detainees in the Boumediene case. Wilner filed with the Court an affidavit of Army Lieutenant Colonel Stephen Abraham, a reserve military intelligence officer and an attorney who had been on active duty in the Pentagon office that oversaw the proceedings of the CSRTs, and who had sat as a CSRT panelist himself in one case.

The affidavit was a bombshell. It contended that the recorders of the CSRTs (the officer presenting the case, analogous to a prosecutor) had little training or experience in investigations or intelligence matters, and that the material they presented to CSRT panelists was often generic, with little information relating to the individual detainee himself. Moreover, Abraham wrote, the dossiers were assembled by inexperienced case writers who had little actual access to relevant information, simply taking what intelligence agencies had forwarded to them, which almost always, in Abraham's experience, lacked specifics and withheld any information that might cast doubt on a detainee's alleged combatant status. The case writers took what they were given, included some of it in their write-ups for the recorders and left some out, all "without any articulable rationale." "What were purported to be specific statements of fact lacked even the most fundamental earmarks of objectively credible evidence," Abraham wrote. Moreover, when a CSRT panel concluded that a detainee was not an enemy combatant, Pentagon superiors sent the case back to the panel to review "what went wrong," a less than subtle instruction to change its decision.

In the one proceeding that Abraham sat on, evidence of the detainee's alleged ties to terrorism or combat was so sketchy that the panel ruled that there was no basis to justify holding him. On review, that decision was "immediately questioned" by the admiral in charge of the CSRT office, who ordered the panel to reopen the proceeding for further argument, which it did. When no further information was forthcoming it stuck to its original decision. "I was not assigned to another CSRT panel," he stated.

Seven days after Wilner filed the Abraham affidavit, the Supreme Court had a bombshell of its own. It revoked its denial of certiorari, granted Waxman's and Wilner's petitions, and set the cases for full briefing and oral argument. It didn't say why. Perhaps, at least in part, it was due to Waxman's appeal to orderly procedure, but it is hard not to imagine that Stevens and Kennedy were so dismayed at the showing that the CSRTs were, as Wilner had labeled them, "an irremediable sham" that they had thrown up their hands and abandoned their earlier view that the detainees should exhaust their CSRT appeals and then try again. Veteran reporter Lyle Denniston, who had covered the Supreme Court for decades as acutely as any journalist, wrote in SCOTUSblog that the Court's decision was "a startling turn of events in the legal combat over the war on terrorism." Not since 1947, he wrote, had the Court so reversed itself on a cert petition.

The briefs filed several weeks later by Waxman and Wilner for the detainees and the solicitor general for the government were clear and cogent, focused on the facts and the law, as each side saw the law, forsaking flourishes and hyperbole to let the issue speak for itself. With the increasing and unmistakable polarization of the Supreme Court in recent years, it has become common for lawyers who practice before it to frame their arguments in ways that will sway the one or two swing votes of justices who are less predictable than their seven or eight colleagues. Everyone knows this happens, but it is never acknowledged in court, and certainly not in the advocates' briefs.

Nonetheless, most court watchers expected that Stevens, Breyer, Souter, and Ginsburg would come down on the side of the detainees, as they all had in *Rasul, Hamdi,* and *Hamdan,* and that Scalia, Thomas, and Alito (who had replaced Sandra Day O'Connor in 2006 and had sided with the government in *Hamdan*) would not. Chief Justice Roberts, who had recused himself in *Hamdan* but had voted with the government when that case had been before him in the court of appeals, might align with the Scalia/Thomas/Alito group as well. That would leave Justice Anthony Kennedy, with O'Connor's retirement now the widely regarded swing vote. In the litigation to date, Kennedy had voted with the detainees, but in measured terms. He had been in the majority in *Rasul,* though he had only concurred in the judgment, refraining from joining Stevens's expansive view of habeas. He had joined Justice O'Connor's opinion in *Hamdi,* and in *Hamdan* he had voted to overturn military commissions but had stopped short of giving the Court a majority for the proposition that conspiracy was not a crime triable by military commissions. All eyes would be on Kennedy.

Waxman began his brief with eloquence:

> The Founders of our nation created a Constitution dedicated to protection of liberty, not one that turns a blind eye to indefinite detention without a meaningful opportunity to be heard. The Suspension Clause of Article I stands as the surest guarantee of liberty and due process by preventing Congress from abolishing habeas corpus or replacing it with a procedure that does not afford a petitioner a meaningful way to challenge his imprisonment. By allowing the indefinite military detention of Petitioners to stand without adequate judicial examination, the court of appeals disregarded the Founders' deliberate protection of the greatest legal instrument they knew.

Waxman argued that his clients were entitled to habeas, that Congress had unconstitutionally revoked it in the Military Commissions Act, and that, once that error was corrected, the unlawfulness of the confinement was apparent.

As it had in the court of appeals, the issue of whether aliens confined abroad could win release on habeas was to plunge the parties into deep historical research on whether British courts by 1788 had or had not gone that far. But this examination of the scope of "constitutional habeas" presented several problems, none of which was acknowledged by the parties, each striving to show that history clearly supported its position. The historical record in truth was sketchy, ambiguous, and often contradictory, leading the lawyers for the detainees and the government alike into a studied parsing of the distinctions among dominions, territories, kingdoms, and realms in eighteenth-century Britain and deconstructing the legal and political status of India and Scotland, then Jersey and Guernsey, and thence into Berwick-upon-Tweed, the Bechuanaland Protectorate in Africa, and the British Concession in Shanghai, in each of which the British writ was—or was not, depending on whose brief one was reading—available. But assuming, however wistfully, that all that could be sorted out, the greater problem was that there was no reliable yardstick for applying the usages of a monarchy with a global empire of territories, protectorates, and colonies to a 1788 American republic, and then applying it further to the odd and unique status of a twenty-first-century US military base perpetually occupied on foreign soil under a 1903 lease.

For the government, disproving the availability of habeas to aliens abroad in 1788 would have been enough, given that the habeas enshrined in the Constitution was the habeas that the Constitution's framers knew and protected, sparse as their writings on the point were at that time. If habeas was not available then, the court of appeals was correct to rule that, as far as the Constitution was concerned, there was nothing for the Military Commissions Act to suspend. The petitioners had a far longer road to victory, first to establish that in 1788 habeas did in fact extend to aliens abroad, and then that Gitmo, had it existed then, would have been subject to it, and then further that the MCA had not merely adjusted federal jurisdiction but had indeed tacitly suspended it, and finally that the CSRTs were not an adequate substitute for it.

However murky the historical record, Waxman at least had a muscular argument that the CSRT procedures fell far short of what a litigant would be entitled to in a habeas proceeding. The detainee's opportunity to present evidence was hamstrung by his inability to know what evidence was being used against him (the government acknowledged that "most of the CSRT conclusions are based in significant part on classified information" not disclosed to the detainee); there was no "neutral and plenary review" of the evidence because the government's evidence was presumptively correct unless the detainee could overcome it; there was no right to counsel; the right to call witnesses was illusory in practice; and even the right to cross-examine witnesses was an empty shell because the case against the detainee consisted of a sheaf of documents—in Waxman's words, a "one-sided body of hearsay and second-hand summaries of evidence"—rather than real testimony from actual witnesses who could be questioned face-to-face about what they knew about a detainee's activities and how they knew it. Perhaps most significantly, Waxman argued, if the CSRT ordered the detainee to remain confined there was no provision in the Military Commissions Act authorizing the appeals court to order his release.

The government for its part—assuming for the sake of argument that the detainees would be entitled to habeas to begin with—answered not by comparing the process the detainee received to what a US habeas petitioner would receive in a federal court, but to what traditionally had been available at law to a captured combatant, which was of course nothing at all: under longstanding laws of war, including the Geneva Conventions, prisoners of war could be detained for the duration of hostilities without access to courts.

That was true as far as it went, but it did not answer the detainees' underlying contention: they were not combatants at all, and never had been, but hapless victims of roundups and bounties. The Court in *Hamdi* had said they were entitled to a fair opportunity to have their story heard, but, Waxman argued, the government had given them none, not in the CSRT or anyplace else. Their CSRT hearing and the court of appeals' limited scope of review under the MCA thus did not give them due process of law that the Court had promised in *Hamdi*. In Waxman's words, the rules "allowed [the government] to avoid meaningful explication of the charges, prevented Petitioners from seeing most of the evidence used against them, forbade them from consulting counsel, and made it virtually impossible for them to identify and proffer favorable evidence."

The solicitor general's brief responded by citing the rights accorded under the CSRT process, which were not insubstantial: notice of the charges, disclosure of the government's evidence (excluding classified evidence); the right to call witnesses, the right to cross-examine. But it was clear that the government was relying on what the law said, while the petitioners were arguing that the process had to be judged not by how it worked on paper but how it was actually conducted, which was quite a different matter, and much to their detriment. The government's brief concluded by resurrecting the position that Stevens and Kennedy had originally taken in denying review of the case, urging the Court to require the petitioners to go through the review of their CSRT proceedings in the court of appeals and if they lost there, then to make their case to the Supreme Court, if they still could, that they had been treated unfairly.

Oral argument on December 5, 2007, was not particularly enlightening. Surely the first time any justices of the Supreme Court had been instructed on the law in Bechuanaland, much of the presentations centered on obscure questions of eighteenth-century British sovereignty, and the more familiar issue of whether the Court should stay its hand and require the detainees to pursue an appeal of their CSRT verdicts, or at least await the outcome of other cases then pending in the court of appeals on whether the CSRTs met *Hamdi*'s requirement of due process for detainees.

The case went behind the red velvet curtains for six months.

On June 12, 2008, the Court handed down a 5-4 decision that appeared to be a complete victory for the detainees. Justice Kennedy, in a seventy-page opinion for a majority that included, not surprisingly, Stevens, Ginsburg, Breyer, and Souter, opened with an extended discussion of habeas corpus, beginning with the Magna Carta, the venerated decree that in 1215 first recognized individual rights under a government of checked powers, and gave the promise that "no man would be imprisoned contrary to the law of the land," as Kennedy summarized it. Habeas gradually became the means by which the lawfulness of imprisonment could be examined by the judiciary, but the writ was suspended so often in times of political turmoil that in 1679 Parliament secured it in the Habeas Corpus Act, which the jurist William Blackstone proclaimed the "stable bulwark of our liberties."

A century later, wrote Kennedy, those who drafted the Constitution in Philadelphia were well aware that "pendular swings to and away from individual liberty were endemic to undivided, uncontrolled power," and so divided the powers of the new US government into three separate branches. In doing so, they took care to create "an essential mechanism in the separation-of-powers scheme" by preserving habeas corpus as "an affirmative right to judicial inquiry into the causes of detention" by the executive. He quoted Alexander Hamilton, writing in *Federalist* No. 84: "The practice of arbitrary imprisonments, have been, in all ages, the favorite and most formidable instruments of tyranny." Hamilton then quoted the influential Blackstone: "Confinement of the person, by secretly hurrying him to jail, where his sufferings are unknown or forgotten, is a less public, a less striking, and therefore *a more dangerous engine* of arbitrary government" (the emphasis is Hamilton's). "The separation-of-powers doctrine, and the history that influenced its design," Kennedy wrote, "therefore must inform the reach and purpose of the Suspension Clause."

As to the specific question of whether habeas corpus historically was available to foreigners detained abroad in time of war, Kennedy mercifully refrained from venturing too deeply into the realm of British colonial law. Instead, he resolved the conflicting narratives of the detainees and the government pragmatically: there are "no certain conclusions," he wrote, no case in which a British or American court either did, or did not because it lacked jurisdiction, issue the writ to such an applicant. "The common-law courts simply may not have confronted cases with close parallels to this one. We decline, therefore, to infer too much, one way or the other, from the lack of historical evidence on point."

With the historical slate scrubbed clean, the majority turned to the government's contention that the United States did not have "sovereignty" over Guantanamo Bay because the still-extant 1903 lease recognized that "ultimate sovereignty" remained with Cuba. Noting that "sovereignty" was a term used and misused "in many senses," Kennedy again declined a definitive answer, this time to the conundrum of which nation was "sovereign." Even accepting the government's assertion that Cuba retained *de jure* sovereignty, Kennedy wrote, "we take notice of the obvious and uncontested fact that the United States, by virtue of its complete jurisdiction and control over the base, maintains *de facto* sovereignty over this territory."

Having thus wrestled both history and elusive sovereignty to a draw, the Court was free to consider its own various precedents on the extent to which the Constitution has extraterritorial application. These cases, mostly dating from 1901, did not, Kennedy acknowledged, present an especially clear picture either, and from this he derived a third pragmatic conclusion: the decisions were based on "practical considerations" rather than doctrinal ones. Still, one case in particular had to be dealt with squarely—the Court's 1950 decision in *Johnson v. Eisentrager*, the one rejecting habeas petitions from German officers convicted of war crimes by a postwar US military tribunal in Europe and imprisoned in occupied Germany. Throughout the Boumediene litigation (and also in the Rasul litigation several years before), the government had relied heavily on that decision for the proposition that aliens confined abroad by US authority simply had no access to US courts on habeas. Indeed, the Court in *Eisentrager* had made a point of saying that the German prisoners were not within "any territory in which the United States is sovereign" and that their crime, capture, trial, and punishment were "all beyond the territorial jurisdiction of any court of the United States," a situation, the government repeatedly stressed, that described the Gitmo detainees exactly (except of course for the trial part).

But the Court rejected the government's contention that this language was "proof positive that the *Eisentrager* Court adopted a formalistic, sovereignty-based test for determining the reach" of habeas. Noting that the German petitioners had already received a full-fledged criminal trial with lawyers and judges and due process to spare, Kennedy concluded that nothing in *Eisentrager* "says that *de jure* sovereignty is or has ever been the only relevant consideration in determining the geographic reach of the Constitution or of habeas corpus." The better view was that "questions of extraterritoriality turn on objective factors and practical concerns, not formalism."

And here he slammed the door shut on the government. If its position were upheld, "disclaim[ing] sovereignty in the formal sense of the term" as the United States had done in the 1903 lease while nonetheless retaining absolute control of the territory, would make it "possible for the political branches [Congress and the president] to govern without legal restraint." But, wrote Kennedy, "our basic charter cannot be contracted away like this." The Constitution gives the president and Congress the power to govern US territory but not "the power to decide when and where [the Constitution's] terms apply." That is the job of courts. For the judiciary to accept that the political branches rather than the courts determine "questions involving formal sovereignty and territorial governance is one thing. To hold the political branches have the power to switch the Constitution on or off at will is quite another." He went on, "The writ of habeas corpus is itself an indispensable mechanism for monitoring the separation of powers. The test for determining the scope of this provision must not be subject to manipulation by those whose power it is designed to restrain."

It was a point of enormous importance, reiterating what Justice O'Connor had written four years earlier in her Hamdi opinion: separation of powers does not mean that the Executive, even with the assent of Congress, can bar the courts from examining the Executive's decisions. It means just the opposite, that each branch of government has specified powers that it must invoke when the other two branches try to overextend their powers. The government's argument, she had written then, does not uphold the separation of powers; it "serves only to *condense* power into a single branch of government" (O'Connor's emphasis).

Justice Kennedy's sharp words, therefore, can be read as more than a rejection of the Bush administration's long-held and vigorously argued position on the legal status of Guantanamo. They rebuke the administration for even taking that position, for disrespecting the separation of powers and failing to understand the consequences of its argument on the very foundation of the Constitution, and thus of the government itself. Habeas corpus is a constitutionally-protected power of the courts to tell the Executive that it has gone too far, that it has exceeded its lawful authority over those whom it has deprived of liberty. It is not for the Executive therefore to manipulate its acknowledged authority to determine "sovereignty" into a shield that bars the Judiciary from inquiring into the lawfulness of the deprivation.

Having thus uncoupled the inquiry from both historical and doctrinal formalism, the Court returned to its point that the extraterritorial reach of habeas must be determined by "objective factors and practical concerns." In the detainees' cases, the objective factors were at least three: "(1) the citizenship and status of the detainee and the adequacy of the process through which that status determination was made; (2) the nature of the sites where apprehension and then detention took place;

and (3) the practical obstacles inherent in resolving the prisoner's entitlement to the writ." As to the first, the status is disputed: the government claims that the detainees are enemy combatants, but the detainees deny it. Yet unlike the military trial of the German detainees in *Eisentrager*, the CSRTs—"the process through which that status determination is made"—had not afforded these detainees a "rigorous adversarial process to test the legality of their detention," nor a detailed statement of the specific facts leading to the charges, nor representation by counsel, nor a practical opportunity to introduce evidence themselves, and to cross-examine the government's witnesses. The limited CSRT procedures thus "fall well short of the procedures and adversarial mechanisms that would eliminate the need for habeas corpus review" by the courts.

As to the second relevant factor, while the detainees are, as in *Eisentrager*, aliens "technically outside the sovereign territory of the United States," occupied Germany was not under the sole, complete, unquestioned, and everlasting control of the United States, as the Guantanamo naval base is. As a practical matter, Kennedy wrote, Guantanamo is not even "abroad; it is within the constant jurisdiction of the United States." (On this point, he was echoing his concurring opinion four years earlier in *Rasul*, which he would have decided in favor of the detainees simply on the basis that Guantanamo is functionally part of the United States and thus, for habeas purposes, no different from any of the fifty states.)

And finally, as to the "practical obstacles" to determining the rights of the detainees, Kennedy acknowledged that there might be some incremental expense in holding habeas hearings for distant petitioners and some marginal distraction for Gitmo's military staff, but the government has presented "no credible arguments that the military mission at Guantanamo would be compromised if habeas corpus courts had jurisdiction to hear the detainees' claims," Kennedy wrote, and "none are apparent to us." Unlike occupied Germany, the naval base is a mere forty-five square miles, "isolated and heavily fortified," and does not concern itself with local governments and populations and sensitive political and diplomatic relationships. Perhaps with an eye toward other detention facilities, such as the one then at Bagram Air Base in Afghanistan, the majority noted that "if the detention facility were located in an active theater of war, arguments that issuing the writ would be impracticable or anomalous would have more weight."

Each of the three "objective factors and practical concerns" thus supported the detainees. "We hold," the Court concluded, that the right of habeas corpus, as protected in the Constitution, "has full effect at Guantanamo Bay. If the privilege of habeas corpus is to be denied to the detainees now before us, Congress must act in accordance with the requirements of the Suspension Clause." Kennedy turned to that question.

Congress could deny the privilege, as the Constitution provided, by suspending habeas "when in Cases of Rebellion or Invasion the public Safety may require it." That was a nonstarter, Congress not having acted on that basis and the government having disclaimed any reliance on it. The question thus became whether Congress, invoking its constitutional authority to determine federal courts' jurisdiction, violated the Suspension Clause by rescinding that jurisdiction over habeas actions filed by Guantanamo detainees, or indeed anyone held in US military custody abroad, as it had in the Military Commissions Act of 2006. That implicated the question, as the majority put it, "whether the statute stripping jurisdiction to issue the writ avoids the Suspension Clause mandate because Congress has provided adequate substitute procedures for habeas corpus."

The government's lawyers, anticipating the complications it would face by the absence of explicit suspension, had long argued that the revocation of jurisdiction was permissible because the Supreme Court had in the past recognized that providing "adequate substitute procedures" for habeas would avoid troublesome suspension issues. To us, it may seem odd that the Court would allow any substitute for a safeguard so important to the constitutional separation of powers, but it had, and the government's argument was that the CSRTs were that adequate substitute. Thus, it implied, the jurisdiction-stripping provisions were simply an adjustment of technical matters in the federal courts, a procedural tinkering with "statutory habeas corpus" that did not deny the core rights of constitutional habeas because the detainees were given CSRT hearings.

Kennedy's opinion quickly cut that argument down to size, essentially ruling that the government was reading far too much into the "adequate substitute" rule. "There are few precedents addressing what features an adequate substitute for habeas corpus must contain," he wrote, and in fact the Court had applied that rule only rarely. And when it had, "the statutes at issue were attempts to streamline habeas corpus relief, not to cut it back." In one case, Congress had acted to allow prisoners to file habeas petitions in the federal district court where they had been sentenced, which would have the records of their trial, not necessarily in the possibly distant district where they were presently confined. In another, Congress had sought to relieve the overcrowded habeas docket of the federal court in the District of Columbia by opening its local courts to habeas petitioners imprisoned there, but the purpose then was "to expedite consideration of the prisoner's claims," Kennedy wrote, "not to delay or frustrate it." In both cases, Congress had acted "to strengthen, rather than dilute, the writ's protections" and had in any event preserved the pre-existing habeas jurisdiction, so that no petitioner's rights were actually curtailed.

The Detainee Treatment Act and the Military Commissions Act were entirely different, because they were plainly intended to circumscribe habeas review and had done so explicitly, by extinguishing it altogether for Gitmo detainees and all other aliens held abroad. Moreover, unlike habeas petitions that seek to review the legality of a conviction and sentence imposed after a criminal trial, these detainees were being held by executive order. They had been given no trial, and thus no appeal or indeed any judicial review, so "the need for habeas corpus is more urgent." The CSRT process, Kennedy wrote, was no "adequate substitute." It places "constraints upon the detainee's ability to rebut the factual basis for the Government's assertion that he is an enemy combatant." He has "limited means to find or present evidence to challenge the Government's case against him. He does not have the assistance of counsel and may not be aware of the most critical allegations that the Government relied upon to order his detention." And with the wholesale allowance of hearsay evidence in government dossiers of generalized allegations from undisclosed sources, "the detainee's opportunity to question witnesses is likely to be more theoretical than real." The process is "closed and accusatorial," all of which leads to "considerable risk of error in the tribunal's findings of fact. . . . And given that the consequence of error may be detention of persons for the duration of hostilities that may last a generation or more, this is a risk too significant to ignore."

The risks posed by these shortcomings, the Court concluded, were not cured by allocating to the court of appeals the jurisdiction to review the CSRTs' verdicts. That authority was appreciably narrower than that accorded in habeas proceedings because it was limited to reviewing whether the CSRT had followed its own rules and procedures, hardly a thoroughgoing inquiry into the legality of the detention. Particularly troubling was the court of appeals' lack of any statutory authority to order the detainee's actual release from custody, or even to receive evidence from the detainee that he had been unable to present in the CSRT hearing itself, though such evidence might be "critical to the detainee's argument that he is not an enemy combatant and there is no cause to detain him." In all, Kennedy wrote, "The role of a [US federal] court in the exercise of its habeas corpus function cannot be circumscribed in this manner." The entire CSRT process, the majority concluded, was well short of anything that could be considered an "adequate substitute" for habeas corpus.

In reaching this conclusion, the Court did not rule that the CSRTs were themselves unconstitutional; they were just inadequate to meet the government's constitutional obligation to provide detainees a full and fair forum as a substitute for habeas corpus. CSRT hearings could continue, and in fact courts could defer consideration of any habeas petition until a detainee had gone through that process. (This reservation did not amount to much; Gitmo had received fewer than three dozen new detainees in the previous four years, and everyone there had already undergone the CSRT review.) Furthermore, the Court added, the government did not have to make habeas available immediately upon capture and detention—"proper deference can be accorded to reasonable procedures for screening and initial detention under lawful and proper conditions of confinement and treatment for a reasonable period of time." But the Court was emphatic that for the detainees before it (and by implication nearly all detainees) six years was far too long to be reasonable. They were "entitled to a prompt habeas corpus hearing," without, contrary to the government's argument, going back to the court of appeals to undergo review of the adequacy of their CSRT hearing.

Kennedy's opinion, however, said little or nothing about how such hearings would be held, including what evidence would be allowed, or whether the government could continue to rely on hearsay evidence, or what evidence would suffice to establish that a detainee was being lawfully confined as an enemy combatant. Nor did he go anywhere near the question of whether a detainee, if he were found to be a lawfully detained combatant, would be entitled to the status of a prisoner of war under the protections of the Third Geneva Convention, including the right under that convention to be released upon the "cessation of active hostilities," whatever that might mean in the context of a global war on terrorism.

In closing, the Court acknowledged that "the law must accord the Executive substantial authority to apprehend and detain those who pose a real danger to our security." But, Kennedy wrote, "security subsists, too, in fidelity to freedom's first principles. Chief among these are freedom from arbitrary and unlawful restraint and the personal liberty that is secured by adherence to the separation of powers." He went on, "Our opinion does not undermine the Executive's powers as Commander in Chief. On the contrary, the exercise of those powers is vindicated, not eroded, when confirmed by the Judicial Branch. Within the Constitution's separation-of-powers structure, few exercises of judicial power are as legitimate or as necessary as the responsibility to hear challenges to the authority of the Executive to imprison a person." He concluded, "The laws and Constitution are designed to survive, and remain in force, in extraordinary times. Liberty and security can be reconciled; and in our system they are reconciled within the framework of the law. The Framers decided that habeas corpus, a right of first importance, must be a part of that framework, a part of that law."

Chief Justice Roberts, writing for the four dissenters in a twenty-eight-page opinion, strenuously objected to the majority's displacement of the review process that Congress had written into the Detainee Treatment Act and the Military Commissions Act. "The majority merely replaces a review system designed by the people's representatives with a set of shapeless procedures to be defined by federal courts at some future date," he wrote. "This decision is not really about the detainees at all, but about control of federal policy regarding enemy combatants." Congress had exercised its authority "to reconcile review of the prisoners' detention with the undoubted need to protect the American people from the terrorist threat," he wrote. "All that today's opinion has done is shift responsibility for those sensitive foreign policy and national security decisions from the elected branches to the Federal Judiciary." Furthermore, the Court's action was at the least "grossly premature" in adjudicating the detainees' rights "without first assessing whether the remedies the [Detainee Treatment Act of 2005] system provides vindicate whatever rights petitioners may claim." Not only did the Court jettison the court of appeals' review of CSRT procedures—"more opportunity and more process, in fact, than that afforded prisoners of war or any other alleged enemy combatants in history"—it wrongly ignored "the distinct possibility that its 'habeas' remedy will, when all is said and done, end up looking a great deal like the DTA review it rejects."

Roberts's prematurity point was in one sense thoroughly orthodox, and in fact had presumably been shared by six of the justices, including Kennedy and Stevens, when the Court had originally denied review in the case to allow the DTA review to play itself out in the court of appeals. But it evidently had lost those two justices by not overcoming their concerns about four factors: the fairness of the CSRT procedures even on paper; the haphazard administration of those procedures in light of the Abraham affidavit (though the majority had not mentioned CSRT administration or the affidavit specifically); the adequacy of the court of appeals' review; and the prolonged detention the petitioners had already endured. So the majority, clearly not persuaded that the DTA review might prove to be an adequate substitute for habeas, was likewise not bothered by Roberts's criticism that it had jumped to unproven conclusions by declining to wait and see.

Justice Scalia, also writing for the four dissenters, added an additional criticism, based on his own historical conclusions. "My problem with today's opinion," he wrote, is that "habeas corpus does not, and never has, run in favor of aliens abroad; the Suspension Clause thus has no application, and the Court's intervention in this military matter is entirely *ultra vires*"—beyond its authority. Never one to restrain his indignation or to temper his prose when more pointed words would do, Scalia wrote that the Court's decision would have "disastrous consequences" because "America is at war with radical Islamists" in which "our countrymen in arms" have been killed, and the "game of bait-and-switch that today's opinion plays upon the Nation's Commander in Chief will make the war harder on us. It will almost certainly cause more Americans to be killed"—a reference to a Senate committee's minority report that "at least 30 of those prisoners hitherto released from Guantanamo Bay have returned to the battlefield" and "the number of the enemy returned to combat will obviously increase." Scalia went on, "What competence does the Court have to second-guess the judgment of Congress and the President on such a point? None whatever. But the Court blunders in nonetheless."

Turning to the law, Scalia found the Court's 1950 decision on German prisoners in *Eisentrager* fully adequate for the proposition "beyond any doubt—that the Constitution does not ensure habeas for aliens held by the United States in areas over which our Government is not sovereign." Even putting aside the "conclusive precedent of *Eisentrager*," Scalia wrote, "it is clear that the original understanding of the Suspension Clause was that habeas corpus was not available to aliens abroad."

Scalia concluded, "Today the Court warps our Constitution" by "invoking judicially brainstormed separation-of-powers principles to establish a manipulable 'functional' test for the extraterritorial reach of habeas corpus" that "blatantly misdescribes important precedents" and "breaks a chain of precedent as old as the common law." "Most tragically," he wrote, the Court "sets our military commanders the impossible task of proving to a civilian court, under whatever standards this Court devises in the future, that evidence supports the confinement of each and every enemy prisoner. The Nation will live to regret what the Court has done today."

The decision in *Boumediene* was the fourth time in four years that the Supreme Court had rejected the Bush administration's detainee policies, and the second time in two years that it had found congressional regulation of detainee matters likewise unconstitutional. It seemed a virtually unqualified victory for the long-imprisoned men at Guantanamo, and indeed it was so received. President Bush said, "We'll abide by the court's decision. That doesn't mean I have to agree with it. It was a deeply divided court, and, I strongly agree with those who dissented." The administration's opponents predictably welcomed the ruling. Senator John Kerry of Massachusetts, the Democratic presidential nominee in 2004: "Today, the Supreme Court affirmed what almost everyone but the administration and their defenders in Congress always knew," he said. "The Constitution and the rule of law bind all of us even in extraordinary times of war. No one is above the Constitution."

Senator Barack Obama, soon to be nominated by Democrats, applauded the Court's decision as "an important step toward re-establishing our credibility as a nation committed to the rule of law."

Events over the next six years, however, were to prove both the promise of habeas corpus and the dire warnings of Justice Scalia wrong. The US Court of Appeals for the District of Columbia Circuit was to see to that, and the Supreme Court watched in silence.

In the first four years after the Boumediene decision, according to a detailed study published in 2012 by Professor Mark Denbeaux of Seton Hall University's law school, the US District Court for the District of Columbia issued decisions in forty-six habeas cases brought by Guantanamo detainees seeking a court order that they be released. The issue in each case was whether the government could justify a petitioner's detention with evidence that he was an enemy combatant and thus subject to confinement under the laws of war and the Authorization for the Use of Military Force.

As the cases progressed, the government's evidence varied from individual to individual, but generally it focused on four factors: whether the detainee had committed hostile acts against the United States; whether he stayed at guesthouses in Pakistan and Afghanistan known to be frequented by al Qaeda and Taliban fighters; whether he had undergone training at an al Qaeda camp; and whether his means and route of travel from his home to the combat zone in Afghanistan matched a profile that, the government contended, was a tell-tale sign of al Qaeda or Taliban affiliation.

In the first two years of this litigation, many detainees succeeded. In every one of the ten cases in which the evidence satisfied the district court that the detainee had actually taken up arms to fight American forces in Afghanistan, the court denied release—such evidence conclusively established that he was indeed an enemy combatant. But when the government's case depended on one or more of the other three allegations, the government fared less well. In a few of these cases, the court found such circumstantial evidence sufficient to prove combatant status, but in most it did not. In all, during those first two years, detainees prevailed in twenty of the thirty-four cases decided—nearly 60 percent, and the government prevailed in the remaining 40 percent. A detainee's chances were strongest when the government either did not allege, or could not prove, participation in actual hostile acts, and had to rely on the more equivocal acts of travel and lodging.

The government filed an appeal in every loss, which kept the detainee at Guantanamo, but for the victors, there was, at last, light at the end of the tunnel. But the tunnel ran through the US Court of Appeals.

The court of appeals, as the district court, had to decide what evidence sufficed to prove a detainee an "enemy combatant," but this somewhat elastic concept had no firm definition in US or international law beyond the obvious inclusion of those who had taken up arms in combat for the enemy. To be sure, the Authorization for the Use of Military Force, passed by Congress shortly after 9/11, was broader than that, authorizing the president to use "all necessary and appropriate force"—certainly including detention—against persons "who he determines planned, authorized, committed, or aided" the terrorist attacks on that day, or "harbored" such persons. But few Gitmo detainees were actually implicated in the 9/11 attacks. So the definition of enemy combatant that the government wanted to apply in the habeas cases went beyond the AUMF to reach anyone "who was part of or supporting Taliban or al Qaeda forces, or associated forces that are engaged in hostilities" against the United States. In other words, it was not necessary that a detainee personally had engaged in hostilities or had been involved in 9/11 to fit the government's definition of an enemy combatant; it was enough if he was part of, or even "supported" the Taliban or al Qaeda, or any of their "associated forces."

But the elasticity of these terms clearly left much room for interpretation. Unlike conventional military organizations, neither the Taliban nor al Qaeda nor any "supporting forces" had formal inductions, identifying documents, or uniforms that could reliably distinguish between those who were and were not a "part of" those entities, much less those who were and were not "supporting" them. Added to this problem was the question of whether, whatever a "part of" or "supporting" might mean, a detainee's route of travel or guesthouse lodgings proved anything about it.

The first case decided by the appeals court of a detainee who had won his habeas case in the district court was that of Mohammed al-

Adahi, a then-forty-nine-year-old Yemeni citizen, in July 2010. The district court had found the government's evidence unpersuasive, though it showed (and Adahi admitted) that he had traveled to Afghanistan in 2001 at the urging and with the help of his brother-in-law, whom the court of appeals described as a "close associate" of Osama bin Laden. Adahi himself had met with bin Laden twice, had been trained at an al Qaeda camp, and had traveled throughout Afghanistan while US forces were fighting there, finally being evacuated to Pakistan in a bus carrying wounded Arab and Pakistani fighters. Adahi had offered an innocent explanation for all this—he described his Afghan travels as a vacation—and the district court, though it did not necessarily buy his explanation, had found each of the facts insufficient to show that he had been an enemy combatant. It ordered him released.

The court of appeals found the lower court's reasoning and its conclusion "incomprehensible" and "perplexing." That court had proceeded on the belief, the appeals court said, that "if a particular fact does not itself prove the ultimate proposition (e.g., whether the detainee was part of al Qaeda), the fact may be tossed aside and the next fact may be evaluated as if the first did not exist." It agreed with the government that "this was a fundamental mistake that infected the court's entire analysis," because it did not consider the cumulative effect of all the evidence taken together. "When the evidence is properly considered, it becomes clear that Al-Adahi was—at the very least—more likely than not a part of al-Qaida." And that preponderance of the evidence was sufficient to prove that Adahi was a properly detained enemy combatant.

The court of appeals called its fact-weighing "conditional probability analysis," a somewhat grandiose label for what was essentially just a process of placing all the evidence in context and then taking it as a whole, rather than assessing each piece independently of all other pieces. But the decision makes sense. Whatever being a "part of" al Qaeda might mean, two face-to-face meetings with Osama bin Laden in Afghanistan when you're at an al Qaeda camp and your brother-in-law is his close associate seems enough to show that you were on his side, a part of his organization, in the fight against American forces.

The court of appeals' analysis reverberated beyond Adahi's own case. It decisively changed the dynamic in the district court. In the twelve cases that the district court decided in the following year, it denied habeas in eleven. And the court of appeals reversed the single case that a detainee had won, and in doing so it all but closed the detainees' road to release.

In that case, brought by Adnan Latif, also a Yemeni, the government's case consisted largely of an intelligence report—the court of appeals redacted the name of the agency that provided it, but it was almost surely the CIA—that Latif had admitted under interrogation that he had been recruited in Yemen and had traveled to Afghanistan, where he fought under Taliban leadership. At his habeas hearing, Latif claimed he had been misunderstood; he had traveled to Afghanistan for medical care. The district court granted habeas because there was a "serious question" as to whether the CIA report accurately recounted what Latif had said to his interrogators; moreover, the Taliban connection was uncorroborated, and Latif had "presented a plausible alternative story to explain his travel."

The court of appeals was not impressed. But rather than simply reversing the decision on grounds that the government had sufficiently proven that Latif had been an enemy combatant, the court ruled that, thenceforth, government reports of the kind introduced against Latif at his hearing "are entitled to a presumption of regularity"—in other words, the government does not have to go beyond the report to prove the facts recited in it. The report itself suffices, and it is then up to the detainee to disprove those facts—if he can.

The presumption of regularity of government reports is a familiar evidentiary construct in American courts, but it has traditionally been extended only to the everyday recording of uncontroversial facts compiled without reference to any dispute: routine financial transactions, contemporary weather information, and the like. It dispenses with the need to call to the witness stand the actual person who recorded the information, who probably would have no independent recollection of the actual event but no reason to have recorded it inaccurately at the time. This treatment does not preclude the opposing party from contesting the truthfulness of the information, but he must do so with contrary evidence of his own; if he does not, or if his evidence is unpersuasive, the information is taken as truthful.

Interrogation reports, particularly when they are being interpreted into English from what the detainee is saying in his own language, don't really fit into that category, because there is a real risk of imprecision or even inaccuracy, particularly if the interpreter is less than expert in one language or the other. In addition, the reports here were not verbatim translations but only summaries, and redacted summaries at that, of what the detainee had (allegedly) said. By its ruling that such reports are to be accepted, and taken at face value if not disproven, the court of appeals was making it significantly easier for the government to prove that the detainee, now habeas petitioner, was indeed the enemy combatant that the government said he was. The detainee is free to say, "I never said that" or "the translation is wrong" and to produce whatever evidence he can in support, but there is no guarantee that the judge will believe the detainee and reject the government's report. And because no witness need be called to attest to the matters in the report, there could be no cross-examination. As a practical matter, therefore, it became the detainee's burden to prove that he was not an enemy combatant.

In addition, the court of appeals arguably expanded the reach of the government's authority to detain. In the Authorization for the Use of Military Force, Congress gave the president the authority to use force against those who had "planned, authorized, committed or aided the terrorist acts" of 9/11, and those who harbored such persons; and in the 2012 National Defense Authorization Act Congress had adopted the government's definition of enemy combatant by including those who, as the government was arguing in court, were "part of or substantially supported al-Qaeda, the Taliban, or associated forces that are engaged in hostilities against the United States." By the end of 2013, the court of appeals found that standard satisfied in the case of Abdul Razak Ali, based on evidence that he had spent eighteen days in an Afghan guesthouse in the company of al Qaeda operatives. The court concluded that hanging out with those operatives was sufficient to prove that Ali was "part of . . . associated forces" of al Qaeda despite the lack of evidence that he had actually done any more than that.

Judge Harry Edwards, writing separately, criticized this "personal associations" test as "well beyond what the AUMF and the [National Defense Authorization Act] prescribe." The "troubling question in these detainee cases," he wrote, "is whether the [court of appeals] has stretched the meaning of the AUMF and the NDAA so far beyond the terms of these statutory authorizations that habeas corpus proceedings like the one afforded Ali are functionally useless."

For detainees seeking to leverage the Boumediene decision into their release from Guantanamo, these decisions of the court of appeals had created formidable obstacles—too formidable, in fact, for them to overcome. Is this what the Court in *Boumediene* had in mind? The cases were obvious candidates for Supreme Court review. All of them collectively broke new ground on how detention could be justified (or not) in the courts, and all of them were turned away by a court of appeals that the Supreme Court had already reversed three times, in *Rasul, Hamdan,* and *Boumediene,* on the rights of Gitmo detainees, a matter of clear national importance.

Petitions for certiorari filed by the detainees accumulated in the Supreme Court's in-box, every one opposed by the Justice Department, now in the administration of President Barack Obama. Court-watchers waited for the justices to announce which case, or group of cases, they would hear to review what the court of appeals was doing. On June 11, 2012, four years less one day after its Boumediene decision, the Court ended the suspense: it turned down every petition.

Journalist Lyle Denniston summed up the situation in SCOTUS blog:

> The practical effect is that the D.C. Circuit Court now functions as the court of last resort for the 169 foreign nationals remaining at the U.S.-run military prison in Cuba, and that court has a well-established practice of overturning or delaying any release order issued by a federal judge when the government objects. . . . In a string of decisions, not one of which the Supreme Court has been willing to review, the D.C. Circuit [has] fashioned its own legal rules for Guantanamo cases.

In the nearly three years since then, the Court has continued its refusal to intervene. As is its custom, it has not explained its denial in any case, nor has any individual justice filed a dissent. As of the end of 2014, no Guantanamo detainee has been released when the government has opposed it. (In one case, the government did not oppose release on habeas corpus, due to the detainee's age and failing health.)

Why? Because the nine men and women who know aren't saying, one can only speculate. A likely hypothesis, or part of one, is that the four justices whom one would expect to have taken issue with the court of appeals' decisions—Stephen Breyer, Ruth Bader Ginsburg, Sonia

Sotomayor (appointed by President Obama in 2009 to replace David Souter), and Elena Kagan (appointed in 2010 to replace John Paul Stevens)—believe that the court of appeals would be upheld by the four steadfast dissenters (John Roberts, Antonin Scalia, Clarence Thomas, and Samuel Alito) joined by Justice Kennedy, and that they have no desire to see those decisions validated by the Supreme Court. The other four justices, according to this hypothesis, are content with the rulings below and see no reason to review them. If the hypothesis is accurate, Justice Kennedy is the one who is letting let the court of appeals' decisions stand. Given his full-throated rejection of the CSRT-DTA process as inherently unfair in *Boumediene*, and his expressed impatience—in 2008—with the prolonged and indeterminate detention of the Gitmo detainees, one would expect that he would be entirely in favor of a thorough and authoritative review, to determine whether the court of appeals is now itself acting unfairly in creating evidentiary rules that have blocked every detainee attempting to vindicate the rights that his opinion for the Court established.

Boumediene has been limited in another way as well. After the Supreme Court handed down its decision in 2008, detainees held by the United States at the Bagram Air Base in Afghanistan pressed their claim for the same habeas rights recognized in that case. The Obama administration's Justice Department firmly, and successfully, opposed any such extension of *Boumediene* to "enemy aliens in the active war zone" of Afghanistan. The US Court of Appeals for the District of Columbia ruled in the government's favor on May 21, 2010. Applying the *Boumediene* factors, the court in *Al-Maqaleh v. Gates* held that although the United States maintained complete control over Bagram, albeit not with the intent to remain permanently, the "practical obstacles" to granting the writ "overwhelmingly" required a different result because "Bagram, indeed the entire nation of Afghanistan, remains a theater of war," and extending habeas to detainees there would "hamper the war effort."

The Supreme Court denied review. The United States turned the Bagram detention center over to the Afghan government in March 2013.

So, in the end—at least the end of the seventh year after *Boumediene*—the court of appeals has accomplished what the Congress failed to do: it has effectively denied habeas relief to Guantanamo detainees, and it has done so with the tacit acquiescence of the Supreme Court. Barring the death or retirement of Roberts, Scalia, Thomas, or Alito, and the confirmation by the Senate of a pro-habeas replacement nominated by President Obama—the latter most unlikely given the Republican majority in the Senate that convened in January 2015—*Boumediene* has become a judicial derelict.

CHAPTER SEVEN

The Obama Administration

The terrorist attacks of September 11, 2001, took place in the first year of the administration of President George W. Bush. It was his decision to invade Afghanistan, to establish military commissions, and to send suspected al Qaeda and Taliban captives to Guantanamo Bay. It was in his administration that the Supreme Court, however close the vote, rebuffed in every case his policies on military commissions, on Guantanamo detention, and on habeas corpus. It was also in his administration that the CIA and some military elements inflicted "enhanced interrogation" on captives, techniques that were widely criticized, at home and abroad, as nothing less than torture. The criticism accelerated after graphic photographs of the abuse of prisoners at Abu Ghraib in Iraq became public in 2004, followed by release of internal Justice Department memos in 2005, and a report of the Senate Armed Services Committee in 2008, and were reinvigorated by the scathing report of the Senate Select Committee on Intelligence in 2014, which removed any doubt that torture was widely condoned and practiced for years after 9/11. (None of the torture matters reached the Supreme Court, or indeed were adjudicated on the merits by any lower court, and so they are beyond the scope of this work.)

In the 2008 presidential campaign, Senator Barack Obama made clear his opposition to the Bush administration's policies and promised that as president he would reverse them. He wasted no time. On January 22, 2009, his first day as president and commander in chief, he signed three executive orders. One ended overt mistreatment of detainees and all interrogations that did not conform to long-standing military procedures; one suspended, for the time being, all military commission proceedings so that their machinery could be thoroughly reviewed; and one initiated an interagency review of Guantanamo and all 240 detainees then in it, by the Departments of Justice, State, Defense, and Homeland Security and the director of national intelligence and the military's Joint Chiefs of Staff, with the goal of closing Gitmo altogether as a detention camp within one year. His election and his first-day orders were widely seen as the beginning of the end for Gitmo, and the end, or at least the fundamental restructuring, of trials by military commission.

President Obama's record in reaching those goals, however, has been decidedly mixed. Military commissions still exist, although their procedures have been considerably reformed by the Military Commissions Act of 2009. His Justice Department has, with notable success, put terrorists on trial in federal courts instead of commissions, but Congress has blocked any transfer of Gitmo detainees to US courts for that purpose (or any other, including continued imprisonment). Guantanamo thus remains, its population in the spring of 2015 reduced to about 125. The torture of detainees there and elsewhere has ended. And for reasons that continue to confound those who saw his election and reelection as a reversal of the Bush policies on detainees, his Justice Department has resolutely opposed, as his predecessor's had, all efforts by detainees to win habeas in the courts.

Military Commissions

When President Obama took the oath of office, military commissions had accomplished next to nothing. Ordained by President Bush in 2001, implemented by the military only in 2004, they had been fatally wounded before their first trial by the Supreme Court's Hamdan decision in 2006 for, among other reasons, Bush's failure to seek or obtain congressional authorization for them. Months later, Congress resuscitated them in the Military Commissions Act of 2006, which provided the necessary assent, but they were hampered by problems that Congress had no way of fixing. Most notably, there was simply no evidence that the majority of detainees had actually committed any war crimes. Participation in hostilities against American forces, where it could be established, sufficed to make them enemy combatants subject to detention, but fighting the enemy in war is not a crime.

For those to whom some connection could plausibly be drawn to the terrorist crimes of 9/11, or at least some important connection to al Qaeda, cases were tainted by the brutal interrogation most had undergone. The 2006 Military Commissions Act precluded the use at trial of any "statement obtained by the use of torture" and allowed other statements "in which the degree of coercion is disputed" only if the military judge found that the statement was "reliable and possessing sufficient probative value" and that "the interests of justice would best be served" by accepting it. That was a wide exception but it gave detainees room to argue that they had been tortured, or coerced into giving false confessions, undermining the value of any incriminating statements. Prosecutors preparing cases had to find a way to refute that attack or proceed without the evidence.

Although fighting the enemy in war is not a crime, Congress in the 2006 Military Commissions Act all but made it so, by giving military commissions the authority to try al Qaeda and Taliban fighters for "material support" of terrorism. Material support, according to the Justice Department in both the Bush and Obama administrations, included fighting with al Qaeda or the Taliban in Afghanistan, or giving support to those who did. Material support of terrorism had first been made a crime in 1994, but it applied only to support given in the United States, thus allowing federal courts to reach domestic supporters of terrorist acts committed abroad or at home, but necessarily excluding conventional military action. Extending the definition to include support given abroad, and extending jurisdiction over it to include the newly approved military commissions, significantly extended its reach. When it came to al Qaeda and the Taliban (and whatever their "associated forces" might be), two presidential administrations, with the support of Congress, had effectively erased the distinction between conventional military action and material support of terrorism.

By the time of President Obama's inauguration, military commissions had concluded exactly one case in the seven years since President Bush's initial order. Following enactment of the 2006 Military Commissions Act, David Hicks, an Australian long held at Guantanamo, pleaded guilty in 2007 to providing material support to terrorism by training with al Qaeda in Afghanistan and going onto the battlefield against US-led coalition forces. Holding a national of a stalwart American ally was an embarrassment, so under a pretrial agreement with prosecutors he was sentenced to nine months of confinement and quickly sent home to Australia to serve it. He was reportedly released after six months.

The commissions had tried two others. As noted in chapter 5, after winning his case in the Supreme Court, Salim Hamdan, bin Laden's driver, was tried under the restructured commissions of 2006, where he was acquitted of conspiracy and convicted of providing material support of terrorism. He was sentenced to sixty-six months of imprisonment, but the military judge deducted the sixty-one months he had already spent at Guantanamo, and four months later the United States released him back to Yemen. The other defendant was Ali Hamza al-Bahlul, convicted on similar charges and sentenced to life imprisonment, about which more below.

After President Obama suspended all commission trials, the Congress, with a Democratic majority in both houses, enacted the Military Commissions Act of 2009, which brought commissions much more closely into line with the Uniform Code of Military Justice procedures for courts-martial, and the DoD placed the prosecutions under the leadership of Army Brigadier General Mark Martins, a West Point graduate and decorated infantry officer who later earned a law degree from Harvard. Unlike his various predecessors, Martins was firmly committed to an open, transparent, and fair commission process.

But legal problems continued to plague commissions. As chapter 5 explained, although Hamdan had been freed, the US Court of Appeals for the District of Columbia in 2012 reversed his material-support conviction on grounds that Congress would not have intended its criminalization of material support in the Military Commissions Act to reach prior conduct if it had correctly understood that it was creating a new crime. This reasoning was not only far-fetched; it did what courts are never supposed to do—it interpreted a statute based not on what Congress did, but on what the court concluded it should have done.

The reasoning of the court of appeals panel did not last long. Two years later, on July 14, 2014, the court took up the case of another Guantanamo detainee, Ali Hamza al-Bahlul, a Yemeni citizen. Bahlul was no cog in the al Qaeda hierarchy, no hapless outlier scooped up on an Afghan battlefield. He was a close aide to Osama bin Laden and had produced, at bin Laden's direction, a video that celebrated the al Qaeda attack on the US Navy vessel *Cole* in Yemen in 2000, killing seventeen American servicemen and wounding thirty-nine. The video was widely distributed as al Qaeda propaganda. Bahlul then became bin Laden's public relations secretary and prepared the "martyr wills" of two of the 9/11 hijackers. He even volunteered to take part in the attacks himself, which bin Laden nixed because he wanted Bahlul at his side. Just prior to 9/11, he and bin Laden left al Qaeda's headquarters for a remote hideaway, where they listened together to news coverage of the hijacked airliners' attacks in the United States. He later fled to Pakistan, where he was captured, turned over to US forces, and sent to Guantanamo.

Bahlul admitted all this; indeed, he boasted of it, calling the video one of the best that al Qaeda had ever done. Charged in 2008 before a military commission with conspiracy, material support of terrorism, and solicitation of others to commit war crimes—all of which were crimes made triable by military commission in the MCA of 2006—Bahlul pleaded not guilty as a protest against the legitimacy of an American tribunal, but he fired his assigned military lawyer and, proceeding alone, sat passively throughout the trial and put on no defense. He was convicted on all counts later that year and sentenced to life imprisonment.

Before the court of appeals, his lawyers from the Office of the Chief Defense Counsel, the military's designated hitters for the defense of Gitmo detainees charged by commissions, naturally relied on the precedent established by that court in its Hamdan decision two years earlier—that because the 2006 MCA was not retroactive, Bahlul could not be validly tried and convicted for acts done years earlier, and thus his conviction on all three charges should be overturned. The Department of Justice, conceding that it stood no chance under the Hamdan precedent, asked the full court of seven judges to hear the case and overrule the court's three-judge panel that had decided *Hamdan*.

The Justice Department acted over the reported objections of Solicitor General Donald Verrilli and chief prosecutor General Martins, both of whom were said to believe that the government should accept the Hamdan defeat and give up the fight to make material support of terrorism a valid charge for pre-2006 acts. But the Justice Department's tactic proved successful. The appeals court heard the case *en banc* (all judges sitting, not just a panel of three) and in its decision handed down on July 14, 2014, it curtly overruled the *Hamdan* conclusion that Congress had not intended to apply the crimes specified in the MCA retroactively. "There could hardly be a clearer statement of the Congress's intent to confer jurisdiction on military commissions to try the enumerated crimes regardless of whether they occurred 'before, on, or after September 11, 2001,'" the full court ruled. "The 2006 MCA is unambiguous in its intent to authorize retroactive prosecution for the crimes enumerated in the statute."

That conclusion required the court to answer the question that their colleagues in *Hamdan* had studiously avoided—whether retroactive application violated the Ex Post Facto Clause. That clause, in the words of Supreme Court Justice Samuel Chase in a 1798 case, prohibits "every law that makes an action, done before the passing of the law, and which was innocent when done, criminal; and punishes such action."

But did that clause even apply in the first place to aliens held at Guantanamo? That question—like *Boumediene*'s question of whether the Suspension Clause applied to the Gitmo detainees—had not been answered by any court, but here the government, unlike in *Boumediene*, put up no argument. It accepted that the prohibition on ex post facto charges did apply, to Bahlul and to all detainees. The court's majority, apparently nonplused at the concession, noted that it was not "obligated" to accept it as conclusive, but that it would, although it was "not to be understood as remotely intimating in any degree an opinion on the question." (By framing the issue in this way, the court avoided creating a precedent on the applicability of the Ex Post Facto Clause to Gitmo detainees, accepting the government's position only for the immediate case and leaving the matter open for actual decision in some future case.)

So, assuming that the Ex Post Facto Clause did apply, was it violated here? The court answered that it was not. As to Bahlul's conviction for conspiracy, the court explained that a federal criminal statute first enacted in 1986 made it a crime for anyone outside the United States to conspire to kill a US national. Bahlul had admittedly done that, and after 1986. The fact that conspiracy was made triable by commission only in 2006 was irrelevant, the court ruled. "The right to be tried in a particular forum is not the sort of right the Ex Post Facto Clause protects" because "such a transfer does not have anything to do with the definition of the crime, the defense or the punishment." The court then went on to conclude, as an entirely independent justification for the validity of the conspiracy charge, that conspiracy had also been a crime "triable by military commission" at least since 1865, when a military commission convicted the accomplices of Abraham Lincoln's assassins of "conspiring to kill and murder" him.

The appeals court acknowledged that in the Supreme Court's Hamdan decision four justices had concluded that conspiracy was *not* a crime "triable by military commission." But four was not a majority, Justice Kennedy having declined to join them on that point, so their conclusion was theirs alone, not the Supreme Court's, and did not bind the appeals court.

His conspiracy conviction upheld, Bahlul fared better when the court of appeals turned to his conviction for material support of terrorism. Because such support, when rendered outside the United States, had been criminalized only in 2006, the Ex Post Facto Clause did prohibit prosecution of Bahlul, because his support necessarily ended with his capture in 2001. His conviction for solicitation to commit a war crime was likewise reversed, on similar grounds.

Although the full court of appeals overturned the three-judge panel's Hamdan decision on retroactivity and upheld the validity of conspiracy convictions, it dealt commission prosecutors a serious setback when it invalidated the convictions for material support of terrorism and solicitation to commit a war crime as ex post facto violations. The material-support charge, especially, had been the prosecutors' means of reaching detainees whose support consisted of fighting with, or assisting, al Qaeda and Taliban forces, however mundane their role. That strategy could not survive the court of appeals' decision.

And then, after further briefing, the court reversed the conspiracy conviction as well, on June 12, 2015. It did not disturb the ruling on ex post facto; rather, it held that military commissions have jurisdiction only to try cases alleging violations of the international laws of war, which conspiracy is not. The court emphasized that any exceptions to the constitutional guarantee of trial by jury must be narrow and specific. Conspiracy must therefore be tried in federal criminal courts, which, as one judge noted, have compiled convictions in "almost 200 'jihadist-related' terrorism and national-security cases" while commissions have convicted only eight, of which only three remained standing.

Regardless of whether the court of appeals' decision in *Bahlul* is the final word on what charges military commissions can validly try, the status and the outlook for commissions is light years removed from what the Bush administration intended them to be when in 2001 it pulled them from the depths of history to make them its centerpiece of bringing terrorists to justice. In fourteen years, the government, in both the Bush and Obama administrations, has spent far more time and resources justifying the existence and procedures of commissions than it has actually trying cases, and its accomplishments have been meager.

1. David Hicks of Australia, by agreement with the government, pleaded guilty in 2007 to material support for terrorism, was sentenced to nine months imprisonment, and was promptly returned to Australia. But in light of the al-Bahlul decision on material support, he asked the US Court of Military Commission Review (a panel of military judges appointed by the Secretary of Defense to hear appeals from military-commission convictions) to reopen his case and overturn his conviction. On February 18, 2015, the court did so.
2. Hamdan was acquitted on the conspiracy charge, and his conviction of material support for terrorism resulted in his release four months later, and in any event was reversed on appeal.
3. Bahlul's convictions for conspiracy, material support, and solicitation were overturned. The government might appeal.
4. Omar Khadr, a Canadian-born son of an alleged Egyptian al Qaeda official, was captured in Afghanistan at age fifteen and sent to Guantanamo, the youngest detainee there. He was charged in 2008 with killing an American soldier with a hand grenade in violation of the law of war (Khadr being a civilian and thus an unlawful combatant) and related charges, including conspiracy and material support for terrorism. Under a plea agreement, he was sentenced to eight years of imprisonment, the first year at Guantanamo and the remainder to be served in Canada. He was transferred to Canada on September 29, 2012. He became eligible for parole in 2013 and some human rights groups have called for his release, citing his age in 2002 and the harsh treatment he received at Guantanamo. As of this writing he remains in a Canadian prison.
5. Ibrahim al Qosi of Sudan was captured in Afghanistan in 2002 and sent to Guantanamo. In 2010, he pleaded guilty to conspiracy and material support of terrorism. Under a plea agreement, he was sentenced to fourteen years with twelve years suspended. He was released and returned to Sudan on July 11, 2012. Unlike Hamdan, he did

not appeal his conviction after his release, and unlike Hicks, he has not to date sought to have his material-support conviction reversed.

6. Noor Uthman Muhammed, also of Sudan, allegedly an al Qaeda training camp administrator in Afghanistan, was captured there in 2002. On February 18, 2011, he pleaded guilty to conspiracy and material support of terrorism, and under a plea agreement was sentenced to fourteen years imprisonment with credit for time served. He was released and returned to Sudan in December 2013. He likewise has not appealed his conviction.

7. Majid Khan, a Pakistani citizen, spent his teenage years in a Baltimore suburb, graduating from high school in 1999. He then joined al Qaeda. Captured in 2003, he was one of the last to arrive at Guantanamo, in 2006. He had been held, and said he had been tortured, at a CIA black site. In February 2012, he pleaded guilty to conspiracy involving the bombing of a Marriott Hotel in Jakarta in 2003. He agreed to testify against Khalid Sheikh Mohammed (below), who allegedly planned the Jakarta bombing. Sentencing was deferred pending his testimony; according to a report in the *Washington Post*, the deal was for a reduced sentence and eventual release to Pakistan. He remains at Guantanamo, presumably being held to testify at Khalid Sheikh Mohammed's trial, whenever that takes place.

8. Ahmed al-Darbi cut a deal similar to Majid Khan's. A Saudi member of al Qaeda, imprisoned at Guantanamo since 2002, he pleaded guilty on February 20, 2014, to terrorism charges arising out of his complicity in an al-Qaeda plan to attack a French oil tanker in 2002. He reportedly has agreed to testify against Abd al-Nashiri in the latter's trial for orchestrating the 2000 attack on the *Cole* in Yemen. After his testimony, Darbi will be sentenced to no more than fifteen years, with credit for time served following his plea, and "it is possible," said General Martins, that he will then be returned to Saudi Arabia to serve the balance of the sentence.

In all, fourteen years have yielded eight convictions, four of which have come on plea agreements in exchange for release (six, if one includes the deferred releases of Majid Khan and Ahmed al-Darbi). The two completed trials to date have resulted in two convictions, but Hamdan's has been overturned in full, and Bahlul's as well.

As of 2015, after years of delay, disruption, and suspension, with little accomplished, and with material-support charges for pre-2006 activity held unconstitutional unless and until the Supreme Court steps in, the commissions are now focused on a handful of "high value detainees"— Khalid Sheikh Mohammed and several others, accused of conspiring to carry out the murders of 9/11 or the attack on the *Cole*. (The others are Walid Muhammad Salih Mubarek Bin 'Attash, Ali Abdul Aziz Ali, Mustafa Ahmed Adam al Hawsawi, and Ramsi bin al Shibh. They are charged with several crimes, including conspiracy, murder, hijacking, and terrorism. In addition to these, there are ten or so additional "high value" detainees whose crimes do not include the 9/11 attacks.)

The proceedings are advancing glacially, with no trial dates in sight. Dru B. Brenner-Breck, a retired Army JAG officer and now president of the private and nonprofit National Institute of Military Justice, wrote at the end of 2014 that, "rather than the rapid progress toward trial anticipated for the Guantanamo military commissions, at the end of the year [2014] the Commissions were further away from their goal of a trial on the merits than when the year began."

Given the reforms of the 2009 Military Commissions Act, General Martins has professionalized the prosecutions, but he can only do so much. He was given a shipwreck, and he is salvaging what he can. Whatever the outcome of the remaining trials, the military commission process has been a failure, and a failure especially acute when one considers the nearly unbroken record of convictions the federal courts have compiled since 9/11.

Trials in US Federal Courts

The Bush administration's strategy for trying terrorists by military commissions was intended to displace federal courts from doing so. The "war council," under the guiding light of Vice President Cheney, was convinced that federal courts were too good for al Qaeda jihadists. There they would have civilian lawyers, civilian juries, and civilian judges, and all the protections accorded to any accused criminal—protections that might give the jihadists a public platform and even lead to intolerable acquittals. When the commission plan was announced in 2001, critics argued strenuously that federal courts are fully capable of trying and judging accused terrorists, and they pointed to trials that had resulted in the conviction and life sentence of Omar Rahman, the "blind sheik," and other Islamic extremists in the World Trade Center bombings of 1993; the 2001 conviction and life sentences of three conspirators in the 1998 bombings of the US embassies in Tanzania and Kenya that left 223 dead; and the conviction and execution of Timothy McVeigh for the catastrophic bombing of the federal office building and courthouse in Oklahoma City in 1995.

The president's Military Order of November 13, 2001, limited commission jurisdiction to persons who were not US citizens. As matters developed, all those who have been referred to commissions have come from Guantanamo. This has left room for Department of Justice prosecutors to bring charges in federal court against other terrorists, would-be terrorists, and conspirators, and they have done so in a number of cases.

The first conviction after 9/11 came in 2002, while the commissions' first rules were being written in the Pentagon. John Walker Lindh, an American who had joined al Qaeda before 9/11 and had fought with the Taliban in Afghanistan, was captured in December 2001. He was indicted in a federal court in Virginia on various charges of conspiracy and material support; he pleaded guilty and was sentenced to twenty years' imprisonment without parole.

Zacarias Moussaoui, a French-born son of Moroccan immigrants, was arrested in Minnesota in August 2001 when instructors in a local flight school became suspicious of his desire to learn how to fly a Boeing 747 without needing to learn how to land it. They called the FBI, which took him into custody on garden-variety immigration charges. Following the September 11 attacks, he was indicted in federal court in Virginia on six counts of conspiracy. An admitted member of al Qaeda, he portrayed himself as 9/11's "twentieth hijacker" had he not been caught, though it has never been clear if this was in fact true, or just his bragging. In 2006, he was convicted by a jury and sentenced by a federal judge to six life terms without parole. He is now at the federal maximum security penitentiary in Florence, Colorado—known as the "supermax" prison—where prisoners are held in solitary confinement for 23 hours a day. So, too, Richard Reid, a British convert to Islam and al Qaeda who attempted to light explosives in his shoe on a flight to the United

States and was sentenced in Boston's federal court in 2001 to three life sentences plus 110 years, also in the supermax pen.

Moussaoui's obstreperous and self-aggrandizing behavior at hearings in 2002 reinforced the belief of the war council that civilian trials for alien terrorists should never happen as long as George Bush was president. But the snail's pace of military commissions and the Supreme Court's invalidation of the entire structure in 2006 revealed the defects in that idea. In his inaugural address, President Obama said, "As for our common defense, we reject as false the choice between our safety and our ideals. Our founding fathers, faced with perils that we can scarcely imagine, drafted a charter to assure the rule of law and the rights of man, a charter expanded by the blood of generations. Those ideals still light the world, and we will not give them up for expedience's sake." On the following day he suspended all commission proceedings pending the outcome of an interagency review of what should be done with Guantanamo detainees.

While the review was under way, on November 13, 2009, Attorney General Eric Holder took a bold step from which he was later forced into a humiliating retreat. He announced that the Department of Justice would put Khalid Sheikh Mohammed and several other detainees on trial in the federal court in New York City for their roles in the crimes of September 11. KSM, as he was often referred to, was by consensus the highest-ranking captive implicated in those attacks; indeed, he repeatedly claimed that he was the mastermind who planned them. He had been captured in 2003 and interrogated (and was waterboarded an astonishing 183 times) at CIA sites abroad before finally being sent to Guantanamo in 2006. By any measure, he was the prize trophy in the bag of captured terrorists. "After eight years of delay," Holder said at his press conference,

> those allegedly responsible for the attacks of September the 11th will finally face justice. They will be brought to New York to answer for their alleged crimes in a courthouse just blocks from where the twin towers once stood. I am confident in the ability of our courts to provide these defendants a fair trial, just as they have for over 200 years. The alleged 9/11 conspirators will stand trial in our justice system before an impartial jury under long-established rules and procedures.

Holder also announced that five other prisoners, implicated in the 1998 *Cole* bombing, would remain at Guantanamo to stand trial before military commissions, a measure probably intended to appease hardliners in Congress who were resolutely opposed to civilian trials. "Today's announcements," he concluded,

> mark a significant step forward in our efforts to close Guantanamo and to bring to justice those individuals who have conspired to attack our nation and our interests abroad. For over two hundred years, our nation has relied on a faithful adherence to the rule of law to bring criminals to justice and provide accountability to victims. Once again we will ask our legal system, in two venues, to rise to that challenge. I am confident it will answer the call with fairness and justice.

Holder's confidence in the federal courts might have been well placed, but his reading of the political landscape was not. His announcement brought outrage from Republicans in and out of Congress, and even some Democrats. (Quotations in this section are taken from reporting of Holder's speech and the Ghailani trial in the *New York Times*.)

Congressman John Boehner of Ohio, leader of the Republican minority in the House:

> The Obama Administration's irresponsible decision to prosecute the mastermind of the 9/11 attacks in New York City puts the interests of liberal special interest groups before the safety and security of the American people. The possibility that Khalid Sheikh Mohammed and his co-conspirators could be found "not guilty" due to some legal technicality just blocks from Ground Zero should give every American pause . . .
>
> This decision is further evidence that the White House is reverting to a dangerous pre-9/11 mentality—treating terrorism as a law enforcement issue and hoping for the best.

Congressman Peter King of New York, a persistent critic of President Obama:

I am outraged by the Obama Administration's decision to move Khalid Sheikh Mohammed, one of the most dangerous terrorists in the world, to American soil to be tried. . . . This decision is not only misguided but extremely dangerous. Detaining and trying these five terrorists only a few blocks from the World Trade Center site where, by Khalid Sheikh Mohammed's design, thousands were brutally murdered puts our Nation—and New York City—at greater risk.

Senator Jim Webb, Democrat of Virginia:

I have never disputed the constitutional authority of the President to convene courts in cases of international terrorism. However, I remain very concerned about the wisdom of doing so. Those who have committed acts of international terrorism are enemy combatants, just as certainly as the Japanese pilots who killed thousands of Americans at Pearl Harbor. It will be disruptive, costly, and potentially counter-productive to try them as criminals in our civilian courts.

Holder did have his supporters. "New York is not afraid of terrorists," said Representative Jerrold Nadler, a New York Democrat. "Any suggestion that our prosecutors and our law enforcement personnel are not up to the task of safely holding and successfully prosecuting terrorists on American soil is insulting and untrue."

New York City mayor Michael Bloomberg agreed: "It is fitting that 9/11 suspects face justice near the World Trade Center site where so many New Yorkers were murdered."

Called to testify before the Senate Judiciary Committee a few days later, Holder defended his decision. "We need not cower in the face of this enemy," he said. "Our institutions are strong, our infrastructure is ready, our resolve is firm, and our people are ready." Senator Jeff Sessions, Republican of Alabama, took strong issue. "It's not cowering in fear of terrorists to decide the best way for this case to be tried is to be tried by a military commission," Sessions told Holder. "I think there are clear advantages to trying cases by [the] military as opposed to what can become a spectacle of a trial, with high-paid defense lawyers and others focused on using that as a forum."

As *New York Times* reporters Eric Lichtblau and Benjamin Weiser summarized matters a week after Holder's Friday the 13th announcement:

> The Obama administration's decision to try [Khalid Sheikh] Mohammed and four other terrorism suspects in a civilian court provoked sharp debate among politicians and lawyers about whether American courtrooms are the proper place for so-called enemy combatants, whose suspected crimes were hatched overseas and who viewed themselves as participants in a war against the United States. Both sides agreed that defense lawyers and prosecutors would face unique problems in what is likely to be a hugely complex and emotion-laden case.
>
> Whatever the case, if it actually makes its way before a jury, it promises to be a trial like no other in memory, an extraordinary clash involving the morality of torture, due process rights of foreign terrorist operatives, and the ability of civilian courts to handle national security cases.

Whatever the criticism, Holder's decision seemed final. But matters came to an explosive head later that year, in the trial of Ahmed Ghailani, a Tanzanian man who had been indicted by a federal grand jury in New York City in 1998 for the bombings that year in the US embassies in Tanzania and Kenya, along with Osama bin Laden and others, three of whom were later convicted. Ghailani, then twenty-four years old, had allegedly procured the pickup truck and the explosives used in Tanzania. Captured in Pakistan in 2004, he had been interrogated by the CIA before being sent to Guantanamo in 2006. Holder had him transferred to New York to stand trial on 282 counts: one count of conspiracy to destroy US property resulting in death, and most of the remaining charges the murder of each victim. Ghailani's defense was that he was a gullible young man duped by crafty al Qaeda operatives. In the course of a six-week trial, US District Judge Lewis Kaplan prohibited the government from introducing the testimony of a key prosecution witness, on grounds that his name had been gained through torture. On November 17, 2010, after a week of deliberation, the New York jury convicted Ghailani on one count of conspiracy, and acquitted him of all other charges.

The verdict drew outrage from Republicans in Congress, who saw in it proof of their fears that federal trials with their strict rules of evidence ("legal technicalities" to some) and civilian jurors were unable to deliver stern justice to terrorists. "This is a tragic wake-up call to the Obama administration to immediately abandon its ill-advised plan to try Guantanamo terrorists" in federal courts, said Representative King, about to become chairman of the Homeland Security Committee in the newly elected House with its Republican majority. "We must treat them as wartime enemies and try them in military commissions at Guantanamo." Republican Congressman Lamar Smith of Texas was similarly dismayed, singling out Judge Kaplan's exclusion of the prosecution witness as demonstrating that foreign terrorists "can [not] be adequately tried in civilian courts. The judge in this case, applying constitutional and legal standards to which all US citizens are entitled, threw out important evidence," he said. "The result is that the jury acquitted on all but one conspiracy count."

The Justice Department stoutly emphasized the positive aspects of the case.

"People who are criticizing this verdict need to remember the underlying facts of this case and the fact that the verdict handed down will lead to a sentence of anywhere from 20 years to life," a Justice Department spokesman said. Others agreed that the trial had been a victory for US justice, a demonstration that terrorists could be held to account in trials without the truncated procedures and curtailment of rights in military commissions. Mason Clutter of The Constitution Project, a supporter of civilian trials, noted the absence of the dire sideshows that critics had predicted—costly security; efforts by the defendant or his lawyers to turn the courtroom into a forum or, worse, a circus; and disclosure of classified information. "The system worked here," Ms. Clutter said. "I don't think we judge success based on the number of convictions that were received. I think we judge success based on fair prosecutions consistent with the Constitution and the rule of law."

Juan C. Zarate, deputy national security adviser for combating terrorism in the Bush administration, gave a more nuanced verdict. "The paradox with these kinds of cases," Zarate said, "has always been that if these individuals are found not guilty, will the American government let them go free, which is the construct of a criminal proceeding? And the answer is no. That is the reality. This case highlights that tension, and will complicate the political debate about how to handle more senior Al Qaeda figures, like Khalid Sheikh Mohammed."

Supporters of civilian trials were encouraged a month later, when Judge Kaplan sentenced Ghailani on his conspiracy conviction to life imprisonment. "The impact on him pales in comparison to the suffering and the horror that he and his confederates caused," said Judge Kaplan at the sentencing. "It was a cold-blooded killing and maiming of innocent people on an enormous scale. The very purpose of the crime was to create terror by causing death and destruction." Holder, surely relieved, praised the sentence, which "shows yet again the strength of the American justice system in holding terrorists accountable for their actions." Critics were unpersuaded. Representative Smith likewise expressed relief but called the acquittals on all the murder charges a "near disaster."

The 2010 elections that sent a Republican majority to the House of Representatives promptly brought an abrupt halt to any more near disasters. Although it has no explicit authority to tell the president or the attorney general where to put criminal defendants on trial, Congress does have the power of the purse. In January 2011, weeks after Ghailani's acquittals, it invoked that power when it passed the National Defense Authorization Act, which allocated funds to the Defense Department for the 2011 fiscal year. In addition to setting out what the military could spend on what, the NDAA told DoD what it could not spend: it barred any funds for the transfer of any detainee from Guantanamo to the United States. This prevented not only any more trials of Guantanamo detainees in federal court, but any transfer of a Gitmo detainee to a state or federal prison in the United States for any reason, thus effectively keeping Guantanamo in business, regardless of what the president wanted.

Holder criticized the no-funds rule as "an extreme and risky encroachment on the authority of the executive branch to determine when and where to prosecute terrorist suspects," and a maneuver that would create a dangerous precedent because "the exercise of prosecutorial discretion has always been and must remain an executive branch function." To no avail. With substantial Republican majorities in the House, Congress has renewed this prohibition in every subsequent year, most recently through 2015. Unable to veto the transfer bans separately from the military appropriations, President Obama has signed the bills while repeating the warning that the ban is "a dangerous and unprecedented challenge to critical Executive branch authority to determine when and where to prosecute detainees, based on the facts and the circumstances of each case and our national security interests . . . particularly where our Federal courts are the best—or even the only—option for incapacitating dangerous terrorists." The ban might also, in his stated view, "violate constitutional separation of powers principles," but to date he has not precipitated any confrontation on that issue, choosing however grudgingly to accommodate his policies to the congressional mandate. With greater Republican majorities in the House elected in 2014, and with a new Republican majority in the Senate as well, the restrictions will likely continue through the remainder of President Obama's term.

But Congress got what it wanted. On April 4, 2011, seventeen months after he announced his plan to put KSM and others on trial in New York, Holder retracted it and referred them for trial before military commissions at Guantanamo. Holder's retreat "marked a significant moment of capitulation in the Obama administration's largely frustrated effort to dismantle counterterrorism architecture left behind" by President Bush, wrote Charlie Savage in the *New York Times*. Holder's regret was palpable. "We must face a simple truth," he said in announcing his decision. The congressional restrictions on transferring Gitmo detainees to the United States "are unlikely to be repealed" and "we simply cannot allow a trial to be delayed any longer for the victims of the 9/11 attacks or for their families who have waited nearly a decade for justice." Advocates for civilian trials were not consoled. "The attorney general's flip-flop is devastating for the rule of law," said Anthony Romero of the American Civil Liberties Union, though in truth it was Congress and not the attorney general dictating the decision.

On October 24, 2013, three years after his trial, Ghailani's conviction was upheld by the US Court of Appeals in New York. The judges there commended Judge Kaplan for "presid[ing] over this challenging and complex case with exemplary care and fairness." But the affirmance, like the conviction and sentence, did not change the determination of congressional Republicans to keep Guantanamo open and the federal courts closed. Ghailani is the only Guantanamo detainee to date who has received a civilian trial. He is imprisoned for life in the federal supermax penitentiary in Colorado.

Although Congress had blocked trials in the United States of anyone at Guantanamo, Holder did not retreat from his determination to try terrorists in federal court whenever he could. Justice Department prosecutors were still able to indict and try al Qaeda affiliates who were captured or arrested and never sent to Guantanamo, and in doing so they have compiled an impressive record of convictions.

In 2004, Rafik Sabir, an American physician, was introduced by a jihadist friend to Ali Soufan, who encouraged him to join al Qaeda. Sabir agreed to think about it, and after a year at a Saudi military hospital, he returned to New York and told Soufan he was ready to join Osama bin Laden to "expel the Jews and Christians from the Arabian Peninsula." As Soufan looked on, Sabir swore an oath of allegiance to al Qaeda and agreed to provide medical training and advice to al Qaeda forces upon his imminent return to Saudi Arabia.

Unfortunately for Sabir, Ali Soufan was an FBI agent: Sabir was arrested and indicted in New York's federal court for conspiring to provide material support to terrorism. Material support was the crime that was later to be thrown out in the appeal of Bahlul, but only because it could not be applied retroactively. That availed Sabir nothing. He was convicted in 2007 and sentenced to twenty-five years.

Other federal cases followed, including:

- Umar Abdulmuttalab tried unsuccessfully to light bombs in his underwear on a flight to Detroit on Christmas Day, 2009. He was sentenced in 2012 to four life sentences, plus fifty years.
- Faisal Shahzad was arrested in 2010 as he boarded a flight to Pakistan two days after his failed attempt to detonate a car full of explosives in Times Square. He pleaded guilty and received life without parole.
- Najibullah Zazi, who drove from Colorado to New York City with a car full of bombs to be set off at rush hour in the subway, pleaded guilty in 2010 to material support of terrorism; he was indefinitely confined, to be sentenced after cooperation with federal prosecutors.
- Sulaiman Abu Gaith, a Kuwaiti imam and the son-in-law of Osama bin Laden who had spent the night of September 11 with the al Qaeda leader and had taped several propaganda videos urging others to join

the fight, was arrested in Jordan and turned over to American officials there. He was tried in New York City in 2014 on charges of conspiring to kill Americans and providing material support to terrorists. He was sentenced to life in prison. Judge Kaplan, Ghailani's judge, told Abu Ghaith at the sentencing: "You sir, in my assessment, are committed to doing everything you can to assist in carrying out Al Qaeda's agenda of killing Americans—guilty or innocent, combatant or noncombatant, adult or babies, without regard to the carnage that's caused." Attorney General Holder: Abu Ghaith's "trial, conviction and sentencing have underscored the power" of federal civilian courts "to deliver swift and certain justice in cases involving terrorism defendants." Preet Bharara, the United States Attorney in Manhattan, whose office had handled the prosecution: "No sentence can restore what was taken from the families of Al Qaeda's victims. But today's sentence ensures that Sulaiman Abu Ghaith will never be free to incite or support mass murder again."

- On May 19, 2014, Mostafa Kamel Mostafa (a.k.a. Abu Hamza al-Masri), a former imam in London, was convicted after a six-week trial in New York on all eleven terrorism-related charges arising out of his complicity in the 1998 kidnappings of sixteen American, British, and Australian tourists in Yemen. Mostafa had close ties to al Qaeda, and had called bin Laden a hero and said, "Everybody was happy when the planes hit the World Trade Center." US Attorney Bharara said that the conviction proved "that in an American civilian courtroom, the American people and all the victims of terrorism can be vindicated without sacrificing our principles." The jury foreman said, "I feel he got a fair trial. There's no doubt in my mind about that."

One remarkable aspect of the federal trials is the readiness of many defendants to acknowledge their al Qaeda ties and admit to the acts with which they are charged, refuting the assumptions of those who claimed that federal trials, with their Miranda warnings and the right against self-incrimination, would be overly protective of terrorists and less likely than military commissions to accept incriminating evidence. The opposite seems to be true. "It is counterintuitive—and I understand that," Preet Bharara said in an interview quoted in the *New York Times* on October 13, 2014, that people one morning want to do everything they can to kill everyone who looks like an American, and destroy cities, and in some cases, prepare to engage in suicide missions or help others engage in suicide missions, and then the next afternoon, when caught, snitch on their plans, snitch on their colleagues, snitch on intelligence that otherwise would have been unavailable to the very same people that they were dedicated to killing. However, it is true; it happens all the time.

Ali Soufan, the FBI agent who nabbed Rafik Sabir, said that in his experience, the "higher the operatives are in the pyramid of the terrorist organization, the easier it is to talk to them. What works on one subject does not necessarily work on the other. But if you know how to do it and you know what buttons to push, intellectually and mentally, these guys will talk." The war council had no clue about that.

In all, the Department of Justice has prosecuted scores of cases of material support of terrorism and related charges, with a conviction rate of about 87 percent, according to the Brennan Center for Justice at New York University School of Law. While these cases cover a wide variety of crimes, many of them only marginally related to al Qaeda, the sheer number of them, the success rate, the lack of any security problems before and during trial, and the hefty sentences, have undercut fears that federal trials would be too dangerous, too protective, too lenient, too solicitous of constitutional rights, and too inclined to acquittal to be entrusted with the administration of justice for terrorists.

Federal courts work. Guantanamo remains.

Guantanamo

January 2015 marked the beginning of the fourteenth year of Guantanamo's existence as what was to be an interim holding facility for al Qaeda and Taliban operatives, a place where they could be interrogated, and a place where they could be tried if necessary. Instead, it has become a permanent jail not only for those who took up arms in the American invasion of Afghanistan in 2001, some of whom did have al Qaeda or Taliban connections, but also others who were not combatants at all. None of the detainees in any event has been accorded the treatment required by the Geneva Conventions for prisoners of war, and none of them, apart from the high-value detainees sent there in 2006 after years of harsh interrogation elsewhere by the CIA, had any involvement in the 9/11 attacks or have produced any particularly useful intelligence. Guantanamo has been reviled throughout the world and has become a rallying cry for jihadists, and very likely a place where some detainees, if not terrorists when they arrived, were radicalized while they were there.

The Guantanamo Review Task Force, convened by President Obama the day after his inauguration, issued its report one year later, on January 22, 2010. According to the report, 779 men had been imprisoned at Guantanamo at one time or another, 749 (96 percent) of them arriving in 2002 and 2003, and only 30 since then, the last one in 2008. Of all these, 530 (68 percent) had been released by the end of 2008. When President Obama took office in 2009, 242 detainees remained, according to the task force. Releases all but came to a stop in 2011–2013, because Congress, in the annual National Defense Authorization Acts that had prohibited any transfers to the United States, had also severely restricted transfers out of Guantanamo to third countries unless stringent assurances of security could be met, and President Obama had curtailed the release of anyone to Yemen, given that country's instability.

In a letter to the *New York Times* published on June 14, 2014, Eric M. Freedman and Brian E. Foster, lawyers representing some Gitmo detainees, provided the following breakdown of the 149 then at Gitmo: 78 had been cleared for release, but remained; 38 more had been classified as "too dangerous to release but unable to be prosecuted;" 7 were being "actively prosecuted" before military commissions; 23 had been referred for trial before commissions; 3 had been convicted by commissions.

About 40 percent of the detainees were Yemeni, and another 10 percent were Afghans. The other half were from a variety of countries, chiefly Saudi Arabia, Algeria, Tunisia, Syria, Libya, Kuwait, and Pakistan. Ninety percent had been captured in Afghanistan or Pakistan. (There were seventeen from China, but these were Uighurs, restive Moslems from China's central Asian region, and the US government conceded that sending them to Guantanamo had been a mistake; the Uighurs had no significant ties to al Qaeda or the Taliban and bore no ill will toward the United States. Their release was long delayed because they faced persecution in China, and they were eventually resettled elsewhere.)

But the task force identified a problem: as of January 2010, there were forty-eight detainees who could be neither prosecuted nor released. These were significant al Qaeda or Taliban officials or operatives, veteran jihadists, or terrorists vowing to take up the fight if released; each posed "a high level of threat that cannot be mitigated sufficiently except through continued detention" and yet prosecution, whether before commissions or federal courts, would not be "feasible." The reason they could not be prosecuted, the task force concluded, was "insufficient admissible evidence to establish the detainee's guilt beyond a reasonable doubt" or the detainee, whatever his actions, had simply never committed a "chargeable offense."

The lack of admissible evidence was real enough. As the task force noted, in many cases there was no evidence that the al Qaeda or Taliban operative "participated in a specific terrorist plot." The Bush administration had tried to work around that void by charging Salim Hamdan with providing material support to terrorism, even if just by driving bin Laden around, but the task force concluded such that material-support allegations in the absence of specific plots were problematic, and the US Court of Appeals for the District of Columbia was to rule two years later that they were *ex post facto*, too.

The other evidentiary problem of "infeasible" prosecutions was more troublesome. Some of the Gitmo detainees, particularly Khalid Sheikh Mohammed and a dozen others of "high value," had been tortured to obtain information, and that information—or any evidence gained as a result of it—was certainly not admissible evidence in federal court, and very likely not even in military commissions. The task force tiptoed around this problem. Noting that the evidence against some detainees might be "tainted," it acknowledged that "while the intelligence about them may be accurate or reliable, that intelligence, for various reasons, may not be admissible evidence." Although it never mentioned torture (or "enhanced interrogations"), the references to tainted evidence that could not be used at trial "for various reasons" seemed an oblique way of saying that the harsh treatment of those detainees had doomed any realistic hope of prosecuting them.

So the task force charged with coming up with the way to close Guantanamo concluded that for the forty-eight of them who could neither be released nor tried, continued detention was the only alternative. (This number, in January 2010, had apparently been reduced to thirty-eight by the time attorneys Freedman and Foster wrote to the *Times* four and a half years later. It is not clear what happened to the other ten, if both figures are accurate.) The task force left open the possibility that future events might someday, somehow, make prosecution "feasible," but it suggested no concrete route to this end, nor has anyone else, for that matter. While the task force did not preclude the transfer of these detainees to US prisons so that Gitmo could be closed, the Congress elected in November 2010 closed off that alternative as well.

On March 7, 2011, President Obama, repeating his intent to reduce and ultimately to close Guantanamo, established by executive order a periodic review of each detainee by a board of "senior officials" from several Cabinet departments, in order to determine who was no longer a threat to US interests and could safely be released—an echo of the Combatant Status Review Tribunals of the Bush administration. But the Periodic Review Board has moved very slowly; the first man was released on November 5, 2014, and the second a few weeks later. Three others are reportedly on the list for transfer, while another three were relegated to continued confinement.

Republicans in Congress have not moderated their opposition to any release of anyone. "The US government must not release terrorist detainees at the same time we have committed US service members to fight ISIL," said Howard McKeon, chairman of the House Armed Services Committee in a letter to the president, referring to the Islamic State terrorist group. It remains to be seen whether the Congress that convened in 2015, with Republican majorities in both houses for the first time in the Obama administration, will use its appropriations power to bar transfer of any detainee anywhere for release or any other reason. The House voted to do so in 2014; the measure died in the Democratic-majority Senate. Congressional Republicans noted the slaughter of French journalists of the satirical magazine *Charlie Hebdo* in January 2015 by renewing their arguments that this was still a dangerous world, and no time to be closing Guantanamo.

"Guantanamo in 2013 is a far cry from Guantanamo in 2002," Jennifer

Daskal, a former national security lawyer in the Justice Department, had written in the *Wall Street Journal* on January 11, 2013. "Thanks to the spotlight placed on the facility by human rights groups, international overseers and detainees' lawyers, there has been a significant, if not uniform, improvement in conditions. The majority of Guantanamo detainees now live in communal facilities where they can eat, pray and exercise together."

Shortly after those words were published, however, conditions at Guantanamo took a sharp turn for the worse. In February 2013, a small group of detainees began a hunger strike that rapidly spread to include some 100 of the 166 prisoners there, most of whom had been cleared for release but were bureaucratically stalled. The reasons for the strike were not entirely clear—some prisoners said they were protesting the guards' periodic searches of their Korans for contraband—but there seems to be consensus among prisoners and their military wardens alike that the primary cause was the keen despair of the prisoners at their situation, a profound fear that their imprisonment was indeed perpetual, that Guantanamo would be not only their prison but their tomb.

That despair was not unfounded. The victory in *Boumediene* had proved hollow, leading to the release of nobody. After President Obama's reelection in 2012, Guantanamo receded not only from the public eye but from the president's own agenda. Congress had derailed the president's vow to close the place. The release of prisoners had come virtually to an end: in 2011, there was one release and three suicides; in 2012 four releases, and another suicide; in 2013, no one had been released for nearly a year. The prisoners resorted to one of the few actions they still could control, by refusing to eat.

The government responded by force-feeding them. Twice a day, striking prisoners were taken from their cells and strapped into a restraining chair, where a rubber tube was inserted into their nose, down their throat and into their stomach, and a liquid nutrient was poured through the tube. Prisoners resisted, and were subdued so the process could be completed.

On April 14, 2013, the *New York Times* printed on its op-ed page the translated account of one prisoner, given to his lawyers over the telephone. Samir Naji al Hasan Moqbel was a thirty-five-year-old Yemeni imprisoned at Guantanamo since his arrest at age twenty-three while looking for promised work in Afghanistan. "I will never forget the first time they passed the feeding tube up my nose. I can't describe how painful it is to be force-fed this way. As it was thrust in, it made me feel like throwing up. I wanted to vomit, but I couldn't. There was agony in my chest, throat and stomach. I had never experienced such pain before." He went on,

> Two times a day they tie me to a chair in my cell. My arms, legs and head are strapped down. I never know when they will come. There is no end in sight to our imprisonment. Denying ourselves food and risking death every day is the choice we have made. I just hope that because of the pain we are suffering, the eyes of the world will once again look to Guantanamo before it is too late.

The hunger strikers' lawyers filed suit in the US District Court in Washington, seeking an order to end the practice. The government answered that it had no choice but to induce forced feeding to preserve the life and health of the prisoners. Judge Gladys Kessler, reviewing the evidence, found it "perfectly clear" that "force-feeding is a painful, humiliating, and degrading process." She nonetheless concluded, with palpable reluctance, that her court did not have jurisdiction to stop the practice. In the Military Commissions Act of 2006, Congress had not only stripped the federal courts of jurisdiction to hear habeas corpus cases from Gitmo, but also jurisdiction to "hear or consider any other action . . . relating to *any* aspect of the detention, transfer, treatment, trial or conditions of confinement" of detainees (emphasis added). The Supreme Court had invalidated the habeas portion in *Boumediene* but had no occasion to consider lawsuits seeking other kinds of relief. Kessler ruled that the prisoners' request to end force-feeding concerned one of the "conditions of [their] confinement" and thus she was barred from granting the injunction, however painful and degrading she found the practice to be.

She concluded, however, with a pointed reminder of who could end the practice.

> Even though this Court is obligated to dismiss the Application for lack of jurisdiction, and therefore lacks any authority to rule on [the

detainees'] request, there is an individual who does have the authority to address the issue. In a speech on May 23, 2013, President Barack Obama stated "Look at the current situation, where we are force-feeding detainees who are holding a hunger strike. . . . Is that who we are? Is that something that our founders foresaw? Is that the America we want to leave to our children? Our sense of justice is stronger than that."

"It would seem to follow," Judge Kessler wrote, "that the President of the United States, as Commander-in-Chief, has the authority—and power—to directly address the issue of force-feeding of the detainees at Guantanamo Bay."

The president soon remarked, "I don't want these individuals to die," and he did not put an end to the practice. The prisoners took their appeal to the US Court of Appeals for the District of Columbia, the court that had given little comfort to Gitmo detainees in a string of cases over the years. In this case, however, it took a significant step: on February 11, 2014, a relatively speedy seven months after Judge Kessler's dismissal of the case, it ruled that seeking a court order to end abusive practices of one's jailers *is* a request for habeas relief, and as such it could proceed under the green light that *Boumediene* had given to habeas lawsuits.

The ruling was significant because the Supreme Court had never ruled in any case that a request for a court order to alter the "conditions of confinement" was a habeas matter. In several cases, in fact, the Court had refrained from going that far. The court of appeals therefore relied on one of its own decisions, forty-four years earlier, that a petitioner claiming that his jailers were subjecting him to threats and beatings was a claim of "unlawful deprivation of liberty" and thus "in effect" a habeas corpus suit. "Habeas corpus," the court had said in that 1970 case, "tests not only the fact but also the form of detention." That "description of the writ's availability," the same court now ruled, "constitutes binding precedent."

But the prisoners' victory on that point yielded them little in the end. "Even if force-feeding burdens fundamental rights," the court went on, "a federal court may step in only if the practice is not reasonably related to legitimate penological interests." Here, the government had asserted its penological interests as "preserving the lives of those in its custody and maintaining security and discipline in the detention facility." These interests could not be dismissed out of hand; indeed, many courts over the years had upheld force-feeding as a legitimate response to hunger-striking prisoners and had refused to order it discontinued. "Petitioners point to nothing specific to their situation," the court wrote, "that would give us a basis for concluding that the government's legitimate penological interests cannot justify the force-feeding of hunger-striking detainees in Guantanamo."

But the court tempered that bad news with a second chance. It sent the case back to the district court for further proceedings, to give the prisoners a chance to show, if they could, that "penological interests" in fact did not justify force feeding. "It is conceivable that petitioners could establish that the government's interest in preserving the lives of those detained at Guantanamo is somehow reduced, or demonstrate that the government has such complete control over Guantanamo detainees that hunger-striking inmates present no threat to order and security, or even show that there are 'ready alternatives' to force-feeding that the government might employ to achieve these same legitimate interests."

That litigation continues, but the crisis has lessened. The Guantanamo command has taken steps to reduce the trauma of force feeding, although the Justice Department defends the practice in court and opposes any judicial intervention. All but 19 of the 106 hunger-strikers resumed eating by the end of 2013. David Remes, a lawyer for some detainees, told Charlie Savage of the *New York Times* on September 23, 2013, "I think the hunger strike ended because the men achieved their objectives. As far as I know, Korans are not being searched. Guantanamo has returned to the national agenda. And President Obama has renewed efforts to close it. And, frankly six months is a long time to be on a hunger strike."

In the closing weeks of 2014, there were signs that the gates of Gitmo were opening, if slowly. In November and December, 21 prisoners were released: Tunisians to Uruguay, Yemenis to Slovakia and Kazakhstan, Afghanis to Afghanistan. This movement, reducing the population to 127, with more transfers promised for 2015, appears to reflect President Obama's renewed determination not to leave office with Guantanamo still operating. Secretary of State Chuck Hagel, notoriously slow to sign off on previously ordered transfers, submitted his resignation in

November, under some pressure, to make way for a successor more in step with President Obama's desire to see the place closed. Obama's evident strategy, according to some reports, is to reduce Guantanamo's population to such a small number of hard-core detainees—perhaps 60 to 80—that even Congress will realize that keeping it open no longer makes economic sense and the remaining hard core can be safely held in the United States. That hypothesis, however, finds little support among Republicans in Congress, who remain resolutely opposed to letting any detainee into the United States, for imprisonment or any other reason.

In an op-ed piece in the *New York Times* on January 5, 2015, a few days after he resigned as the State Department's "special envoy" for closing Guantanamo, Cliff Sloan, presumably reflecting the Obama administration's views, issued an unequivocal call for the closing of the facility. The "eye-popping cost" of some $3 million per detainee annually is forty times the cost of a supermax prisoner in the United States. He dismissed the claims of former Vice President Cheney and others that released prisoners would readily attack the United States here or abroad. That was "an outdated view of the risk posed by many of the remaining detainees," Sloan wrote. "The deep stain on our standing in the world is more dangerous than any individual approved for transfer." The 59 (of 127) approved for transfer are not "the worst of the worst," he wrote, "but rather people with the worst luck." But while "the road to closing Guantanamo is clear and well lit," he warned that "it will take intense and sustained action to finish the job," including an end to Congress's "absolute and irrational ban on transfers to the United States for any purpose, including detention and prosecution." Sloan did not discuss military commissions, but if Guantanamo is closed the commissions would have to find quarters in the United States, or be dissolved and have their score of accused terrorists turned over to the Justice Department for federal trials. The rest—the three or four dozen in the can't prosecute/can't release group—would presumably be moved to a US civilian prison or military base. Neither prospect seems likely at all.

"Guantanamo frays and damages vitally important security relationships with countries around the world," Sloan wrote. A "high-ranking security official from one of our staunchest allies on counterterrorism" (whom Sloan did not identify) told him, "The greatest single action the United States can take to fight terrorism is to close Guantanamo."

In his State of the Union speech on January 20, 2015, President Obama said, "As Americans, we have a profound commitment to justice—so it makes no sense to spend three million dollars per prisoner to keep open a prison that the world condemns and terrorists use to recruit. Since I've been President, we've worked responsibly to cut the population of Gitmo in half. Now it's time to finish the job. And I will not relent in my determination to shut it down. It's not who we are."

Republicans did not applaud.

On December 19, 2014, House Speaker John Boehner had made clear where Republicans stood on the closing issue. He said bringing terror suspects to the United States "would be both dangerous and deeply unpopular" with Americans, and that "House Republicans will continue to do all we can to protect our national security and support our men and women in uniform," adding that he "looked forward" to "working with the president" on that.

So after thirteen years, Guantanamo remains in operation, its population as of May 1, 2015, reduced to 122, of whom 55 have been cleared for release, according to the Department of Defense. Those 55 at least have some hope; they know the United States wants them gone. Those who have been referred for trial (except for KSM and his high-value co-defendants) may have some chance to cop a plea and be sentenced to time served, as Hicks and Khadr and others before them have done.

Those in the can't prosecute/can't release category face what Justice O'Connor in *Hamdi* called "the substantial prospect of perpetual detention." If the Guantanamo Review Task Force report is accurate, and there is no reason to think it otherwise, those men were not innocent travelers, religious pilgrims, unlucky wedding guests, or riflemen fighting an invading army. They are trained terrorists, loyal al Qaeda operatives, planners and plotters of death delivered to innocent victims, and the financiers and propagandists who support and enable them. None deserves sympathy.

But is perpetual detention, by executive order without charge or trial, acceptable in a nation ordained by framers of a Constitution for whom unchecked executive action was anathema from a president no less than from a king, and for whom judicial review of any such action was, in Blackstone's words, "the stable bulwark of our liberties"? For as long as Guantanamo exists, so too do those questions.

CHAPTER EIGHT

Conclusion

In the weeks that followed the carnage of September 11, 2001, President George W. Bush made momentous decisions, three in particular. The first was to invade Afghanistan, depose the Taliban regime, and commit the US military to destruction of Osama bin Laden and his al Qaeda network. The second was to bring suspected Taliban and al Qaeda captives to the naval base at Guantanamo to be held and interrogated. The third was to establish military commissions for those charged with crimes, precluding any trials in US civilian courts.

The first was undeniably the most important and most justified, given the starkly demonstrated ability of al Qaeda terrorists to commit mass murder in the United States. But as to the other two decisions, the verdict should be clear. They were ill conceived to begin with and they have proven to be failures. Worse, they have been failures that have contorted American ideals, polarized American politics, repelled American allies, and radicalized America's enemies.

All of the issues presented in the Supreme Court's decisions in the cases examined here could have been avoided, and should have been. They were sown by the two regrettable, fateful, and altogether avoidable mistakes of the Bush administration. The first was to establish a holding ground for captives at Guantanamo that would be divorced from American law, including the Third Geneva Convention, a treaty ratified by the United States and virtually every other nation in the world, which requires the humane treatment of those captured in armed conflict. The second was to order a system of trials administered by the military that would be divorced from the requirement of the Fifth Amendment of the Constitution that no one—not only citizens but "no person"—"be deprived of life, liberty, or property, without due process of law."

In both respects, the Bush administration vigorously and relentlessly opposed every effort by the Supreme Court, and by federal courts at every level, to examine the legality of those tactics according to the Constitution's most fundamental principles of American government: separation of powers; checks and balances that enforce that separation; independence of the judiciary; and due process. Throughout his administration, the Congress reinforced his efforts, passing laws that would formalize a regime of closed trials and choke the jurisdiction of federal courts. Barack Obama, the reluctant inheritor of these policies, promised to end them, but in the face of continued congressional recalcitrance his efforts to close Guantanamo and end military commission trials have been only partially successful. Guantanamo, its population now much reduced, remains in operation, and the military commissions plod toward distant trials that seem never to get any closer.

President Bush could have accomplished everything he wished, without doing the least violence to any of these fundamental principles of the Constitution, with a simple announcement in the weeks after 9/11 that would have gone like this:

"We have today launched our invasion of Afghanistan to find and kill or bring to justice those responsible for these unspeakable crimes against our country, and those who are assisting or harboring them. We are engaged now in a war against terrorists and their enablers, whom we will not dignify by calling them warriors. They are treacherous criminals who have slaughtered innocent Americans without the slightest regard for the Geneva Conventions and other rules of warfare that protect civilians by confining armed conflict to armed forces. Those whom we capture will be interned and interrogated, as armies have always done and as the Geneva Conventions explicitly permit.

"Some may believe that these criminals captured in combat, or elsewhere after their escape, are prisoners of war entitled to the protection of those Conventions. I disagree, but I will leave to others the debate on that point of law. Whether they are entitled or not, the United States will deal with them in strict compliance with those Conventions, and particularly the provisions dealing with the treatment of prisoners, while they are in our custody. They will be placed under military control and treated humanely, given the basic food, clothing, sanitary conditions, and medical attention that Geneva requires. They will be held under conditions of uncompromising security. Those who have been complicit in these crimes against our nation and our people will be identified and brought to trial. As to the rest, the International Committee of the Red Cross, the official and traditional arbiters of compliance with Geneva, will have the required access to our facilities to ensure that we are in fact in compliance, and the confidential reports of its findings will be given due consideration by me and by our military commanders. As Geneva requires, those whom we confine, unless they are placed on trial, will be released at the cessation of hostilities. When that day will come, or what will signify its arrival, are questions no one can answer now. This war will be a long one, not because we wish it but because those who have instigated it will do all in their murderous power to prolong it.

"We will certainly interrogate these prisoners to gather all useful intelligence as to how and by whom these crimes were planned and committed, and to learn what similar atrocities are now being plotted against us, so that we can act swiftly and decisively to end them by any means necessary. Such interrogation is a fundamental aspect of our right to self-defense and is in no way forbidden by the Geneva rules. I accept that those rules do not require captives to give any information beyond identifying themselves, but neither do they inhibit our lawful questioning or the willingness of the captives to provide information.

"We have no need to engage in so-called 'enhanced' interrogations, much less to inflict torture, on those we capture. Torture is unconditionally forbidden not only by international treaties that we have advocated and ratified but by the laws we have enacted through our democratic processes. I reaffirm now our adherence to those principles and those laws. Even if the course of torture were open to us, we would reject it because experience demonstrates that torture produces only answers to end torture, not the useful or reliable information we seek.

"Our military has specialists trained in effective and lawful techniques of gathering intelligence, and our Federal Bureau of Investigation and other agencies have a long record of successful interrogation of our nation's enemies, and criminals of all kinds. Such success requires the creation of an environment that leads the subject to cooperate willingly and to provide useful information. We know how to do that and we will do that.

"I have instructed the secretary of defense and the Joint Chiefs of Staff to take immediate steps to prepare a suitable and secure American military facility where those we capture can be interned and interrogated in compliance with our needs, our international obligations, and our laws. Given the nature of war, it can be expected that some of those whom we relegate to this facility will claim to be, and may in fact prove to be, not combatants but innocent travelers or other bystanders who have not taken up arms against us and have no connection to terrorist activities. I have instructed the secretary and our military to implement, as we have before, the detailed regulations dating from the days of the war in Vietnam that provide a tribunal of impartial military officers to hear and decide the claim of any prisoner that he is not a combatant and should be released. Where the evidence is unpersuasive, the prisoner will continue to be held. Where it is clear that he is not our enemy, he will be released. We have no reason, no need, and no time to continue holding such persons.

"It is also foreseeable—and it is my intent, shared by all Americans—that some of those whom we capture will not be innocent bystanders or mere foot soldiers who have taken up arms against our invading forces but those who are complicit in the crimes of 9/11 that we seek to condemn and punish, or who have conspired with or assisted or protected those who have. For those there will be swift and sure justice. They will be charged with their crimes and brought to trial under secure conditions in our federal courts, which have a notable record of conducting fair and public trials with due process of law that result in convictions of the guilty and long sentences befitting their crimes. We have too much at stake to give anyone, friend or foe, now or later, reason to doubt the integrity of the process by which these criminals will be imprisoned or, if the law allows, executed. Our federal courts are the fairest in the world. I have no doubt that they will render justice as they have for over two centuries.

"I commit our nation today to a serious, prolonged and coordinated campaign by our military forces, our intelligence agencies, and our law enforcement officers, with a clear objective: to redress these crimes, to prevent their recurrence, and to bring to justice those who have done them. We have the ability and the will to do so. Our Constitution and our laws, the bulwark of our liberties for over two hundred years, will serve us well, as the world will see. I welcome its support, as I know I have yours. God bless the United States of America."

Had that speech been given, none of the cases we have examined would have arisen. There would have been no *Rasul*, no litigation over the status of Guantanamo, even if the prisoners were brought there, because the government would have no reason to claim, as it did, that Guantanamo's locus and lease gave it some unique insulation from judicial review. It would need only demonstrate to the courts that those at Gitmo were being held lawfully, in accordance with the requirements of the Geneva Conventions, and the courts' role would have been at an end.

There would have been no *Hamdi*, no controversy over the right of any prisoner to have a fair hearing on his status, because the "competent tribunal" required by Geneva for that purpose was already defined by military regulations and needed only to be activated to provide that hearing and render a decision. There would have been no *Hamdan*, because military commissions would have remained a forgotten relic last seen in the aftermath of World War II half a century ago.

Most significantly, there would have been no *Boumediene*, because those who are captured in armed conflict and held captive in compliance with the Geneva Conventions are lawfully interned. Geneva does not give prisoners of war the right to petition civilian courts, whether to review their detention or the conditions or confinement or for any other purpose. Compliance with Geneva's requirements is entrusted to the International Committee of the Red Cross, which inspects POW camps and advises the government on what it must do to be in compliance with those requirements. Geneva does not give POWs the right to consult with a lawyer, at least not unless and until they are charged and tried by their captors for a serious crime before or during their confinement. So even if a detainee in this hypothetical Guantanamo, or a member of his family, should somehow connect with a lawyer to file a habeas petition, a court would dismiss it, because detention of captured combatants in compliance with Geneva is authorized by law. Those who are not conventional combatants—including those in the infrastructure of terrorist organizations—would be charged and tried in American courts like any other criminal and would be no concern of international law.

The Geneva Conventions are not a bothersome interference with American law; they *are* American law. The Constitution says so: "This Constitution, and the Laws of the United States which shall be made in Pursuance thereof; and all Treaties made, or which shall be made, under the Authority of the United States, shall be the supreme Law of the Land." Had President Bush listened to someone beyond Vice President Cheney and the little war council, he would have understood that Geneva was all the authority he needed to hold detainees in isolation, indefinitely, and without lawyers, for as long as armed conflict continued.

The president, in this hypothetical speech, would make his point that terrorists are contemptible criminals who don't deserve the status of warriors and the treatment required of war prisoners. So long as they were being held and treated as Geneva requires prisoners of war to be held and treated, it would make no difference what label the president put on them, or whether he was complying with Geneva voluntarily or because he was required by law to do so. The ICRC, as the monitor of the Geneva Conventions, concerns itself with the treatment of captives, not with what the president calls them.

The president would be giving up little in this speech. Of course a detainee might refuse to cooperate with his interrogators. But the fact is that many held at Guantanamo, and elsewhere, have talked freely, and some have not, which is what happens in any police station. Police and prosecutors know how to make cases without the cooperation of the accused. The Constitution's due process right against self-incrimination often makes that necessary, and prisons are full of criminals who have invoked that right. And where the objective is to gather intelligence to prevent future terrorist attacks, experience has shown that "enhanced interrogation"—torture—produces nothing of value; claims to the contrary in the post-9/11 years have not withstood examination.

President Bush, of course, did not give that speech. He was assured by Cheney and a few lawyers—though there is no record that he spent any time discussing matters—that isolated Gitmo would preclude judicial oversight, that enhanced interrogation would produce useful intelligence, and that military commissions would lead to certain convictions. All those assurances proved false, as any thoughtful and experienced lawyer beyond the closed doors of the White House could have predicted.

What then of President Obama? He faced two problems, neither of which, unlike President Bush's problems, was of his making. First, when he took office in January 2009, Guantanamo had been festering for seven years, and its population was reduced to a hard core of 240, many of whom could not be safely released, either because there was no stable government willing to accept them or because they were, as his task force reported a year later, verified al Qaeda operatives or other terrorists whose release would be dangerous. Second, the military commissions were a mess.

As to Guantanamo, its closure is long overdue. The reasons for its creation—displacing federal courts, enabling unchecked interrogation of terrorists, creating a focus for the "global war on terrorism"—were ill-considered to begin with and in any event all expired years ago by any measure. Meanwhile, the idea that these inmates are "detainees" has become a mockery. Thirteen years is not detention; it is imprisonment. And barring an about-face by a Republican majority in Congress, Guantanamo is facing a long future. The wardens of its population, however reduced, require expensive construction of deteriorating facilities. Its isolation and limited medical facilities (it has no MRI equipment, for example) and the congressional prohibition on transfer of detainees to the United States even for medical care means that doctors must be brought there, which is inconvenient and expensive, not to mention inadequate for proper care of its aging prisoners. Hunger strikes have necessitated the repugnant practice of forced feeding. Detainees who cannot be released because they are too dangerous could be transferred to conventional US prison facilities with appropriate levels of security and medical attention, but Congress has prohibited even that for five years and is likely to continue. Detainees cleared for release could be sent home, or to other countries—President Obama has lifted the moratorium on Yemen—but Congress has placed steep restrictions on any release, and while some two dozen were released in the last weeks of 2014, the restrictions remain formidable.

President Obama did what he could with the commissions. The Democratic-majority Congress in 2009 revised the rules to bring them largely up to court-martial standards, and his attorney general announced later that year that only the half dozen or so high-value detainees would be tried by commission, the rest to go to federal court. But Congress put an end to that idea. So the commissions lumber on, as unproductive as they have always been, with little to show beyond some plea bargain releases, even as federal courts have compiled a long and continuing record of convictions and life sentences for terrorists.

Of course the whole commission structure should be dismantled. As with Gitmo itself, everything that led to its creation—greater security, restricted rights, speedy process, certain convictions—was a mirage. There is no one at Gitmo, including the high-value detainees of al Qaeda, who could not be tried in federal courts. The president was right when he said at a 2013 news conference, "I think all of us should reflect on why exactly are we doing this. We've got a whole bunch of individuals who have been tried who are currently in maximum security prisons around the country. Nothing has happened to them. Justice has been served. It's been done in a way that's consistent with our Constitution, consistent with due process, consistent with the rule of law, consistent with our traditions."

Yet the Obama administration cannot be exonerated as a well-meaning effort to do the right thing only to be foiled by an obdurate and shortsighted Congress, whatever truth may lie at the core of that assessment. Upon taking office he could have, but did not, instruct his Justice Department to refrain from inflexibly opposing every post-*Boumediene* habeas petition filed in the district courts, and from maintaining that opposition, successfully, even to the court of appeals and the Supreme Court.

Nor, despite his initial burst of action after inauguration, has he kept Guantanamo and commission issues particularly high on his agenda. No doubt the need to address health-care reform, immigration, a wounded economy, two wars, and a continuing threat of terrorism, in addition to a hostile Congress since 2011, has kept his plate full, but presidents have to prioritize and seldom do they enjoy the luxury of sufficient time for everything that needs their attention. Unlike health care, the economy, and terrorist threats, Gitmo and its commissions are far away and out of sight; they don't affect the day-to-day lives of Americans. President Obama's desire to end the processes left to him by his predecessor is real enough, as is congressional opposition, but his actions have been sporadic and largely ineffective.

Whatever President Obama's shortcomings, however, the course was irretrievably set by President Bush during his eight years in office. As he faced the most momentous decisions of his presidency, there is little indication that he or the small group of advisers who had his ear gave any thought, or indeed had any real awareness, that those decisions would bring each of the branches of American government—executive, legislative, and judicial—into confrontation and conflict with each other. This outcome, however, is of an order different from the political controversy that those decisions created.

By dividing the responsibilities of governance among three branches, the Constitution invites confrontation and conflict—or at least a creative and constructive tension. Indeed, that was, within reasonable limits, the whole idea. No branch was to be independent, supreme, or unrestrained. Each had its own powers, but none of those powers could be exercised by any branch in disregard of the proper roles and responsibilities of the other two. And even that structure was created for a federal system of governance that limited the powers of the national government altogether and left the remaining powers, considerable if largely unspecified, to the states.

In some respects, but in some respects only, this separation of powers in the national government is marked by bright boundaries. But control of the military lacks any such clarity. The president is famously the "Commander in Chief of the Army and Navy," but the Constitution gives Congress the responsibility to "declare War," "make Rules concerning Captures on Land and Water," "raise and support Armies," "provide and maintain a Navy," and "make Rules for the Government and Regulation of the land and naval Forces." So the president as commander in chief plainly does not have supreme or unchecked control over military affairs; indeed, the Constitution, literally read, makes him only the military's highest-ranking officer, a sort of six-star general and admiral of all the fleets.

Hamilton said as much in *Federalist* No. 69: "The President is to be commander-in-chief of the army and navy of the United States. In this respect his authority would be nominally the same with that of the king of Great Britain, but in substance much inferior to it. It would amount to nothing more than the supreme command and direction of the military and naval forces, as first General and admiral of the Confederacy." If the president, then, commands the armed forces but Congress makes the rules to govern and regulate them, where are the boundaries that mark the difference between commanding, governing, and regulating?

Deciding boundaries whose lines wander and cross like this is the job of the judiciary. In the military context, for example, it was this boundary-drawing by which the Supreme Court in the 1952 Youngstown case ruled that the president, though commander in chief, lacked the power to seize the nation's steel mills to ensure production needed by the military fighting a war, because he did not have the assent of Congress to do so. In striking down the president's action, the Supreme Court was exercising its constitutional power to decide "all Cases, in Law and Equity, arising under this Constitution" and "the Laws of the United States," though—separation again—"under such Regulations as the Congress shall make." That regulatory power, combined with the exclusive authority of Congress to "constitute Tribunals inferior to the supreme Court," enabled Congress to impose the habeas-stripping provisions of the Detainee Treatment Act and the Military Commissions Act—until the Supreme Court said that it did not.

British prime minister William Gladstone might have been a bit hyperbolic in calling the American Constitution "the most wonderful work ever struck off at a given time by the brain and purpose of man," but only a bit. The separation of powers and the checks and balances inherent in it and necessary to its operation transformed a brilliant concept into a government and political system that stabilized a young nation, survived a traumatic civil war, fostered a global economic and military power, and brought unrivaled prosperity to its people. The Constitution written by the founders is hardly perfect—it excluded women and preserved slavery—but at its core the allocation of powers and the separation of authority to exercise them created a constructive confrontation that has proven a remarkably durable and effective system of governance.

The four decisions of the Supreme Court from 2004 to 2008—*Rasul, Hamdi, Hamdan,* and *Boumediene*—are among the most important and sustained demonstrations of this preeminent strength of the Constitution. Each is a judicial nullification of powers asserted by the executive. *Rasul* rejected the Bush administration's attempt to transform a remote US military base into a zone where the president and the secretary of defense could act with impunity, free of judicial oversight. *Hamdi* ruled that the due process of law did not allow an executive regime of confinement that deprived prisoners of any opportunity to contest the lawfulness of their confinement before impartial decision makers. *Hamdan* struck down military trials ordered by the president because, among other things, he had acted without the assent of Congress. And *Boumediene* upheld the venerable right of habeas corpus that the president sought to deny to aliens in captivity, and in doing so solidified that writ as the surest foundation for the judiciary's check on executive power over individual liberty.

Yet none of those decisions is a sweeping assertion of judicial supremacy. *Rasul* stands only for the proposition that the executive cannot use its base in Cuba to shield its actions from the normal judicial oversight that would attend its actions on bases in the United States. It did so by applying an established rule that a prisoner, whatever his location, can seek judicial review of his imprisonment by bringing suit where his custodian is found, and said nothing about the scope of that judicial review for Gitmo detainees. *Hamdi*, though ruling that due process of law entitled one deprived of his liberty by the military for a substantial period to receive a fair hearing on the legality of continued detention, invited the military itself to provide that process, and under rules devised by the executive that might well depart from rules applicable to civilians. *Hamdan* struck down the military commission system devised by the executive, not because commissions were impermissible as such but because these commissions were not authorized by Congress, and disregarded laws passed by Congress and treaties ratified by Congress. Justice Breyer said that Congress could fix things, and Congress promptly passed a military commissions law that the president signed.

And the Court's majority in *Boumediene*, after duly examining centuries of judicial precedents, concluded that habeas corpus as the framers understood it in 1788 did not necessarily exclude alien captives, and that its important purposes would best be served by applying "objective factors and practical concerns, not formalism," giving due weight and deference to the "Executive['s] substantial authority to apprehend and detain those who pose a real danger to our security." *Boumediene*, for all its undoubted significance in extending habeas rights to Guantanamo detainees and for all the fulminating by Justice Scalia that it would cause Americans to be killed, gave those detainees nothing more than the rights of prisoners at any penitentiary in the United States, and perhaps not even that much. The Court's consistent refusal over the ensuing years to review any of the court of appeals' decisions denying habeas relief in individual cases suggests that it was more concerned with affirming the right itself, and less concerned with evidence, presumptions, and proof that would be applied in the everyday adjudication of individual cases.

And one should not overlook Padilla's case—the companion to *Rasul* and *Hamdi* in 2004—in which the Court declined a confrontation with the president over his authority to arrest an American citizen in Chicago and relegate him to Gitmo-like isolation in a military jail.

To call attention to the limits of the Court's decisions is not to minimize the political impact of those decisions. Each one significantly altered the course that the president had set in what he called the "global war on terrorism." Each one significantly expanded the rights under American law of enemy detainees. Indeed, prior to 2004 detainees had been accorded no judicial rights at all. In the 1942 case brought by Quirin and other Nazi saboteurs, the Court had upheld the jurisdiction of military commissions over the prisoners' claims that they had a constitutional right to trial by jury. In 1946, the Court had ruled that General Tomoyuki Yamashita, tried and convicted before a US military commission in the Philippines on a unique and unprecedented charge of failing to control his troops in wartime, was entitled only to a decision on whether that commission had been lawfully convened; finding that it had, the Court declined to consider whether the commission had deprived him of due process in its charge or in its procedures, and let stand his conviction and death sentence. In 1952, in the Eisentrager case, the Court had declined to review the convictions of the German officers convicted by commission (though with considerably more process of law than Yamashita had received). As to habeas corpus, no prisoner of war had ever been bold or imaginative enough to seek his freedom by petitioning a US court for it, not that it would have done much good.

The importance of the Court's decisions thus should not be underestimated. Still, neither should they be seen as arrogant trespass, knocking down the Executive's powers on grounds that courts know what is best for the American state and the American people. Indeed, the only time that the Court could be thought to have even raised its voice throughout these cases is in Justice Kennedy's opinion in *Boumediene*, when he criticizes the government for, as he put it, asserting that its acknowledged authority to determine questions of sovereignty empowered it to turn the Constitution on and off. Taken as a whole, the opinions—notwithstanding Justice Scalia's bombastic *Boumediene* dissent—are measured efforts to identify and reject specific aspects of Executive orders and policies that conflict with the Constitution, laws, and treaties of the United States, in which the Court always specifies the limits of its rulings.

Of the hundreds of pages of jurisprudence in the Court's decisions in these four cases, the most important teaching on the separation of powers is found in Sandra Day O'Connor's plurality opinion in *Hamdi*, when the Court restricted presidential power to deny captured combatants recourse to contest their status before impartial officials. The government had argued that, once the Court acknowledged the commander in chief's inarguable military authority to detain enemy soldiers captured on the battlefield, its role was done—separation of powers mandated that it not intrude on the president's territory by adjudicating rights of those captives. O'Connor wrote:

> We necessarily reject the Government's assertion that separation of powers principles mandate a heavily circumscribed role for the courts in such circumstances. Indeed, the position that the courts must forgo any examination of the individual case and focus exclusively on the legality of the broader detention scheme cannot be mandated by any reasonable view of separation of powers, as this approach serves only to *condense* power into a single branch of government [the emphasis is O'Connor's]. We have long since made clear that a state of war is not a blank check for the President when it comes to the rights of the Nation's citizens [referring to the Court's Youngstown decision]. Whatever power the United States Constitution envisions for the Executive in its exchanges with other nations or with enemy organizations in times of conflict, it most assuredly envisions a role for all three branches when individual liberties are at stake.

"Thus," she wrote, "while we do not question that our due process assessment must pay keen attention to the particular burdens faced by the Executive in the context of military action, it would turn our system of checks and balances on its head to suggest that a citizen could not make his way to court with a challenge to the factual basis for his detention by his government, simply because the Executive opposes making available such a challenge."

Separation of powers, O'Connor wrote, is a "delicate balance of governance." Indeed it is. And in the process of governance, it is the judicial branch, and the Supreme Court if need be, that must in the end determine when fealty to the separation principle leads to exaggeration of it, freeing one branch to *condense* power and turn back the restraints on that power that maintain the balance on which the government depends. Thus the tension in the Constitution emerges not only when indistinct boundary lines between the powers of the three branches must be discerned and applied, but also when one branch, most often and most visibly the judiciary, must draw the line beyond which another branch would be throwing the government off balance.

In 2004, 2006, and 2008, that is what the Supreme Court did.

GLOSSARY

Italicized terms are defined elsewhere in the glossary.

Al Qaeda. International terrorist network led by Osama bin Laden and based in Afghanistan prior to the US invasion. Responsible for, among others, the 1993 bombing in New York's World Trade Center; the 1998 bombings of the US Embassies in Kenya and Tanzania; the 2000 attack on the US Navy ship *Cole*; and the attacks of September 11, 2001. Bin Laden was killed on May 2, 2011, by a US Navy SEAL team in Abbottabad, Pakistan.

Amicus curiae ("friend of the court") brief. A legal brief submitted to a court by one or more persons, nonprofit groups, trade associations, public officials, or others who are not a party to the case. Amicus briefs are intended to present arguments or perspectives on the case that might be ignored, or not adequately briefed, by the parties themselves.

Army Regulation 190-8. The regulations issued by the Department of Defense for "Enemy Prisoners of War, Retained Personnel, Civilian Internees and Other Detainees," requiring that a panel of three US military officers hear and consider the matter of "any person not appearing to be entitled to prisoner of war status who has committed a belligerent act or has engaged in hostile activities in aid of enemy armed forces, and who asserts that he or she is entitled to treatment as a prisoner of war, or concerning whom any doubt of a like nature exists."

Authorization for the Use of Military Force (AUMF). Resolution approved by Congress on September 14, 2001, authorizing the president to "use all necessary and appropriate force against those nations, organizations, or persons he determines planned, authorized, committed, or aided the terrorist attacks that occurred on September 11, 2001, or harbored such organizations or persons, in order to prevent any future acts of international terrorism against the United States by such nations, organizations or persons."

Boumediene v. Bush. The case decided by the Supreme Court on June 12, 2008, ruling that detainees at Guantanamo were entitled to *habeas corpus* to have courts pass judgment on the legality of their detentions.

Combatant Status Review Tribunals (CSRTs). Panels of military officers convened at Guantanamo, following the Supreme Court's 2004 decision in *Hamdi v. Rumsfeld*, to consider, as to each detainee, evidence that he was an unlawful enemy combatant. Ninety-three percent were ruled enemy combatants whose continued detention was justified. Not to be confused with *military commissions*.

Court-martial. Literally, a military court. American service members are subject to trial by court-martial under the detailed provisions of the *Uniform Code of Military Justice*, which generally provides due process protections comparable to those in federal (civilian) criminal trials. Courts-martial are distinct from *military commissions*.

Courts of appeals. The federal courts that hear appeals from decisions of a *district court*. In this context, the US Court of Appeals for the Second Circuit (New York); the US Court of Appeals for the Fourth Circuit (Virginia), and the US Court of Appeals for the District of Columbia Circuit (Washington, D.C.).

Defendant. The person against whom a lawsuit is filed. In criminal cases, the accused. In habeas corpus cases, the defendant (the government official responsible for custody) is called the respondent.

Detainee Treatment Act (DTA) of 2005. Legislation enacted by Congress in 2005 that among other things purported to strip US courts of jurisdiction to hear *habeas corpus* cases brought by detainees at Guantanamo. In *Hamdan v. Bush*, the Supreme Court ruled that the DTA did not apply to that or other cases pending at the time the act was passed. Largely superseded by the *Military Commissions Act (MCA) of 2006*.

District courts. The trial-level federal courts that sit in each state; the court in which a lawsuit is first filed and that renders the first decision in the suit.

Eisentrager. See *Johnson v. Eisentrager.*

Geneva Conventions ("Geneva"). Four treaties, last revised in 1949 and widely adopted, that govern legal aspects of war. GC I and II require that the sick and wounded on land and sea, respectively, be protected and cared for; GC III imposes detailed requirements on *prisoners of war,* including food, shelter, medical care, and eventual release; GC IV extends certain protections to civilians, particularly those in occupied areas or detained by a hostile power.

Habeas corpus ("habeas"). "The Great Writ" and "the great bulwark of our freedoms." The traditional means by which American courts can inquire into the legality of anyone who is imprisoned and order his release if the detention is unlawful. The Constitution provides that habeas corpus may only be suspended in cases of invasion or rebellion. Held by the Supreme Court in *Boumediene v. Bush* to be a right to which Guantanamo detainees were entitled.

Hamdan v. Rumsfeld. The case decided by the Supreme Court on June 29, 2006, in which it invalidated the *military commission* structure as it had existed to that point, ruling that it did not have the authorization of Congress and was inconsistent with the *Geneva Conventions* and the *Uniform Code of Military*

Justice. The decision led to the enactment of the *Military Commissions Act of 2006.*

Hamdi v. Rumsfeld. The case decided by the Supreme Court on June 28, 2004, holding that an American citizen detained as an enemy combatant could be held under the traditional laws of war and the *Authorization for the Use of Military Force,* but could not be held incommunicado indefinitely. The decision accorded to detainees the right to have claims of wrongful detention heard and decided by an impartial decision maker, such as a panel of military officers who could hear evidence and render a decision. The decision led to *Combatant Status Review Tribunals.*

Johnson v. Eisentrager. The case decided by the Supreme Court in 1950, holding that several German military officers, tried and convicted by a *military commission* and imprisoned in postwar Germany, were not entitled to *habeas corpus* to review their convictions.

Military commissions. Historically, ad hoc panels of military officers convened to hear evidence and reach verdicts in cases where the accused is not subject to trial by court-martial. Few rules governed their procedures. Until 9/11, there had been no military commissions since World War II. They were reestablished by President Bush in his Military Order No. 1, November 13, 2001. See *Hamdan v. Bush; Military Commissions Act of 2006; Military Commissions Act of 2009.*

Military Commissions Act (MCA) of 2006. Legislation enacted by Congress in 2006, in response to the Supreme Court's decision in *Hamdan v. Bush,* that gave congressional assent to trials by military commission, formalized the creation of commissions and the procedures of the trials, and stripped courts of jurisdiction to hear *habeas corpus* claims brought by detainees at Guantanamo and elsewhere. Held by the Supreme Court in *Boumediene v. Bush* not to have "suspended" the right to habeas corpus, despite its language, because suspension would be unconstitutional. Largely superseded by the *Military Commissions Act of 2009.*

Military Commissions Act of 2009. Reform of military commission procedures, enacted by Congress in the Obama administration.

Padilla v. Rumsfeld. The case decided by the Supreme Court on June 28, 2004, holding that Padilla, a US citizen arrested in Chicago and held in military custody in South Carolina, must file his *habeas corpus* petition in the federal court in that state, not in New York. The decision avoided a ruling on whether the president had authority to order the arrest and confinement without trial of US citizens in the United States. The Supreme Court denied Padilla's later *petition for certiorari* in 2005.

Petition for certiorari ("cert petition"). The formal request to the Supreme

Court asking that it hear and decide an appeal from a *court of appeals* (or the highest court of a state). If the Court agrees, it takes the case by granting the petition for certiorari and sets the case for full briefing and oral argument.

Plaintiff. The person who files a lawsuit in court. In *habeas corpus* cases, the plaintiff is called the petitioner.

Prisoner of War (POW). A combatant captured and interned in armed conflict and entitled to the protection of the Third *Geneva Convention*. To qualify as a POW, a combatant must be a member of a party's armed forces, or if not, a combatant in a related and organized unit ("militia" or "volunteer corps," today, partisans, guerrillas, or the like) led by a responsible commander, wearing a uniform or other fixed insignia, carrying arms openly, and adhering to the laws of war.

Quirin, Ex parte. The case decided by the Supreme Court in 1942, holding that several German saboteurs who were landed in New York, by submarine, without uniforms, could be tried by military commission, notwithstanding that one was an American citizen. (The saboteurs were all convicted, and several were promptly executed.)

Rasul v. Bush. The name given to the cases decided by the Supreme Court on June 28, 2004, holding that detainees at Guantanamo were not barred from filing *habeas corpus* petitions in federal courts. *Rasul* did not rule on what relief, if any, the detainees were entitled to, only that they could file their petitions notwithstanding the confinement at Guantanamo.

Solicitor General of the United States (SG). The solicitor general (and his or her staff) represents the United States in cases before the Supreme Court. Generally considered the third-ranking official in the Department of Justice (after the attorney general and the deputy attorney general).

Taliban. The extreme Islamist government of Afghanistan, until being deposed by US and coalition forces in the invasion of 2001. Protected *al Qaeda*.

Uniform Code of Military Justice (UCMJ). Enacted by Congress in 1951 (in Title 10, US Code) and updated from time to time, the UCMJ defines the crimes that can be tried by court-martial and the procedures that courts-martial must follow. The procedures are more detailed and provide greater protection to the accused than *military commissions*.

Youngstown Sheet & Tube Co. v. Sawyer. The 1952 case decided by the Supreme Court, invalidating President Truman's seizure of steel mills during the Korean War. Justice Robert H. Jackson wrote that the authority of the president is at its maximum when he has the authorization of Congress to act, but at its "lowest ebb" when he "takes measures incompatible with expressed or implied the will of Congress."

CHRONOLOGY

2001

September

11—al Qaeda hijacks four aircraft and crashes them into the World Trade Center in New York, the Pentagon in Virginia, and a field in Pennsylvania, killing nearly 3,000 people

14—Congress approves the Authorization for the Use of Military Force (AUMF), authorizing the president to use "all necessary and appropriate force" against those who participated in the 9/11 attacks, or harbored them, to prevent future attacks

November

13—President Bush issues Military Order #1, establishing military commissions and authorizing detention of captives at US Naval Base, Guantanamo Bay, Cuba

December

27—Secretary of Defense Donald Rumsfeld announces that those captured in Afghanistan ("detainees") will be held at Guantanamo

2002

January

11—First detainees arrive at Gitmo

February

7—President Bush declares in a memo that al Qaeda and Taliban detainees are unlawful enemy combatants and not entitled to treatment as prisoners of war (POWs) under the Geneva Conventions

15—More detainees arrive at Gitmo; total now 300

19—Plaintiffs in the case that becomes known as *Rasul v. Bush* file their lawsuit in the federal district court in Washington, D.C., under the procedures for habeas corpus, seeking release or family visitation rights

March

21—Rumsfeld issues Military Commission Order No. 1, establishing procedures for the conduct of trials by military commission

April

Yaser Hamdi transferred from Gitmo to naval brig in Norfolk, Virginia

May

8—Jose Padilla arrested by FBI at O'Hare airport in Chicago; soon afterwards sent to New York as a "material witness," and counsel appointed

10—Federal public defender Frank Dunham files habeas petition in US District Court in Virginia on behalf of Hamdi

29—US District Court in Virginia (Judge Robert Doumar) issues the first decision in Hamdi's case, ordering Department of Defense to give Dunham unimpeded access to Hamdi

31—US Court of Appeals for the Fourth Circuit stays (temporarily blocks) further proceedings in the district court

June

9—Department of Defense designates Padilla an enemy combatant and transfers him to US Naval Base, Charleston, South Carolina

11—Donna Newman, counsel for Padilla, files petition for habeas corpus in federal district court in New York

14—In Hamdi's case, Fourth Circuit stays all proceedings in the district court until further notice

July

12—Fourth Circuit reverses Judge Doumar's order allowing public defender Dunham to have access to Hamdi and sends the case back to Doumar to take evidence on the reasons for Hamdi's detention

30—US District Court (Judge Colleen Kollar-Kotelly) issues its decision in *Rasul v. Bush*, ruling that detainees at Guantanamo are ineligible to file habeas corpus petitions because they are outside US jurisdiction

August

Interrogations intensify at Gitmo

16—After a hearing, Judge Doumar orders that the US government provide full details on the circumstances of Hamdi's capture and initial interrogation leading to his internment at Guantanamo

December

2—US Court of Appeals for the District of Columbia Circuit in *Rasul v. Bush* affirms Judge Kollar-Kotelly's decision denying habeas relief to detainees

4—US District Court in New York (Judge Michael Mukasey) rules that his court has jurisdiction and that Padilla is entitled to a hearing on the lawfulness of his detention

End of year: 537 detainees at Guantanamo (end-of-year numbers are unofficial and based on best available information)

2003

January

8—US Court of Appeals for the Fourth Circuit reverses Judge Doumar's orders and rules that Hamdi is lawfully detained

July

Approximately 600 detainees at Gitmo; high-water mark

September

2—Detainees file petitions for certiorari in the Supreme Court in the cases known as *Rasul v. Bush*

October

1—Hamdi files petition for certiorari

November

10—Supreme Court grants petitions for certiorari in *Rasul v. Bush*

December

18—US Court of Appeals for the Second Circuit (New York) orders that Padilla be released within thirty days unless the government indicts him on criminal charges

End of year: 568 detainees at Guantanamo; only 45 more will arrive

2004

January

9—Supreme Court grants petition for certiorari in *Hamdi v. Rumsfeld*

16—Solicitor general files petition for certiorari in *Rumsfeld v. Padilla*

February

20—Supreme Court grants petition for certiorari in *Padilla*

April

20—Supreme Court hears oral argument in *Rasul*

28—Supreme Court hears oral argument in *Hamdi* and *Padilla*

June

28—Supreme Court issues decisions in *Rasul, Hamdi,* and *Padilla*

July

Combatant Status Review Tribunals (CSRTs) begin at Guantanamo

9—Salim Hamdan is charged with conspiracy and other crimes before the first military commission

September

2—Hamdan files petition for habeas corpus in US District Court for the District of Columbia

November

8—In *Hamdan,* US District Court rules that military commission proceedings are not lawfully authorized and Hamdan cannot be tried by commission unless the procedures are conformed to law

End of year: 476 detainees at Guantanamo

January

19—In one group of cases that would become known as *Boumediene v. Bush*, the US District Court in Washington, D.C. (Judge Joyce Hens Green) rules that Guantanamo detainees have a right to habeas corpus and can be released if they can prove that they are not unlawful combatants

31—In a second group of cases that would also become part of *Boumediene v. Bush*, the US District Court in Washington, D.C. (Judge Richard Leon) rules that Guantanamo detainees have no right to habeas corpus

July

15—In *Hamdan*, US Court of Appeals for the District of Columbia reverses district court and rules that military commissions can proceed

August

8—Hamdan files petition for certiorari in Supreme Court

November

7—Supreme Court grants certiorari in *Hamdan v. Rumsfeld*

December

30—President Bush signs Detainee Treatment Act of 2005

End of year: 460 detainees at Guantanamo

March

28—Supreme Court hears oral Argument in *Hamdan*

June

29—Supreme Court issues decision in *Hamdan*, invalidating military commission structure as it then existed

October

17—President Bush signs Military Commissions Act of 2006

End of year: 434 detainees at Guantanamo; only 6 more will arrive

February

20—In *Boumediene v. Bush*, the US Court of Appeals for the District of Columbia reverses Judge Green and upholds Judge Leon, ruling that Guantanamo detainees have no right to habeas corpus

March

5—Boumediene files petition for certiorari in Supreme Court

April

2—Supreme Court denies certiorari in *Boumediene v. Bush*

June

29—Supreme Court vacates its April 2 denial of certiorari in *Boumediene v. Bush* and grants certiorari

December

5—Supreme Court hears oral argument in *Boumediene*

End of year: 316 detainees at Guantanamo

2008

June

12—Supreme Court issues its ruling in *Boumediene,* reversing the court of appeals and holding that detainees have a right to habeas corpus

August

6—Hamdan convicted by military commission of material support for terrorism, acquitted of conspiracy; sentenced to sixty-six months with credit for sixty-one months in captivity; returned to Yemen in November (see October 2012)

November

3—Ali Hamza al-Bahlul convicted by military commission of conspiracy and material support of terrorism (see July 2014)

End of year: 285 detainees at Guantanamo; last one arrived in May

2009

January

21—Barack Obama is inaugurated

22—President Obama orders all military commission trials halted pending a review by an interagency task force and orders Guantanamo to be closed within one year

October

28—Congress enacts Military Commissions Act of 2009

November

13—Attorney General Eric Holder announces that Khalid Sheikh Mohammed and other high-value detainees will be transferred to the United States for trial in federal courts (see April 2011)

End of year: 234 detainees at Guantanamo

2010

January

22—Report of the Guantanamo Review Task Force

July

In the wake of *Boumediene,* US District Court for the District of Columbia has to this point ordered release on habeas corpus of some 34 detainees

13—Court of Appeals for the District of Columbia issues its decision in *Al-Adahi v. Obama*, the first of several cases that reverse the district court and deny release to detainees

November

17—Ahmed Ghailani convicted in US District Court in New York on one count of conspiracy, and acquitted on all other charges arising out of bombing of US Embassy in Tanzania; later sentenced to life imprisonment (see October 2013)

End of year: 210 detainees at Guantanamo

2011

March

7—President Obama establishes Periodic Review Board to determine which detainees are no longer a threat and can be cleared for release (see November 2014)

4—Holder reverses decision to try Khalid Sheikh Mohammed and others in New York and refers them for trial by military commission at Guantanamo

End of year: 206 detainees at Guantanamo

2012

October

16—Court of Appeals for the District of Columbia reverses Hamdan's conviction for material support of terrorism

End of year: 201 detainees at Guantanamo

2013

February

Hunger strike begins at Guantanamo and continues for several months

July

8—US District Court for the District of Columbia (Judge Gladys Kessler) rules that force-feeding of hunger strikers is a "painful, humiliating and degrading process" but rules that the Military Commissions Act of 2006 has stripped her court of jurisdiction to order an end to the practice (see February 2014)

October

24—Ghailani's conviction and life sentence upheld by US Court of Appeals for the Second Circuit in New York

End of year: 190 detainees at Guantanamo

February

    11—US Court of Appeals overturns Judge Kessler's dismissal of force-feeding case but rules that force-feeding may be justified by "legitimate penological interests" and sends case back to the district court for hearings on that issue

July

    14—US Court of Appeals for the District of Columbia reverses Bahlul's conviction of material support of terrorism and upholds his conviction for conspiracy

November

    5—release of first detainee following review by Periodic Review Board

November and December—17 detainees are released

End of year: 130 detainees at Guantanamo, including 62 who have been cleared for transfer

BIBLIOGRAPHICAL ESSAY

Note from the Series Editors: The following bibliographical essay contains the major primary and secondary sources the author consulted for this volume. We have asked all authors in the series to omit formal citations in order to make our volumes more readable, inexpensive, and appealing for students and general readers. In adopting this format, Landmark Law Cases and American Society follows the precedent of a number of highly regarded and widely consulted series.

For those who would like to read the full opinions in the decisions discussed in this book, the following are the official citations to each case. The cases can be found in any public or university law library, or the library of any federal court, or any computer with a subscription to Westlaw.com, or on the website of the court itself. The Supreme Court's site is www.supremecourt.gov; websites for the appeals courts can be found by entering the name of the court in any search engine. Many of the opinions can also be found on unofficial but reliable online sites, such as Cornell University's Legal Information Institute at law.cornell.edu, or SCOTUSblog.com. The briefs filed in the various cases are not all available on all sites (other than Westlaw.com) and may not be on file in all libraries.

When quoting judicial decisions in the text, I have omitted the formality of ellipses to indicate minor deletions between sentences, and have sometimes omitted internal quotation marks signifying quotations from earlier cases. None of the actual judicial text has been changed, except when clarifications are in order, in which case my edits are enclosed in [brackets]. I also at times use the legal shorthand of referring to the litigant (as in "Rasul urged the Court..." or "Hamdi's brief") though it is of course the litigant's lawyers who are writing and speaking.

Also, the Supreme Court's official transcript of oral arguments has only recently begun to name the justice who asks a question. Where it does not (as in the Hamdi case) the identity is sometimes evident from the lawyer's answer ("Yes, Justice Souter...."). I have identified the questioner when that inference can be drawn here, or when the questioner was named in contemporary news accounts. I have omitted some superfluous questions and answers within the quoted excerpts. My edits within quotes are in [brackets].

Supreme Court decisions are published in United States Reports, indicated in standard legal citation form by "U.S." as in *Hamdi v. Rumsfeld*, 542 U.S. 507 (2004). Decisions of the various US Courts of Appeals are published in Federal Reporter, 3rd Series, indicated by "F.3d."

These are the citations to the Supreme Court's opinions:

Rasul v. Bush, 542 U.S. 466 (2004). As noted in the text, two groups of Gitmo detainees filed their cases in the district court in Washington, D.C. *Rasul v. Bush* involved British and Australian detainees; *al-Odah v. United States* was brought by Kuwaitis. Each group had its own lawyers, and the cases were considered and decided together in the district court, the court of appeals, and the Supreme Court. The Supreme Court's decision, applicable to both cases, listed Rasul's name first, and so it has become generally known as *Rasul* (or "the Rasul case"), and I follow that usage here.

The other Supreme Court cases are *Hamdi v. Rumsfeld*, 542 U.S. 507 (2004); *Rumsfeld v. Padilla*, 542 U.S. 426 (2004); *Hamdan v. Rumsfeld*, 548 U.S. 557 (2006); and *Boumediene v. Bush*, 553 U.S. 723 (2008). The opinions of the Supreme Court contain the citations to the lower courts' decisions in each case. The Court's order granting the government's application to transfer Padilla to civilian custody is *Hanft v. Padilla*, 546 U.S. 1084 (2006), and its order denying certiorari in those later proceedings is *Padilla v. Hanft*, 547 U.S. 1062 (2006).

Other Supreme Court cases discussed in the book include *Youngstown Sheet & Tube Co. v. Sawyer*, 343 U.S. 579 (1952); *Ex Parte Quirin*, 317 U.S. 1 (1942); *In re Yamashita*, 327 U.S. 1 (1946); *Johnson v. Eisentrager*, 339 U.S. 763 (1950); and *Toth v. Quarles*, 350 US 11 (1955).

The more recent cases on detainees, following the Supreme Court's 2008 Boumediene decision, are *Aamer v. Obama* (force feeding), US Court of Appeals for the D.C. Circuit, 742 F.3d 1023 (2014); *Al-Maqaleh v. Gates* (habeas at Bagram), US Court of Appeals for the DC Circuit, 605 F.3d 84 (2010); *Ali v. Obama* ("personal associations"), US Court of Appeals for the DC Circuit, 736 F.3d 542 (2013); *U.S. v Ghailani* (terrorism conviction), U.S. Court of Appeals for the Second Circuit, 733 F.3d 29 (2013); *Hamdan v. U.S.* (proceedings following Supreme Court decision), US Court of Appeals for the D.C. Circuit, 696 F.3d 1238 (2012); and *Al Bahlul v. U.S.* (overruling Hamdan conviction), US Court of Appeals for the D.C. Circuit, 767 F.3d 1 (D.C. Cir. 2014).

The texts of the four Geneva Conventions—the Third Convention is the one that applies to prisoners of war and military detainees—can be found at the site of the International Committee of the Red Cross, https://www.icrc .org/en/war-and-law/treaties-customary-law/geneva-conventions. The US military's regulations for tribunals to decide who is or is not a prisoner of war are found in Section 1-6 of Army Regulation 190-8, "Enemy Prisoners of War, Retained Personnel, Civilian Internees and Other Detainees," http://www .apd.army.mil/pdffiles/r190_8.pdf.

The commentary on post-9/11 legal issues—detention at Guantanamo, the habeas corpus litigation, the military commissions and many related topics— is of course voluminous. Scholars, politicians, journalists, and lawyers have written so much in books, law reviews, and journals of politics and foreign affairs, not to mention countless blogs, that it would take a lifetime to read it all. I can only highlight the sites that I have found to be particularly accurate, comprehensive, and authoritative in their information and analysis. They include *SCOTUSblog* (scotusblog.com)—the preeminent source for information and savvy discussion of Supreme Court cases, featuring Lyle Denniston's unfailingly perceptive analysis; and *Lawfare* (lawfareblog.com)—daily, detailed and informed coverage of law and policy touching on armed conflict, national security, and related topics. Its affiliated authors Benjamin Wittes and Robert M. Chesney, assisted by Larkin Reynolds and Harvard Law School student researchers, have published, under the auspices of the Brookings Institution, *The Emerging Law of Detention 2.0: The Guantanamo Habeas Cases as Lawmaking* (May 2011), an essential guide to the D.C. Circuit's treatment of habeas petitions after *Boumediene*, though not yet updated for more recent cases. *Jurist .org*, from the University of Pittsburgh School of Law, is a voluminous daily bulletin of developments in this field, and many others. *The American Journal of International Law*, though not online except to members of the American Society of International Law, is a respected source of authoritative analysis of these and other international law issues. ASIL's site, www.asil.org, does have some helpful shorter publications that are publicly accessible. Another good source of contemporary news and analysis, with much free content, is the Council on Foreign Relations, www.cfr.org.

The best daily reporting of news about Guantanamo, the legal cases involving detainees, and actions and responses of the president, the attorney general, and Congress, is found in the *New York Times*, both in its daily editions and on a number of online features at nytimes.com. Charlie Savage of that newspaper has been particularly diligent and accurate in reporting events. For an informed inside view of the Bush administration's creation of military commissions, see two articles by Tim Golden in the *New York Times*: "After Terror, a Secret Rewriting of Military Law" (October 24, 2004) and "Administration Officials Split over Stalled Military Tribunals" (October 25, 2004). Adam Liptak, who covers the Supreme Court for the *Times*, and Linda Greenhouse, who brought an acute eye to that beat for many years, are also valuable resources for factual and analytical reporting. The *Miami Herald*'s Carol Rosenberg has been covering Guantanamo since the day it opened for detainee business and her stories are perceptive and clear-eyed.

An invaluable resource in researching the array of post-9/11 legal issues are the publications of the Congressional Research Service, a service for members of Congress. Its expert staff has prepared many comprehensive, objective, and rigorously nonpartisan analyses, frequently revised and updated. Not the easiest documents to locate, but try the Federation of American Scientists

(www.fas.org/sgp/crs) or the US State Department's site, http://fpc.state
.gov/c18185.htm). The following CRS reports are particularly informative. The
dates are for the most recent revision as of January 1, 2015.

On detainee matters generally: *Judicial Activity Convening Enemy Combatant
Detainees: Major Court Rulings* (September 9, 2014); *Wartime Detention Provisions
in Recent Defense Authorization Legislation* (June 23, 2014); *Detention of US Persons
as Enemy Belligerents* (January 23, 2014); *The National Defense Authorization Act for
FY 2012: Detainee Matters* (April 10, 2012); *Closing the Guantanamo Detention Center:
Legal Issues* (May 30, 2013); *Interrogation of Detainees: Overview of the McCain
Amendment* (October 23, 2006); *Terrorism, Miranda and Related Matters* (April 24,
2013).

On military commissions, courts-martial, and federal trials: *Terrorism and
the Law of War: Trying Terrorists as War Criminals before Military Commissions*
(December 11, 2001); *The War Crimes Act: Current Issues* (January 22, 2009); *Military
Justice: Courts-Martial, an Overview* (August 12, 2013); *The Military Commissions
Act of 2006: Background and Proposed Amendments* (September 8, 2009); *Selected
Procedural Safeguards in Federal, Military, and International Courts* (September 18,
2006); *Comparison of Rights in Military Commission Trials and Trials in Federal
Criminal Court* (February 28, 2013); *The Military Commissions Act of 2006: Analysis
of Procedural Rules and Comparison with Previous DOD Rules and the Uniform Code
of Military Justice* (September 27, 2007). The quotation in chapter 7 from Dru
Brenner-Breck, on the slow, indeed negative, progress of military commission
trials in 2014 is from her essay, "War Crimes Trials at Guantanamo Bay: Key
Developments in 2014," in *The War Report* (2015), published by the Geneva
Academy of International Humanitarian Law and Human Rights.

The report by the task force ordered by President Obama on his first day in
office, addressing the issues posed by the anticipated closing of Guantanamo,
is the most complete and authoritative information on Guantanamo detainees
as of that date. *Final Report, Guantanamo Review Task Force (January 22, 2010)*,
http://www.justice.gov/ag/guantanamo-review-final-report.pdf.

The website mc.mil is the official US Government site for information
on the military commissions system and its various cases. It got off to a good
start, but some of its case information is now long out of date, and inaccurate
in some details.

Among the many books on post-9/11 legal developments, the following are
the ones I have found to be the most authoritative and objective.

Bravin, Jess, *The Terror Courts: Rough Justice at Guantanamo Bay* (New Haven,
CT: Yale University Press, 2013). The best account of the development of the
Bush administration's military commission policies. Winner of the American
Bar Association's Silver Gavel Award in 2014.

Fisher, Louis, *Constitutional Conflicts between Congress and the President* (Lawrence: University Press of Kansas, 6th ed., 2014) is the definitive work on the subject, placing war powers in the context of the Constitution's separation of powers.

Goldsmith, Jack, *The Terror Presidency: Law and Judgment Inside the Bush Administration* (New York: W. W. Norton, 2007). Goldsmith was the assistant attorney general, Office of Legal Counsel, and undid many of the earlier misguided decisions of that office. His later book, *Power and Constraint: The Accountable Presidency after 9/11* (New York: W. W. Norton, 2012), is also enlightening.

Greenberg, Karen, *The Least Worst Place: Guantanamo's First 100 Days* (New York: Oxford University Press, 2009). A detailed account of the opening months of Guantanamo, and a sympathetic portrayal of Brigadier General Michael Lehnert, USMC, whose policy of adherence to the rule of law and to the treatment of detainees as human beings did not long survive his departure in the spring of 2002.

Hansen, Jonathan M., *Guantánamo: An American History* (New York: Hill and Wang, 2011). A history of the Bay and its base from the 1500s through 2011, with emphasis on nineteenth- and twentieth-century American domination.

Klaidman, Daniel, *Kill or Capture: The War on Terror and the Soul of the Obama Presidency* (New York: Houghton Mifflin Harcourt, 2012) focuses on the Obama administration's policies on detainees and terrorism.

Mahler, Jonathan, *The Challenge:* Hamdan v. Rumsfeld *and the Fight over Presidential Power* (New York, Farrar, Straus and Giroux, 2008). An informed account of the Hamdan litigation.

Margulies, Joseph, *Guantánamo and the Abuse of Presidential Power* (New York: Simon & Schuster, 2006). A perceptive and pointed analysis, as of 2006, by a lawyer instrumental in seeking judicial review of the Guantanamo detainees, integrating the then newly released Bush administration memos on torture with the events at Gitmo and the Supreme Court's decision in the Rasul and Hamdi cases.

Mayer, Jane, *The Dark Side* (New York: Doubleday, 2008). Peerless reporting on the Bush administration's policies after 9/11.

Rose, David, *Guantánamo: The War on Human Rights* (New York: New Press, 2004). A British journalist's concise account of Guantanamo, based on extensive interviews with newly released detainees in 2004.

Smith, Clive Stafford, *Eight O'Clock Ferry to the Windward Side: Seeking Justice at Guantánamo Bay* (New York: Nation Books, 2007). A veteran defense lawyer tells the stories of several of his thirty-five detainee clients and describes his own experiences in representing them.

Wert, Justin J., *Habeas Corpus in America: The Politics of Individual Rights* (Lawrence: University Press of Kansas, 2011) is a complete guide to the history of habeas corpus.

Report of the Constitution Project's Task Force on Detainee Treatment, April 2013. An independent, bipartisan account, from published sources and interviews of some participants, of the development and implementation of detainee policy.

For a thorough and expert article analyzing recent developments in habeas corpus (published prior to the Supreme Court's decision in *Boumediene*), see Richard H. Fallon, Jr., and Daniel J. Meltzer, *Habeas Corpus Jurisdiction, Substantive Rights, and the War on Terror*, 120 Harvard Law Review 2029 (June 2007).

Though hardly objective, Moazzam Begg's book *Enemy Combatant: My Imprisonment at Guantanamo, Bagram and Kandahar* (New York: New Press, 2006) is the account of a British prisoner released in 2005. As I was finishing this text, *Guantanamo Diary*, by Mohamedou Ould Slahi and Larry Siems, the account of a Mauritania detainee who has been at Guantanamo for thirteen years—and is still there as of this writing—was being published.

Louis Fisher's account of the Quirin trial, *Nazi Saboteurs on Trial: A Military Tribunal and American Law* (Lawrence: University Press of Kansas, 2005), is a complete account of that episode and the issues it raised. On the subject of commissions, I might also mention my earlier book, *Yamashita's Ghost: War Crimes, MacArthur's Justice, and Command Accountability* (Lawrence: University Press of Kansas, 2012), the story of one of the first war crimes trial after World War II, by a US military commission sitting in Manila, of General Tomoyuki Yamashita, for crimes committed in the Philippines while he was the nominal commander of Japanese forces there in 1944–1945.

Beginning in 2006, Professor Mark Denbeaux of Seton Hall University Law School and a team of students and colleagues have published a series of objective and documented reports on the detainees at Guantanamo, some of which demonstrate the inaccuracy of the government's accounts of detainees. Essential reading for a full understanding of Gitmo: http://papers.ssrn .com/sol3/cf_dev/AbsByAuth.cfm?per_id=543402#reg; http://law.shu.edu/ Faculty/fulltime_faculty/Mark-Denbeaux.cfm.

For analysis of the Combatant Status Review Tribunals, see Denbeaux's report, "An Analysis of the Proceedings of the Government's Combatant Status Review Tribunals at Guantanamo," law.shu.edu/publications/guantanamo Reports/final_no_hearing_hearings_report.pdf.

"The Response," a thirty-minute video written by Sig Libowitz and directed by Adam Rogers, is an excellent dramatization of a CSRT hearing, based on actual transcripts. Available on DVD. http://www.theresponsemovie .com/about/credits-and-bios/filmmakers.html.

Books about the Supreme Court generally are somewhat afield of this work, but those who, like me, enjoy reading about the Court can do no better than anything written by Anthony Lewis, including *Gideon's Trumpet* (New

York: Vintage, 1989); *Make No Law* (New York: Vintage, 1992); and *Freedom for the Thought We Hate* (New York: Basic Books, 2010). And for a short (very short) introduction to the history and operation of the Supreme Court, Linda Greenhouse, *The US Supreme Court: A Very Short Introduction* (New York: Oxford University Press, 2012).

.